To: President Anthony Monaco
President of Tufts University

From: Winston Dookeran
Greetings from Trinidad & Tobago.

With admiration and
best best wishes.

Winston Dookeran
13 May, 2023

THE CARIBBEAN ON THE EDGE

The Caribbean on the Edge

*The Political Stress of Stability,
Equality, and Diplomacy*

WINSTON DOOKERAN

UNITED NATIONS

UNIVERSITY OF TORONTO PRESS
Toronto Buffalo London

ISBN 978-1-4875-2944-4 (cloth)   ISBN 978-1-4875-2946-8 (EPUB)
                                   ISBN 978-1-4875-2945-1 (PDF)

Library and Archives Canada Cataloguing in Publication

Title: The Caribbean on the edge : the political stress of stability, equality, and
    diplomacy / Winston Dookeran.
Names: Dookeran, Winston C., author.
Identifiers: Canadiana (print) 20210365641 | Canadiana (ebook) 20210365676 |
    ISBN 9781487529444 (hardcover) | ISBN 9781487529468 (EPUB) |
    ISBN 9781487529451 (PDF)
Subjects: LCSH: Caribbean Area – Politics and government – 21st century. |
    LCSH: Caribbean Area – Foreign relations – 21st century. |
    LCSH: Caribbean Area – Economic conditions – 21st century.
Classification: LCC JL599.5.A58 D66 2022 | DDC 320.972909/05 – dc23

We wish to acknowledge the land on which the University of Toronto Press
operates. This land is the traditional territory of the Wendat, the Anishnaabeg, the
Haudenosaunee, the Métis, and the Mississaugas of the Credit First Nation.

This book is an updated and revised version of *The Caribbean on the Edge:
An Anthology of Ideas and Writings*, by Winston Dookeran, published in 2018 by the
Economic Commission for Latin America and the Caribbean (ECLAC). |
The views expressed in this book are those of the author and do not necessarily reflect
the views of ECLAC.

University of Toronto Press acknowledges the financial support of the Government of
Canada, the Canada Council for the Arts, and the Ontario Arts Council, an agency of the
Government of Ontario, for its publishing activities.

**Canada Council   Conseil des Arts
for the Arts   du Canada**

ONTARIO ARTS COUNCIL
CONSEIL DES ARTS DE L'ONTARIO
an Ontario government agency
un organisme du gouvernement de l'Ontario

UNITED NATIONS

Funded by the   Financé par le
Government   gouvernement
of Canada   du Canada

In commemoration of seventy years of the Economic Commission for Latin America and the Caribbean (ECLAC)

In remembrance of my two younger brothers, Tyrone and Harold, so that the memories of their lives will be inscribed for all time and the joy of our moments together will never be erased

Contents

Section 3: Pathways in Analytical Leadership

Figures, Tables, and Boxes

Boxes

Foreword

The Caribbean on the Edge presents a comprehensive analysis of the development challenges faced by the countries of the Caribbean. The book compiles and adapts the author's many contributions on Caribbean development and on the evolution of critical thinking and frameworks built around the region's development path. Through plans and strategies suggested over the course of many years, the book offers a unique opportunity to reflect and build on the successes and shortcomings of various paths pursued. It is an indispensable reference for the ongoing efforts to address old and new challenges and devise a sustainable future for the Caribbean.

Moreover, the author's reflections, developed over time, benefit from his enduring engagement with the region. These perspectives have become even more urgent today. The COVID-19 pandemic is, undoubtedly, the most complex development challenge that Caribbean countries have had to face, affecting their peoples and economies in recent years. In 2020 economic growth declined sharply owing to the collapse of the tourism sector and a drop in energy prices. In addition, the region remains highly exposed to the impacts of climate change and has already suffered the devastating effects of natural disasters, extreme weather events, biodiversity loss, sargassum deposits, sea-level rise, and ocean acidification. This is manifested in the four hundred disasters that occurred between 1990 and 2019. The pandemic thus exacerbates deep structural inequalities and imbalances that are undermining the Caribbean development trajectory.

These unprecedented times offer an opportunity to reflect on how the Caribbean can "build back better" and recover in a sustainable way. Despite the lessons learned and some of the progress achieved over the period covered in the book, many challenges remain. Vulnerability to external shocks is a lingering threat and access to development financing is challenging. The countries of the Caribbean do not have concessional financial support and receive very little official development assistance. Concessional financial support to the Caribbean is an imperative, regardless of whether its countries are considered to be middle income. Moreover, despite some advances, past plans and strategies have not brought about structural changes. Structural change should be at the heart of a long-term growth process to make equality a reality.

At ECLAC we have embarked on and continue to pursue our "Caribbean first" strategy, a commitment to supporting Caribbean countries on their path towards a sustainable recovery with greater equality. This focus on recovery, regeneration, and enhanced resilience to sustainably overcome the impact of COVID-19 will put the Caribbean back on track to shape a better tomorrow for all its people.

International solidarity is urgently needed. Concessional support for the Caribbean is critical in response to the crisis unleashed by the pandemic, and if these countries are to adequately confront the economic and climate vulnerabilities affecting them. We have made concrete recommendations to the international community for supporting the Caribbean towards building back better: a debt-relief initiative through a debt-for-climate-change-adaptation swap, which includes the creation of a resilience fund; a debt service standstill and a change in the eligibility criteria used by international financial institutions for granting concessional funding; state-contingent bonds, especially with hurricane clauses; green and blue bonds; and liquidity support via the issuance of special drawing rights. Moreover, there is a need to open political spaces at an international level so that the voices of Caribbean and all small-island developing states (SIDS) may be heard. The challenges of low-income countries – but also those of middle-income countries, especially SIDS – need to be addressed by the international community.

With ten years left to fulfil the 2030 Agenda for Sustainable Development, there are warning signs that, without an important push, the goals of reducing poverty and unemployment, enhancing women's empowerment, achieving food security, and improving health and sanitation may not be attained. It is thus time to rally international solidarity, accelerate action, and embark on new pathways to realize the 2030 Agenda and to achieve sustainable growth in the region.

Alicia Bárcena
Executive Secretary
Economic Commission for Latin
America and the Caribbean (ECLAC)

Preface

The Caribbean, a magnet for voyages of discovery over the centuries from Europe, Asia, and Africa to the "new world," has often been viewed as a crucible of globalization. In this time of turbulence in the global economy and political landscape – protectionism, isolationism, terrorism – as the North Atlantic powers turn "inward" and the geo-economic axis shifts in a new era of great power competition, the Caribbean, always on the edge of geography, is at a policy standstill pondering which way and how to turn.

Always an open society where harmony and discord work together, the Caribbean Sea has been a source of hidden wealth and a place that peoples from all continents call home. From Castro's Cuban revolution and 160 years before in Haiti's black rebellion for true independence, the region aptly reflects the dictum that "no island is an island."

Now, in a period of tense stability in the Caribbean space, the old premise that inspired development and diplomacy thinking has become brittle in the face of new global threats facing the Caribbean in its quest to move from survival to sustainability. Can the Caribbean stand up to recurring risks ahead and forge a confident pathway for sustainable development? Will the Caribbean heed the urgings of UN Deputy Secretary General Amina Mohammed to make our institutions "fit for purpose and effective implementation" and "maximize this time for global action"?[1]

The Caribbean on the Edge traces the ideas that evolved in development and diplomacy over the last decade in policy and academic circles, points to the missing gaps in data and strategy, and identifies the way towards a new relevance in analytical leadership. In a time of persistent uncertainty, fragile eco-structures, the politics of "populism," and limits in institutional leadership, this work sets the analytical baseline for a road map to the changing of globalization for the countries on the edge of history in the Caribbean Sea.

This edge was succinctly described by P.J. Patterson, former prime minister of Jamaica: "Everywhere, there is a growing acceptance that the old and traditional style of governance is obsolete ... And the new order for which we yearn has yet to be established as a result of constant cataclysmic changes virtually with each passing day ... There is still an ongoing search to create a brand-new paradigm for the exercise of political power and the management of national economies."[2] The more recent impact of the COVID-19 pandemic on Caribbean countries has reinforced this assertion, challenging even more frontally the theoretical frameworks and policy action necessary for the survival and resilience of Caribbean society and economy.

The analytics of development sought to close the gap between political logic and economic logic, and in so doing increased the political stress levels in governance and management of the nation state. Analytical tools to measure and understand the issues of inequality and poverty were tested, and opened "an intellectual bridge to fill the gap between expectations and performance," in Patterson's words (xii). Political stress testing was added to the indicators of development indices, as politics was increasingly seen as an obstacle to Caribbean advancement. With the region's societies being open ones, in various manifestations, and in the ever-changing global politics of today's era, the practice of diplomacy was challenged simultaneously on several fronts within the region and beyond, generating a fertile arena for students of diplomacy of countries on the edge.

Countries on the edge, particularly if they are small, are often in a state of crisis – subject to systemic external shocks, environmental risks, and vulnerabilities – but generally do perform well on quality-of-life indicators and the promise of stability and serenity. *Crisis and Promise: Politics and Convergence* (2015) is the title of my book on this theme, in which noted scholar Paula Morgan wrote in the preface: "the issues and contestations are common to the new nations which climbed out of imperialism's early experiment in global capitalism half a century ago to craft viable parameters of nation statehood ... [a] comprehensive offering ... [that] combines bedrock pragmatism with a fierce insistence on the higher ground and transcendent aspirations and ideals."[3] This book explores the notion that "leadership and institutions" matter in the performance matrix of Caribbean countries, focusing on the promise of convergence of the wider region to secure the economic space for sustaining resilience in an ever-changing world order.

Shifting the Frontiers: An Action Framework for the Future of the Caribbean,[4] resulting from the Forum on the Future of the Caribbean (2015) – aptly entitled "Disruptive Thinking, Bold Action, and Practical

Outcomes" – detailed uplift approaches for models of Caribbean development. Professor Clement Sankat stirred the imagination of the large audience of mostly young scholars in a "what if" articulation of what the future could look like if certain policy choices were adopted: "what if we removed every barrier to trade, what if we ensured the free movement of people, what if we created a Union of Caribbean State … what if we build a robust production capability that opens itself to the wider world … what if, collectively, we subscribe to a Caribbean Future Vision?" Vice-chancellor Hilary Beckles called for "rekindling the revolution" and a return to our philosophical source, while Professor Amitav Acharya disturbed the orthodox thinking on diplomacy by articulating "the view from a multiplex world." This gathering inspired me to begin building the analytical blocks that led to the chapters in *The Caribbean on the Edge.*

This book is about the policy analytics that shape that different order. Tracing the evolution of the school of thought that influences policy prescriptions over time, the chapters cover ideas that shape the framework, identifies the missing links in thinking, and points out pathways in analytical leadership on issues of development, governance, and diplomacy. In so doing, it sets the stage for designing a framework that is aligned to current realities as the region rides the huge tidal wave washing ashore from the Caribbean Sea.

The early chapters place the policy analysis in a historical context and identify the recurring themes of trade-off between regionalism and sovereignty, managing political tensions, and strategies to expand the region's economic space. These themes remain relevant in today's environment, and the chapters provide insights on how to shift the paradigm to expand the reach of Caribbean economies. In doing so, they identify the missing link of politics in development and spell out how that remains a key gap as one negotiates the future ahead. Later, the challenge of reconciling political and economic logics is considered, with its implications for policy initiatives in energy, finance, and growth across generations and demography.

The focus then shifts to examine the development experience in different regions with lessons for the Caribbean development integration process, inclusive growth, and the waves of reforms in institutions and strategy. The issues of diplomacy, as it affects the Caribbean, in global governance, multilateralism, and international finance, are developed as a prelude to the challenges of the future.

In looking at the years ahead, policy analysts will be considering the key issues of the limits of integration, the scope for convergence, the quest by small countries to capture space in global markets, and the perennial issues of financing of development for macroeconomic to structural demands in order to design a framework for the future. In looking at structural change, the book offers evidence-based analysis of financing with reference to income inequality and higher education. These topics are linked to Piketty's recent work on capital in the twenty-first century,[5] and provide an opportunity for a fresh approach to an old challenge that has always been a source of tension in the political history of nations.

The concluding chapters apply a "political stress" frame in the world of diplomacy for small states in the changing world order of things. These chapters look at the phenomenon of global populism, the link between domestic politics and foreign policy, and the leverage of small states in today's time, where multilateralism is not central in big power rivalries. The challenges and opportunities for small states in Europe and the rest of the world provide the Caribbean with lessons in navigating pathways for a resilient diplomacy. The chapters also call for a strategic recalibration to regional diplomacy, and raises the issue of permanent crisis management facing small economies of the world as they search for economic confidence and an international voice.

The book ends, in the epilogue, by citing the "the lazy orthodoxies prevailing ... [the] tectonic changes around us ... [and] the scope to unlock the 'policy paralysis'" threatening the Caribbean, and the need for political stress-testing in the analytics of the tense stability in the region, the rising expectations of a society facing more inequalities and poverty, and limited space for global action. In a timely sense, *The Caribbean on the Edge* is a fitting companion to my next edited publication, *Frontiers, Flows, and Frameworks: Resetting Caribbean Policy Analysis in the Aftermath of the COVID-19 Pandemic,*[6] which links the analytics of development in this volume to the policy agenda in the years ahead, giving expression to the tectonic changes of this time.

Winston Dookeran

Acknowledgments

Ines Bustillo, director of the ECLAC Office in Washington, DC, in her gentle and persuasive manner urged me to produce this book, and I owe her a loud word of gratitude for the idea and for her unstinting support. Alicia Barcena, executive secretary of ECLAC, has the distinction of being a global leader in the practice of development today, and it was her foresight that brought me to Washington, as I benefited enormously from her leadership, and her deep desire to place the Caribbean on a sustainable development path. For this, I am grateful. Tamara Lorenzo made an extraordinary effort in a short time to assist me, and wrote the introduction to this work; I thank her for both and for her patience and perspiration in bringing home this effort. Helvia Velloso and Daniel Perrotti of the ECLAC Office in Washington in their own writings added to the contents, and I am grateful to them, as well as to Raquel Artecona, for all the conversations in the lunch room and in the corridors of our office.

I was fortunate to share many ideas with my colleagues at the University of Toronto. Donald Ainslie, principal of University College, encouraged me always and showed his support and humility – in an unbelievably hectic schedule – by being present at the launch of *Crisis and Promise*, on which occasion the title of this book was touted. Several faculty members shared their ideas willingly with me: Nelson Wiseman, John Kirton, Melanie Newton, Donald Kingsbury, and Christina Kramer were always on my side in this endeavour, and their insights were of great value to me. So too were the support and insights of Andy Knight of the University of Alberta and Amitav Acharya of American University in Washington, DC.

The Honourable William Graham kindly introduced me to his colleagues in the world of diplomacy. Bonnie McElhinny, principal of New College, opened the doors at her college. Giovanni Di Cola, special adviser, Office of the Deputy Director General, International Labour Organization, sent me comments, for which I am thankful. Charles Gargano, former United States ambassador to Trinidad and Tobago, was gracious in sharing his experience in the Caribbean; and Jorge Heine, former Chilean ambassador, quipped to me that "if it is not written, it has not happened" for (i.e., motivated) the students of the future. In that vein, Jeffrey Taylor, dean and professor at my alma mater, the University of Manitoba, offered to share this work with the students there, and formally invited me to present it, for which I am truly gratified and honoured.

I also wish to acknowledge the continuous support of Yvonne Mac Neill, Cecille Sioulis, Susan Dick, and Zehra Ladak at University College, University of Toronto; and Fiorella Figallo, Paola Celio, Rex Garcia-Hidalgo, and Nyanya Browne of the ECLAC Office in Washington, DC, for all they so willingly did to make this project happen.

At the University of the West Indies, where the final touches to this book were completed, I thank Michelle Seeraj for being so patient with me with during final editing and production of the manuscript, as the editorial assistant. But it was Steven Bloomfield, now associate director at Watson Institute for International and Public Affairs, Brown University, who, during my time as a visiting scholar at Harvard, encouraged me to write on Caribbean issues and introduced me to Donald Halstead and Alan K. Henrikson, who were integral in publishing the prelude to this volume, *Choices and Change: Reflections on the Caribbean* (Inter-American Development Bank, 1996).

Finally, I owe a debt of gratitude to the peoples of Chaguanas, St Augustine, and Tunapuna, who offered me the opportunity to be their member of Parliament in Trinidad and Tobago, and to Basdeo Panday, A.N.R. Robinson, and Karl Hudson Phillip for their encouragement in my public life.

THE CARIBBEAN ON THE EDGE

Introduction

TAMARA LORENZO

The Caribbean on the Edge compiles and adapts different chapters written by the author during the last decades on the topic of Caribbean development. On the one hand, the document provides the reader with the opportunity to travel in time, acknowledging the evolution of academia, paradigms, and frameworks regarding the Caribbean. On the other hand, it shows the reader that many of the action plans and strategies suggested through the years are still relevant and that many of the challenges and structures of Caribbean nations have not changed radically over the years, once again stressing the urgent need for action.

The book covers a wide array of topics within Caribbean growth and development, as it also takes on different approaches. The first couple of chapters are rich in historical background, providing information and analysis bringing the reader up to date with the different Caribbean challenges, while the last couple of chapters are mostly focused on strategies and action plans to achieve the previously identified objectives.

The analysis provided is not only theoretical but is constantly being supported with country-specific examples. Most of these examples focus on the experience of Trinidad and Tobago, the economy with the largest GDP in the Caribbean; however, in more than one chapter the author uses the development examples of European small states, and several chapters look at worldwide trends and experiences, trying to extract some of the best practices from around the globe and to adapt them to Caribbean needs.

The strategies suggested include financial recommendations – such as integration of the financial system, resource clustering, product integrations, changes in higher education and in the financing of it, fostering of knowledge economies, and even shifts in diplomatic approaches. Given this extensive range of topics, the policy recommendations of this work could be adopted not only by government officials, economists, academic scholars, and students but also members of the private sector and Caribbean entrepreneurs.

The document is divided into three different sections. Section 1, "Confronting the Framework," provides background and historical context for the following discussion of Caribbean development. Through detailed analysis, it establishes the main challenges and prerogatives when it comes to the region's growth and introduces some of the main themes that have been repeatedly present throughout discussions on Caribbean development. Such topics include the trade-off between regionalism and sovereignty, country size, political tensions, and trade policies. Moreover, the section provides some initial insights on how to move forward in the search for a new paradigm and on expanding the reach of the Caribbean economy.

Chapter 1 defines the Caribbean as an open frontier and raises the issue of identity and the search for a Caribbean state. In chapter 2, the author provides recommendations supporting an open-regionalism approach, establishing that "open regionalism includes some preferential elements, import barriers are low and it allows for the open-ended participation of its members in other trade agreements and regional schemes, so that these various groupings will function as building blocks towards global accords and an open and more transparent international economy." Chapter 3 explores four significant issues that, in the author's words, "are likely to weigh heavily on the region's economic fortune." He immerses himself in studying the role of small states in global competition, the need to build a knowledge-driven economy, to expand the region's economic space, and to finally address the urgency of adapting the Caribbean to the new global environment. Chapter 4 sets out a framework for a macro planning response to the COVID-19 pandemic, as the old economic paradigm is being severely tested. A loop-type cycle of shocks model underlines the discourse on a set of policy initiatives aimed at averting a deep dive in the economy and setting the frame for funding that may catalyse growth in these unpredictable times.

Section 2, "The Missing Link in Thinking," expands on the relationship between politics and development. The author considers "politics as a key ingredient in the search for answers in development thinking and practice." Furthermore, he introduces the distinctions – as well as associations – between politics, governance, political economy, growth, and development, while addressing several questions, such as: What is the key link between politics and development? What is the right balance between political economy and development, and what is the path to achieving it? What are the components of good governance? Can development be attained without growth? He also pursues Frances Stewart's question: Is there a great transformation in development economics ahead of us?

Chapter 5 builds upon the World Bank's *Growth Report* (May 2008) to analyse the development experiences of different regions, extracting lessons learned from around the world. The chapter briefly summarizes the first and second waves of reforms, studying how the predominant international paradigm shifted from an initial – almost exclusive – focus on macroeconomic stability to one that considers the importance of institutions. Inequality is a recurrent theme throughout the section, given that this unequal distribution created by markets is what leads to winners and losers, a situation that, in the author's opinion, needs to be corrected by the political economy. Chapter 6 further considers the new challenges in global governance, international finance, and multilateral diplomacy, together with the limitations of integration processes around the world. It picks up on Daron Acemoglu and James A. Robinson's development strategy focused on inclusiveness and provides recommendations on how to move forward from the current economic strategy towards a more inclusive one. Chapter 7 returns to the need for a new development paradigm able to reconcile and synchronize the political and economic logics focusing on equality and financial sustainability. This chapter uses the example of Trinidad and Tobago's overdependence on the hydrocarbon sector to show how political and economic changes are essential to bring the country towards sustainable growth. The strategy explored by the author involves tax efficiency, fiscal effectiveness, and jobs.

Section 3, "Pathways in Analytical Leadership," stresses action: its chapters are rich in strategies and action plans framing the path for Caribbean engagement with the world in the near future. Chapter 8 initially argues that the process of Caribbean integration has reached its limits; as a direct response, the author suggests a new framework referred to as Caribbean convergence. In his words, "Convergence is not about creating something new, nor is it opposed to CARICOM integration. Rather, it is about bringing new political and economic dynamics to the process of Caribbean integration by reworking the existing frameworks in innovative and flexible ways." The chapter goes through the main pillars and strategies of the convergence framework and provides recommendations for specific actions aimed at increasing Caribbean convergence.

Since the rise of financial liberalization, financial markets have been becoming increasingly important. So, what is the role of financial markets in development? This is the main question engaged in chapter 9. Will there be a shift of power from policymakers to financial markets? The core of the chapter consists of providing possible Caribbean responses to financial liberalization. Some suggestions are: establishing a Caribbean-wide regulatory system, diversifying the financial sector, and conducting reforms aimed at strengthening banking supervision. In terms of monetary policy, the author explores the strategies of inflation targeting and flexible exchange rates in the Caribbean, and finally identifies some common challenges for small states in today's financial global context.

Chapter 10 explores two different approaches to tackling inequality and attaining sustainable growth. Part A looks at building knowledge economies and examines the role of higher education in building such societies in today's globally competitive environment. It argues for a reform program for higher education, an enabling regulatory framework, and new models of financing of higher education. The chapter looks at worldwide trends in the finance of higher education, and the findings of an OECD/UNESCO study (2002) in developing countries. Various financing proposals are identified in the search for more accessibility to tertiary education, and issues of political governance and challenges to academic values, as the university competes in the marketplace, are discussed.

Part B describes what happens to income distribution during intensive changes in the gross domestic product due to external market conditions. It deals specifically with an open-market petroleum-based economy, Trinidad and Tobago, and reviews changes in national product and income levels and the income distribution pattern over the twenty-year period 1957–76. An examination of the spatial, occupational, and temporal aspect of the distribution pattern points towards the elimination of structural dualism in the economy as the surest path towards greater income equality in Trinidad and Tobago.

Chapter 11 adds more contemporary components to the discussion by addressing the new waves of populism and protectionism that have risen across the world during the last couple of years. This chapter studies new trends in global politics, quoting opinions from different authors regarding the future of the liberal order. The author himself states that "the challenge to the liberal order is not really a challenge to the values underpinning that order as much as it is a correction to the excesses of that order and the consequential shift in the structure of global power." The chapter does not provide specific recommendations but urges the reader to be aware of new mechanisms emerging in regionalism and to consider what these changes could imply for small states.

Lastly, chapter 12 revisits the dynamics between politics and economics, this time from a global economic perspective. The author goes through the political effects of the global financial crisis, addresses current risks in the global economy, and identifies the crossroads in choosing the economic path for the future. He also discusses the Foundation for Politics and Leadership as a central forum and important milestone in achieving a framework for an action agenda for small states. Finally, he stresses the need for a paradigm shift in economic leadership and draws upon different authors to study the evolution of small states in Europe.

While the empirical and policy analysis in these pages is centred on the Caribbean region, that analysis draws on comparisons of small countries in Europe and the Pacific, pointing towards a theory of small states and thus expanding the frontiers of our knowledge to fashion new political models, engender change and deepen the democratic process. At the heart of this book is the deep quest for good governance that underlies the thinking in the chapters' diagnostic and prescriptive analyses. At the same time, the models and data were applied uniquely to small states and states on the edge of geography and history, as seen in a Caribbean perspective.

The Evolution of ECLAC's School of Thought and Its Influence on the Caribbean

DANIEL E. PERROTTI, ECLAC WASHINGTON OFFICE

ECLAC's Structuralism Thesis

Several authors track the origin of Latin American structuralism to the publishing of the following documents: "Theoretical and Practical Problems of Economic Growth," "The Economic Development of Latin America and Its Main Problems," and "Economic Study of 1949."[1] These works use historical analysis to highlight the various problems and circumstances leading Latin America to a point where economic development constituted nothing more than a distant expression of desire.

Structuralism identifies the configuration of a global economic system – based on natural comparative advantages – as one of the main causes of the regional delay in development. This configuration established well-defined roles for the different countries, making a distinction between centric – or industrialized – countries, mainly the United States and Europe, and peripheral countries, constituted by Latin America and other regions. This second group is highly dependent on and influenced by the decisions of industrialized nations.

The characteristics of centric countries were reflected in mature industrial structures, with societies that enjoyed higher standards of living than those in the periphery in terms of both income and the variety and availability of consumption products. In these countries, productive activities had adequate financing, through domestic savings channels and/or capital flows, which allowed them to stay in the lead with state-of-the-art technologies in capital goods, maximizing labour productivity, and spreading large markets of goods and services (in both quality and quantity of supply and purchasing power of demand), capital accumulation, and increases in the potential growth of the economies, consolidating a virtuous socio-economic circle.

The reality in periphery countries was quite different. There were minor similarities with the centre countries, especially in those areas of exports that reflected the natural comparative advantages of periphery countries, where economic agents of large size – relative to the rest of the economy – provided the centre countries with a large part of their raw-material requirements (for further industrialization, consumption, and export). In contrast, the rest of the productive structure, and most of the society, faced significant economic and social weaknesses in a scenario of high-productive heterogeneity.

The fragile industrial structures developed in the region during the two world wars and the Great Depression were focused on developing domestic markets, competing with imports under disadvantageous conditions, such as deficient technologies and services, and low worker skills, which meant lower efficiency in the productive processes. In addition, as mentioned above, the production of basic goods of these local industries was absorbed in a domestic market where purchasing power was significantly lower than that of the developed countries, affecting the potential economies of scale of these industries. Moreover, local elites preferred the consumption of more sophisticated imported goods, mirroring the consumption patterns of elites in developed countries.

The social impact was even worse. The productive structures of the periphery had a negative impact on income distribution given the low levels of labour productivity, uncompetitive markets, and high levels of available labour force – mainly coming from increasing rural-to-urban migration. These characteristics decreased the purchasing power of workers, lowering the chances for a successful market for domestic consumption.

In this context, the Economic Commission for Latin America and the Caribbean (ECLAC) pointed out that the relationship between the centre and the periphery was characterized by an imbalance: distribution of the benefits of economic progress showed a clear asymmetry between the different types of countries. This asymmetry was reflected in the lower purchasing power – terms of trade – of goods exported by Latin American countries versus those purchased in developed countries. It was understood that, in the absence of an active intervention by periphery countries, this asymmetry would tend to be permanent.

Another regional factor generating special concern was inflation. Orthodox approaches claimed that the causes of Latin American inflation derived from the quantity theory of money in its monetarist version. ECLAC presented an alternative explanation, according to which certain rigidities in the productive areas resulted in supply restrictions, triggering inflationary pressures. Ultimately, inflation was considered part of the structural imbalance of economies, for which monetarist solutions would be ineffective.

ECLAC's reasoning, based on the reality observed in Latin America, contrasted with the analysis of the neoclassical approach, which assumed that terms of trade while exchanging primary exports – from periphery countries – for manufactured goods – from centre countries – would generate a long-term tendency favourable to the periphery. This theory was based on the idea that increasing productivity in industrial countries would tend to lower the prices of their goods, while agricultural products, with limited productive resources such as land, would show a rising tendency in prices. These desirable consequences contrasted with a reality in which the products exported by the region revealed income elasticity lower than unity, while imports had higher income elasticities.

The Industrialization Period

ECLAC's perspective concluded that the invisible hand,[2] rather than promoting regional development, only aimed to maintain the Latin American status quo. Given this, it became clear that government intervention was necessary. However, what type of intervention would foster development? Certainly, from the beginning of the First World War, and more intensely in the interwar period, Latin American countries began to modify their perception of the role of the state in their economies. Governments introduced regulatory and interventionist policies and expanded their – until then – limited framework of action, mainly in reaction to the rise of protectionism and nationalism in centre countries as a result of the wars and the Great Depression.

This incipient and fragile industrialization – observed only in a few countries – showed certain unfavourable biases, such as difficulty in attracting financial resources, management problems, lack of economies of scale, and shortages in economic infrastructure. In addition, important technological clustering could be observed in those few firms linked to foreign companies. However, the economic clusters with the highest accumulation of domestic capital (large landowners) were reluctant to get involved in industrial activities and investments; instead, they were conceiving a return to the primary agro-export insertion model.

For ECLAC, the solution was straightforward. State intervention was required, not as a reaction to specific external events, but as a systematic and rational way of responding to a global economic structure that was causing undesirable and permanent effects in the region. It was a rational intervention with a clear objective: Latin American industrialization.

The proposal consisted of two differentiated phases. The first phase would substitute imports of basic consumer goods and byproducts from light industries, in addition to the substitution of certain productive inputs. During the second phase, efforts would focus on domestic production of capital and durable consumer goods, through the development of base industries, with greater technological content.

The external bottleneck was a key factor to be solved in the transitional period towards industrialization. In its early texts, ECLAC highlighted how the tendency to a permanent deterioration in trade affected the balance of payments, stressed by the need for imported goods and services, as well as intermediate inputs. Prebisch expected that the industrialization process would require an import of inputs and capital goods not previously seen in the region; for that purpose, he proposed active government policies minimizing the costs during the process of change in the Latin American productive matrix. In particular, he pointed out the need to reduce the consumption of non-essential imported goods.[3]

It was hoped that, as industrialization progressed, domestic production would reduce external dependence, while promoting an expansion in productivity and propagating the fruits of growth over a large part of the population. In the long term, the regional situation was expected to be more comparable with that of centre countries than with peripheral ones, reflecting better standards of living for a vast part of the population, as the vulnerabilities in the external sector would be overcome.

This approach implied a long-term perspective that, unlike the neoclassical perspective – which emphasized efficiency in a context of static equilibrium – assumed that costs in short-term efficiency derived from distortions created in the period of industrialization promotion would be far outweighed. In the medium- and long-term, ECLAC's vision proposed a virtuous model of accumulation, in which the macroeconomic aggregates would come with favourable and well-diversified social indicators.

During this period, ECLAC emphatically promoted planning to provide coherence and cohesion to support public policies. The best example of this was the creation of the Latin American and Caribbean Institute for Economic and Social Planning (ILPES) in 1962. Several courses and seminars were provided, manuals were created, and technical support missions were carried out in situ.

In addition, the planning process needed basic economic statistics. In this regard, ECLAC would also forge a role as a pioneering institution, this time in the collection and consolidation of national accounts, presenting annual reports on economic series. Likewise, with ECLAC's creation of the Latin American and Caribbean Demographic Center

(CELADE) in 1957, statistics and population projections would be integrated regularly into its work.

Other activities of regional institutions during this period concerned the promotion and guidance of proposals for regional and sub-regional integration (such as those of the Latin American Free Trade Association, or LAFTA, and the Central American Common Market). The support came from the structuralist understanding that industrialization processes reflected gains from economies of scale available for market sizes greater than those within the physical borders of the countries; thus integration was a desirable solution. Similarly, ECLAC put forth the proposal for creation of the United Nations Conference on Trade and Development (UNCTAD), which would address issues of trade inequalities between industrialized and underdeveloped countries. This was also the period in which ECLAC introduced its thesis on dependence and on structural heterogeneity, with proposals to modify Latin America's structure via income redistribution policies (including agrarian reforms).

Macroeconomics and Shocks Period

ECLAC's school of thought during the seventies was essentially focused on a new development "syntheses" between promoted social homogenization and pro-export diversification, with sustainable production and consumption patterns. ECLAC also pointed out efficiency problems related to faults in commercial and industrial policies. Economic studies of the period – particularly those of 1975 – detailed a number of issues to be improved, such as excessive protectionism against large-scale projects, low productivity, and non-productive use of capital inflows. ECLAC's proposals focused on strengthening industrialization and promoting exports as mechanisms to combat the difficulties of the region's international insertion. Towards the second half of the decade, ECLAC prioritized macroeconomic analysis and issues related to foreign debt. It also published the first documents that explicitly dealt with environmental problems.

In the eighties – a decade that would later be called the "lost decade," given its contraction in per capita GDP – ECLAC, driven by the needs and urgencies of the existing situation, became focused on technical analysis and proposals to attend short-term issues. In particular, those issues concerned the implementation of adjustment and stabilization policies, offering alternatives with greater gradualism and fewer social impacts ("expansive adjustments") with respect to the proposals promoted by the mainstream. It also prepared studies on proposals for the renegotiation of foreign debt, to alleviate pressures from the external sector.

The Productive Transformation with Equity Period

During the nineties, ECLAC became an institution concerned about a "productive transformation with equity," characterized by a focus on a long-term approach. Technical progress was promoted as the strategy to eliminate poverty and external vulnerabilities, but with a renewed vision that proposed commercial openness to avoid techno-logical isolation. This new vision also highlighted the need to advance on legitimate competitiveness, as opposed to the spurious competitive-ness derived from simple manipulation of the nominal exchange rate. ECLAC maintained a posture in favour of gradual reform in search of greater efficiency, but highlighting the need to reconcile the reform with a long-term vision, minimizing the social costs.

The Rights Approach Period

During this period, ECLAC maintained its long-term approach but ex-panded and deepened the set of economic and social variables studied in previous decades. Thus, for example, assessments of equality no longer focused only on income, but instead became part of a multidimensional perspective based on the rights approach. Something similar happened with the measurement of poverty, with multidimensional aspects added to calculations. Likewise, topics related to minorities – such as gender, ethnicity, and youth – were incorporated in greater detail. Other issues, already examined in previous decades, acquired renewed emphasis, like the governance of natural resources, planning, environmental issues, and aspects of the investment cycle and financing for development. ECLAC also placed new emphasis on the study of alternatives to compensate for the asymmetries of globalization, with the goal of allowing for a regional insertion within a framework of equal distribution and social cohesion. Moreover, a common denominator of much of the intellectual efforts of the institution in recent years has been to establish the welfare and de-velopment of human beings – together with their social dimensions and interactions with nature – as the centrepiece in the pursuit of sustainable growth in Latin America and the Caribbean.

SECTION 1

Confronting the Framework

1 Caribbean Development: Setting the Framework[*]

The Caribbean as an Open Frontier

The Haitian anthropologist Michel-Rolph Trouillot once described the Caribbean as an open frontier where harmony and discord work together; where the boundaries of culture are not easily defined, and where memories of "roots" refuse to allow the past to be silenced or the society to be cancelled, a reminder of Europe's distant history of centuries-old rivalries and war time conflicts.

The Caribbean is a place where the old and new worlds meet, where African, Asian, and European peoples have converged, and where the east-west and north-south fault lines sometimes surface. There has been a silent yearning for a Caribbean identity over the years, at one time reflected in the West Indian Federation. "The peoples of CARICOM and their Governments must no longer think in narrow terms of a 'Commonwealth Caribbean' but in wider terms of a 'Caribbean Commonwealth,'" declared the West Indian Commission, in their 1992 report *Time for Action*.[1]

Two years later, in the search for new economic and political space, the Association of Caribbean States was set up, with membership of all countries whose shores are washed by the Caribbean Sea. Cuba is a member; the United States is not. The platforms defining Caribbean economic and political space over the last forty years include the triangular trade of the pre-independence period, the era of multinational

---

[*] The text in this chapter was adapted from Winston Dookeran, "Caribbean Development: The Premises of an Emerging Agenda," *Iberoamericana: Nordic Journal of Latin American and Caribbean Studies* 28: 1–2 (1998): 25–53.

corporations and United States hegemony, and more recently, the IMF-World Bank structural adjustment programs. Out of this framework came theories of exploitation, neocolonialism, and marginalization and the export of protest diplomacy. There followed heavy moral and political overtures for protection, special consideration, aid, trade, and investment support from the developed world.

This approach may have been acceptable in the 1960s and 1970s, given the state of development thinking and the geopolitical structure of the world economy in that period, but it is no longer sustainable. For decades, the plantation economy of the hinterland has adjusted only to persistent low-level equilibrium, resulting in low levels of employment and incomes. Although the region's resource-based industries were integrated into the global economy, this resulted in economic enclaves within the domestic economy, without sufficient development benefits. Caribbean countries remain highly sensitive to exogenous factors such as shocks, exchange rate manipulation, and crisis, all of which can adversely affect their critical foreign exchange, their largely export-driven public revenues, and their competitiveness.

The financial and economic geographies of the world have altered and have facilitated new flows of international capital. Now there is an increasing divergence between political and economic boundaries. There are now no privileged spaces. Yet there is a high demand for Caribbean countries to create a new generation of exports to reduce the cost of doing business and to expand its production frontiers. How? And what are the options? Two further questions arise: Is our development strategy correct? Is our understanding of world politics insightful?

The Changing Perspectives

Objectives of Development

Caribbean development, always challenged by the dichotomy between growth and development, has been premised on the argument that growth is a necessary condition for development. Now the sequence may have changed, as development has become a necessary condition for growth. What then did we do and what do we mean by development? In previous decades, development was seen as simply increasing GDP. Joseph Stiglitz contends that today, economists and planners have a broader set of objectives that lead to a quite different development strategy. He argued that the objectives of development should be widened and the role of the state be changed to create a partnership between government and the markets, which involves a catalytic role for governments in creating markets, and elaborated that "successful development entails sustainable, equitable, and democratic development; that the development had to be sustainable environmentally, socially, politically, and of course economically; and that such sustainable development necessarily involved a societal transformation."[2] I argued for a more balanced approach between the state and the market than was reflected in the Washington Consensus, which focused on minimizing the role of government, with government interventions centred on price mechanisms. I suggested that the government had many more instruments at its disposal – and it should make use of these additional instruments. Stiglitz argues that "it has long been recognized that a market system cannot operate solely on the basis of narrow self-interest."[3]

As economists have long recognized, GDP accounting can no longer adequately capture changes in standards of living. Improved education and health care, the abatement of pollution, and the generation of externalities must all be taken into account if we are to arrive at a meaningful estimation of living standards. There has been a change in thinking about development strategies: a change in objectives.

This broadened set of objectives leads to quite different development strategies. In sketching the outline of an agenda for economic development for the coming century, Stiglitz concludes that "it includes a wider set of objectives than development agendas of the past" and "a changing role for the state – a partnership between government and markets – that involves a catalytic role for government in helping to create markets."[4] This will require that a new regulatory structure and framework be designed to protect the public interest in these wider set of development objectives.

Having the relevant policies in place and getting the prices right is not enough. The states can create markets, they helped regulate markets, and they used markets to achieve their development objectives. The sequence of reforms can affect not only the performance of the economy in the short run, but also the momentum for the continuation of reforms. The simple lesson to emerge from this discussion is that incentives matter: that they matter in both the public and the private sector, that the government should make more extensive use of incentive mechanisms for guiding its own behaviour, and that government should take actions to improve the incentives within the private sector.

Development, as we recognize today, is more than the accretion of physical or human capital. It also includes closing the knowledge gap between rich and poor economies. And it includes other transformations, such as those that result in the creation of social capital, the quality of growth rates, and changes in the structure and behaviour of economic organizations. Alberto Alesina asserts, based on a cross-country data analysis, that countries with large public sectors and "poor" institutions are gravely harmed in the development process.[5] Now the external environment is an "endogenous" factor and influences significantly the political economy of "high and low growth" in both advanced and developing countries. In Stiglitz's view, the coming decade will see enormous growth in the developing world and a reduction in poverty. It will be a struggle. The challenges are great, but the opportunities are enormous.

Regionalism and Multilateralism

The forces transforming the global environment are moving the international system in two seemingly contradictory directions. On the one hand, the world is moving towards multilateralism and global integration with a strong commitment to open markets and international institutions. On the other hand, it is entering a new era of regionalism, as nations seek to guarantee their markets. Policies, strategies, and institutions that are not in harmony with international regimes may not be tenable. The meshing of local policies with the external policy environment is an emerging issue that may have prompted Robert Putnam to design a "two-tier framework" to analyse the domestic component of foreign policy.[6]

The issue is more complicated with the resurgence of regionalism, as pointed out by Jagdish Bhagwati.[7] The first round of regionalism collapsed in the 1960s, primarily because the United States was intent upon following a multilateral course. Now, regional thrusts are seen as a stepping stone to multilateral goals, thus widening the interest in the regional agenda going beyond trade and investment issues into matters of security, common regulatory systems, environment and labour standards, and institution-building. This broadened agenda has set the stage for a new kind of "moving integration" where the boundaries keep shifting, new frontiers keep emerging, and the economic equations within the integration areas are changing. We are now in a dynamic integration process calling for a new model of integration.

In this rethinking process, regionalism is not about developing "self-contained" blocs; it too must synchronize its formation in a global context. As Bhagwati noted; "regionalism need not necessarily be a stumbling block towards a multilateral trading system."[8] The World Trade Organization is the most recent example of the evolution of a global institutional framework, a trend that poses major reform requirements for other international bodies in the field of development. Development banks are likely to face new demands for change in a more competitive global financial setting. Indeed, political leaders and other executives of the public interest can no longer define interests primarily in terms of their geopolitical boundaries, but must increasingly do so in regional and global terms.

The Issue of Sovereignty of the Nation State

However, as difficult as integration might be, collaboration on agreed-upon agendas and shared responsibility for the promotion of common interests do not mean that the nation state will disappear, or that national sovereignty will be lessened. Indeed, this issue has sparked much debate in the Caribbean recently, as nation states in the region strive for common-interest positions as a means of pooling their "sovereignty" for wider regional and global trade-offs. If entered into wisely, such agreements will increase economic well-being at home and enhance governments' ability to govern. The establishment of regional common interests and joint problem-solving processes, far from limiting the state's power, may therefore heighten national autonomy, particularly when these agreements are entered into with a view to how one can benefit from greater integration with the external world while at the same time supporting the multilateral process.

Political Systems Are Undergoing Stress

Governments in both the developing and developed world are, in an increasingly laissez-faire global environment, facing the progressively more difficult task of managing their national economies in order to improve macroeconomic performance; provide increased levels of public investment for job creation, education, and health care; and develop policies and institutions that will address the issues of poverty and inequity. Political systems are undergoing stress, as the economic forces for integration outstrip those systems' capacity to make the requisite political adjustments. They are likely to endure only insofar as they are able to adapt.[9]

In the Caribbean and other developing regions, this scenario is further complicated by structural adjustment policies, which many argue are undermining the conditions for development. Others fear that building the requisite regional institutions for addressing these problems will result in a loss of national identity and sovereignty. Furthermore, as regionalism is by definition discriminatory, economists and decision makers are concerned about the possible trade-diverting effects of the future regional landscape.[10]

Size Is Not an Issue

We in the Caribbean have rationalized that our smallness constrains development, but in fact size is not itself an issue. The city states of Hong Kong and Singapore have achieved high levels of prosperity without significant natural resources, preferential trade accords, or proximity to the United States and European markets. They determined their cultural strengths and built on them, developing policies and strategies that unleashed the microeconomic forces for growth, and complementing these with the macroeconomic framework. This was a matter of clear goals, skilful strategies, and sound policymaking, not market size.

China, on the other hand, with its historically unique form of government, large internal market, and substantial resources, was unable to modernize its economy outside the global framework; nor have other large nations, including India, Indonesia, Brazil, Russia, Pakistan, Bangladesh, Nigeria, and Mexico, been able to do so, though many have excellent resource bases.[11] The point, then, is that the political and sociological legitimacy of the nation state is not threatened by changes in operational sovereignty per se; rather, today's world requires that the nation state cede more of its operational sovereignty in order to retain its legitimacy and viability.

The Emerging Frameworks

Open Regionalism

Regionalism is an inescapable feature of the landscape. Open regionalism encourages nations to form sub-regional trading blocs in ways that facilitate linkages with others, thus synthesizing the globalization and regionalization trends. It allows for the open-ended participation of its members in other trading arrangements and regional schemes, so that these various groupings will function as building blocks towards global accords and an open and transparent international economy.

Open regionalism is seen as a way of achieving a development model in which economic growth and social equity are enhanced simultaneously. Accordingly, the horizontal expansion of aggregate demand as a result of market integration would be compounded by vertical expansion of demand, owing to country-level social integration. In this connection, integration agreements between countries not only may be compatible with the goal of steadily increasing international competitiveness, but may also be instrumental in achieving it. Their purpose is to usher in a more open, transparent international economy. In other words, integration is seen as a constituent of a future international economy free of protectionism and barriers to the exchange of goods and services.

The open regionalism approach should be designed with certain characteristics in mind: it should contribute to a gradual reduction of intra-regional discrimination, to macroeconomic stabilization in each country, to the establishment of suitable payment and trade-promotion mechanisms, to the building of infrastructure, and to the harmonization or non-discriminatory application of trade rules, domestic regulation, and standards. Moreover, reduction of transaction costs and discrimination within the region could be reinforced by sectoral arrangements or policies to take advantage, in turn, of the synergistic effects of integration.

The Rise of Regional Economies

Kenichi Ohmae asks whether "nation states – notwithstanding the obvious and important role they play in world affairs – [are] really the primary actors in the world economy." Indeed, as Ohmae suggests, it is doubtful whether, in today's world where economic borders are progressively disappearing, "nation states are the best window on the global economy; whether they provide the best port of access to it; whether arbitrary, historically accidental boundaries are genuinely meaningful in economic terms; and, if not, what kinds of boundaries do make sense?" In other words, what exactly are "the sufficient, correctly sized and scaled aggregations of people and activities" with which to tap into the global economy?[12]

As Ohmae notes, one way to answer these questions is to observe the flows of what he calls the four "I's": investment, industry, information technology, and individual consumers. Taken together, the mobility of these four I's makes it possible for viable economic units in any part of the world to attract whatever resources are needed for development. They need not look for assistance only to pools of resources close to home. Nor do they need to rely on the formal efforts of governments to attract resources from elsewhere and funnel them to ultimate users. This makes the traditional "middleman" function of nation states – and of their governments – largely unnecessary. Because all the global markets for the four I's "work just fine on their own, nation states no longer have to play a market clearing role. Global solutions will flow to where they are needed without the intervention of the nation states. On current evidence, moreover, they flow better precisely because such intervention is absent."[13]

In essence, therefore, as Ohmae argues, "region states are economic not political units, and they are anything but local in focus. They may lie within the borders of an established nation state, but they are powerful engines of development because their primary orientation is towards – and their primary linkage is with – the global economy. They are, in fact, among its most reliable ports of entry." Indeed, what defines the region states is "not the location of the political borders but the fact that they are the right size and scale to be the true natural business units in today's global economy. Theirs are the borders – and the connections – that matter in a borderless world."[14]

The "Flying Geese" Metaphor in Economic Growth

Tadayoshi Ito put forward a very interesting observation that the pattern of development takes place through a "flying geese" formation.[15] Based on his study of East Asian countries, he concluded that the Asian economies are like a group of geese flying in V-formation. Japan, flying at the front, is flanked by Hong Kong and Singapore, followed by the Republic of Korea and Taiwan. Behind them are Malaysia and Thailand, the Philippines and Indonesia. The order of the formation is that of the stage of industrialization and per capita income.

The argument is based on shifting comparative advantage. As rich countries shift their production to technologically advanced new products, lower value-added versions of these products are produced by neighbouring less developed, lower-cost countries that, taken together, generate a dynamic process of development. As an example of this type of phenomenon, one can look at Japanese investment behaviour in East Asia in electronics and autos industries. Japanese investment behaviour in their manufacturing sectors shifted from Japan in the late 1970s, first to Hong Kong, Singapore, Taiwan, and Korea, then to Malaysia and Indonesia, and now to China.

Is this pattern likely to be replicated in other regions of the world? In other words, would economic take-off now take place in clusters of economies rather than through national economies or satellite economies? In the new economic geography, the regional economy diverges from the established political boundaries; it now appears that it is the regional economy, not the national or even satellite economy, that will become the basic unit upon which a dynamic process for economic growth and development can be predicated.

Ito goes on to argue that for countries with little natural resources, like Japan, Korea, and most East Asian economies, growth means industrialization. Two indicators of the level of economic development are agriculture's share of GDP and machinery's share in exports. As economic growth increases, a resource shift takes place to the manufacturing sector, and in this process the product composition of exports changes. Production and exports shift from textiles and light industrial products to more sophisticated goods such as machinery, steel, and automobiles.

Is this sequencing appropriate for Caribbean industrialization? Empirical evidence of industrialization performance does not support this process of resource shift. The early thinking on this matter focused on the "value-added" concept, where more returns are being sourced from the existing resource use, leading to downstream and linkage industries. As a result, specialization and resource shift were given lower priority in the development of industry in the Caribbean. According to Dennis Pantin (1995), CARICOM developed an industrial allocation scheme to target specific "light industries" in the smaller Caribbean economies. This scheme has had limited results.[16]

What is emerging is the distinction between a strategy for economic development based on the value-added idea as opposed to a strategy based on "resource shift." Many sunset industries in the Caribbean have been retained based on the argument that new investment could diversify the outputs and create a dynamic for growth based on the old expenditure patterns. To some extent, this explanation is attractive because of its political appeal. There are no real losers, only winners. The need for de-industrialization to precede re-industrialization is clearly addressed in the "resource shift" idea, where dynamic development will be sustained only through major shifts in national expenditure from "sunset" to "sunrise" industries.

Ito argues that the key lesson that can be learned from the experience of East Asia is to understand how incentives have worked in that environment, and the efficacy of government intervention in these economies. In both respects, the countries in the cluster region employed a common policy approach that facilitated the emergence of the flying geese formation in economic change. By comparison, there are wide spaces in policy coordination among Caribbean countries; in spite of valiant attempts to establish common approaches in external trade matters and monetary cooperation, it would seem that the flying geese metaphor in a Caribbean context may require an integrated policy framework at both the policy and operational level. The framework must be based on new pillars of growth that are sustainable through the working of the market system, including perhaps the issue of a policy framework for the knowledge-based economy. This remains a major challenge to the political economy of development in cluster economies.

Widening the Scope for Economic Reform

In most Caribbean countries the first generation of reforms – macroeconomic policy, trade reform, financial reform, and privatization – are in process. The current aim is to make a permanent shift towards growth following adjustment. There is now a need to go beyond the adjustment process into an agenda of second-generation reforms. The situation in each country differs; Trinidad and Tobago, for instance, has embarked on a highly complex process of change that has not yet run its course. Will the present policy matrix sustain external balances and deepen the process of structural change? What are the key elements of a second-phase program that will maintain the momentum of growth and development?

Nancy Birdsall saw the key elements as the three "E's": export, education, and enabling government. She described these as the missing ingredients for the economic success of the Caribbean. She argues that the growth of exports encourages the rapid growth of employment and eventually wages, which raises the demand for labour and contributes to relative equality of incomes. Exporting may also create a second advantage in that it forces countries to be globally competitive, thereby generating rapid productivity gains.[17] Birdsall's second key variable, education, needs to be accorded a high priority because it contributes not only to wage and productivity growth but also to fertility decline, which makes higher investment in education per child possible.Her third element is an enabling government: in her view, government should be viewed not as an engine of growth but as an enabler or catalyst of private-sector growth. In particular, governments need to create a predictable and reliable environment for investors, and thus an environment friendly to the business sector. Birdsall's "missing links," now perhaps part of the old orthodoxy, necessitate a development framework that will provide these missing elements.

The growth of an economy depends on how stabilization efforts and structural reforms work in a particular setting. The environment takes into account microeconomic behaviour, the functioning of factor markets, and the performance of the regulatory system. The interplay of micro- and macroeconomics, says an ECLAC publication,[18] is the new challenge to policy-makers in the Caribbean and Latin America. Growth alone is not enough. There are also conditions on the microeconomic and systematic levels that are essential for creating externalities that will internalize the transformation process with a special objective of increasing the income of the poorest.

The setting goes beyond the national economy. The strategy to capture global technology flows, to be competitive in an integrated regional economy, and to respond to the global business cycle will determine the growth rate and the income level at which the economy may reach a "steady-state" equilibrium. That equilibrium may produce an externality that opens or closes the gap between private and social returns to investment, depending on how the management of social policy takes place. The missing challenge in strategic economic programming in many Caribbean countries is to design a logistics that will link

- short-run macroeconomics and medium-run growth;
- public institutions and the production and trade structure;
- micro- and macroeconomics;
- the national and global economy; and
- economic and social efficiency and political feasibility.

This leads to the construction of an agenda for second-generation reforms that in broad outline may cover, inter alia, the management of the public sector, a prospectus for "unshackling" the private sector, choices and change in financial and monetary management, and sustainable social programming.[19]

Sustaining the Integration Efforts

ECLAC's study *Open Regionalism in Latin America and the Caribbean* emphasizes two critical aspects of integration: one dealing with technical change and the other dealing with social integration. It argues that technical progress in integration requires government to play a catalytic role in Latin American and Caribbean economies in order to build appropriate business structures and information networks that are required to facilitate technological change. With respect to social integration, ECLAC argues for a strategy that will change production patterns with social equity, and in this respect outlined a series of measures in microenterprise development aimed at reducing marginalization and increasing participation of lower-income people in the actual business of development.

In the search for a new integration paradigm, three main pillars upon which such a strategy can be designed have been identified.[20] The first concerns the search for external economies of scale. In the midst of a world that is now less dependent on physical resources and commodities, the identification of such an industrial strategy remains a key area of enquiry. The development of geographically compact economies is another pillar where strategic niches can be built upon and corporate partnerships and alliances can be encouraged. The third pillar upon which the integration paradigm can be constructed is the search to extend the range of Caribbean economies so that regional capacity can be enhanced to play a competitive role in world commerce. These considerations, along with the concept of dynamic integration alluded to earlier, are but a starting point in the building of an integration approach.

Development in the Caribbean entails a comprehensive political economy of change, including the development of endogenous growth capacity to drive the economy. Only then can the region benefit from the new and flexible world economy, in which ends and means are readily adjusted to changing opportunities in different countries. This will require an integration model that transcends trade and converges at the institutional level, and facilitates backward and forward macro- and micro-economic linkages. Eventually, a virtuous cycle should be created, in which the region can expand its political space and gain greater negotiating strength in the international arena. Merging into a greater political economic whole should help to free individual states from rent-seeking power bases, bring about greater economic efficiencies, and allow governments to concentrate on governance.

Sustainable development is an affirmative political-economic process, linking economic logic – the measures needed to pursue economic efficiency in both the international and domestic spheres – with political logic in a synergism that allows them to reinforce one another. Merely opening the economy to the outside will not induce sustainable growth; to the contrary, it will result in further social and economic destabilization. As integration progresses and the state reduces its direct role in the economy, public policy will have an even greater impact on society. There will be winners and losers; to address this situation, the government must be strong enough to manage the transition and alter the opportunity structure, so that lower- and middle-income groups will not bear disproportionate burdens. The government's challenge is to ensure that poverty issues are systematically addressed with visible effect.

The issue of the competitiveness of the Caribbean economy has now emerged as a key requirement for the successful integration of these economies into the global economic system. Serious issues do arise in determining the path and process for improving competitiveness. These issues include matters of macroeconomic policy, changes to the structure of specific industries, the financing of infrastructure development, and institutional systems to promote competitiveness.

In the new agenda for global trade, the issue of an international agreement on competition policy has emerged. The argument is that the determination of trade barriers does not ensure that markets are genuinely contestable. The WTO currently does not require its members to meet competition policies; there is thus no entity responsible for ensuring that global markets are competitive. A single set of rules could, in principle, provide more coherence than the current system.

The negotiation of these rules covers a wide range of topics:

- elimination of antidumping and countervailing duties rules
- antitrust laws
- business practice that restricts market access
- creation of an international competition office
- implications for preferential tax treatments
- constraints on domestic competition policy
- the possibility that competition rules will outlaw market-sharing agreements

Whatever the agenda items, it is clear that an international competition policy will directly affect trade and commercial practice, and will have differential effects on different groups of countries. It may well lead to the categorization of countries on the basis of their degree of integration with the world economy. It may also be that an incremental approach is the most viable way to incorporate competition policy within the international trading system. The Caribbean region's framework for negotiations is now an urgent assignment.[21]

Managing Political Tensions

The Politics of Development

Fragmentation and social incohesion at both the national and regional levels have raised questions about the readiness of Caribbean states to confront inescapable global realities and challenges emanating from a dynamic environment. In the post-independence period, political development and the forging of relevant social institutions have received little attention. A formula to harness and exploit the potential of multi-ethnic, multicultural societies remains elusive despite increasing evidence that politics and culture can have positive impacts on the development process. Replacing many of the old theories and approaches are paradigms that recognize the need for inclusiveness in promoting social stability and addressing problems of equity. The imperative now is to forge new forms of governance involving greater national consensus and wider community participation in decision making. There is much to learn from countries that have moved ahead.

Management of the regional integration process in the Caribbean community has been stymied over fear of loss of national sovereignty and a wavering commitment to transfer sovereignty to a regional entity. Overcoming these obstacles is a huge diplomatic challenge with political overtones. Political skills have been in short supply, and increasingly not even the rhetoric can hide the failure and the disappearing vision.

Is the Westminster System under Stress?

Political systems are undergoing stress, as the economic forces for integration outstrip their capacity to make the requisite political adjustments. Consequently, they are likely to endure only insofar as they are able to adapt. There is the fear that building the requisite regional institutions for addressing regional problems will result in a loss of national identity and sovereignty.

Anthony Payne notes that the emergent forms of politics in the post-independence Commonwealth Caribbean have been shaped by the historical legacy of British colonialism, that this inherited political order has been adapted to Caribbean conditions in a creative and distinctive way, and that the resulting system, which can be described as democratic, offers the region a workable, although far from flawless, basis on which to defend its political practice into the 1990s and beyond.[22]

Despite the dominance of the Westminster model, however, Arend Lijphart questions which form of democracy is the most suitable for countries like Grenada and others in the Eastern Caribbean area. His answer is that the consensus model of democracy – characterized by such features as power sharing, proportional representation, multi-partyism, and federalism – should be given serious consideration as the major alternative to the Westminster or majoritarian model, because most of the Caribbean countries are plural or deeply divided societies.[23]

According to M.G. Smith, "it is perfectly clear that in any social system based on intense cleavages and discontinuity between differentiated segments, the commitment of values or social relations between those sections will be correspondingly low."[24] He argues that a plural society is one in which sharp differences of culture, status, social organization, and often race characterize the different population categories that comprise it. Smith's definition is roughly similar to Lijphart's, that plural societies are ones "that are sharply divided along religious, ideological, linguistic, cultural, ethnic, or racial lines into virtually separate sub-societies with their own political parties, interest groups, and media of communication." In Lijphart's view, because the Caribbean states tend to be deeply divided societies, the consensus model of democracy appears more suitable for them than the majoritarian model. Consensus democracy can almost be said to have been especially designed to manage the tensions inherent in such societies.[25]

The Challenges of Regional Security[26]

"Security" is a highly contested concept with a variety of definitions and usage. However, it is generally considered as part of a country's "high politics." As some experts believe, non-military developments can pose genuine threats to long-term security and quality of life. Traditional concepts of sovereignty cannot cope with significant transborder flows of narcotics, money, AIDS, arms, and immigrants. However, no country can combat these threats alone, and new regional and international rules and institutions will be needed to cope with the non-military threats facing most nations. Moreover, not only are states no longer the only critical actors in the international arena, but non-state actors abound, and some of them wield considerable power, often more than states.

There are three structural and operational features of the still-transforming global environment with direct implications for the region:

- the changed structure of military and political power
- alterations in economic relationships
- policy reprioritization

As Jorge Dominguez rightly observed, the Caribbean now has lesser military importance in world affairs.[27] However, the end of the Cold War does not negate the strategic value of the Caribbean. The region's strategic significance is reflected in economic, geographic, and communications attributes that have transcended East-West geopolitics. Also, the Caribbean is of strategic importance not only to states but also to non-state actors, notably drug barons.

As the relevance of military threats and alliances declines, geo-economic priorities are becoming increasingly important in state actions as countries seek new alignments to advance economic prospects. The transition to a new world economy is already marked by conflict, and the accompanying uncertainties will pose major challenges for the region. The mega bloc phenomenon with its multiple implications occurs at a particularly unpropitious time for the region, given the significant impact of the global and regional turbulence, which includes depressed banana, bauxite, and sugar production, high public debt, and high unemployment.

The military-political changes caused by the end of the Cold War have had tremendous causal and consequential links to the third general feature of the new strategic environment that is critical to the Caribbean: policy reprioritization. Reprioritization by these countries is the result of several factors. These include budgetary constraints, economic recession, shifting foreign policy focus, the demand by domestic constituents for more attention to domestic concerns, and leadership changes that may cause policy revaluation. In tangible terms, this has meant reduced aid, aid relocation, preferential trade readjustment, reduced foreign investment guarantees, and diplomatic downgrading of some Caribbean countries.

The Caribbean as a "Buffer Zone" in Diplomacy

The Caribbean must work within the realities of the new global economy, and a policy environment must arise to provide a development buffer zone, as we strive to emerge on a higher international platform. In this context, the establishment of the Association of Caribbean States can be seen, not as an integration process per se, but as an attempt to strengthen the region's negotiating position in international diplomacy. This poses an opportunity for the Caribbean to move away from its traditional posture of protest diplomacy towards a more affirmative stance, in which vital interests are identified and promoted in anticipation of changing balances in world politics.

These ideas lend credence to the notion that a non-sovereign "regional state" – one that could exhibit the same sort of cooperation in world affairs that the Scandinavian countries often demonstrate, and perhaps move towards regional cooperation on economic policy matters, the funding policies of international financial organizations, and cooperation within the United Nations and other multilateral organizations – may well be more appropriate to the conduct of international relations than the nation state.

Towards a Multitrack Trade Policy

The term "globalization," popularly used in the 1980s, really reflects the investment surge of that decade. During 1985 to 1990, global investment averaged nearly 30 per cent per year, four times the rate of world output and three times the rate of trade. Most of this investment was in capital- and technology-intensive sectors. Technology flows between the first and second half of the 1980s increased from a negative growth rate of 0.1 to 22 per cent.

These outflows reflect underlying structural forces as the revolution in information and communications technology altered the production function of firms and industries on an economy-wide basis. The investment surge, fueled by technology flows, had a profound effect on the structure of world output and trade. At the same time, the movement towards new trading pacts accelerated.

US trade policy, long rooted in the strong advocacy of multilateralism and the GATT, shifted to a multifaceted trade policy: multilateralism, regionalism, bilateralism, and unilateralism. US trade policy continued to emphasize the need for a multilateral trading system, eventually leading to the establishment of the World Trade Organization.

At the same time, track two of US policy pursued further relations through regional arrangements like NAFTA and FTAA as well as bilateral ones like the arrangements concluded with Israel as well as the Caribbean Basin Initiative. The third track, based on a unilateral focus on Section 301 of the US Trade Act of 1974, and the special 301 provisions in 1989, became a dominant aspect of the "trade politics" between the United States and Japan.

At the December 1994 Summit of the Americas in Miami, Florida, the democratic countries of the Western hemisphere announced their intention to form a hemispheric free trade area to be known as the Free Trade Area of the Americas (FTAA). In particular, they committed to (1) begin immediately to eliminate barriers to trade and investment; (2) conclude the negotiations no later than 2005; and (3) make concrete progress towards the attainment of this objective by the end of this century.

In the absence of a single path to the FTAA, many alternative strategies are evolving simultaneously. Existing trade arrangements and the proliferations of new initiatives may either hinder or contribute to the eventual creation of the FTAA.

Existing bilateral agreements seek both to liberalize and to facilitate trade. The proliferation of such agreements, however, has created a confusing array of rules of origin and regulation. This overlapping of agreements is more likely to hinder trade than to promote it. The simplification that is expected to result from a single FTAA would be a significant benefit.

Substantial economic liberalization has been achieved in the majority of countries in Latin America and the Caribbean, although the state of preparedness to participate in and benefit from the FTAA varies widely. However, as Richard Bernal notes:

> By the early 1990s, a new "Latin American consensus" had emerged, based on competitive markets, macroeconomic stability through reduction of public sector deficits, opening of the external sector to foreign

competition, and reducing the role of the state by privatization and deregulation. The extent of trade liberalization reflects a variety of structural economic features, policy orientations and political perspectives. Further complications arise from limited and tentative political support for economic reform and liberalization, partly due to the fact these policies were prompted by the frustration with import-substitution and protectionism during the 1980s. The circumstances in which the more complex stages of liberalization must be implemented are made difficult by more unequal distribution of income and increased incidence of poverty that have accompanied economic reform and liberalization. The recent experiences of Venezuela and Mexico reveal the fragility of the process.[28]

Whether the Latin American and Caribbean countries are able to take advantage of access to the larger hemispheric market or to larger regional groupings to expand exports will depend on both government policies and the private sector's readiness and ability to compete effectively. Even where an economy has comparative advantage, it can be offset by the lack of a competitive advantage. Economic reform, liberalization, and adjustment are necessary preconditions for participation in the FTAA. Trade liberalization, on the other hand, is a necessary but not sufficient condition. Governments must of necessity address the economic, social, and political difficulties of adjustment if the goal of hemispheric free trade is to be realized.

The Bridgetown Declaration–US Caribbean Summit

The Bridgetown Declaration, an agreement signed in Barbados on 1 May 1997 between the United States and fifteen Caribbean countries, was an attempt to strengthen cooperation in responding to challenges of the coming millennium. The Declaration recognizes the important link between trade, economic development, security, and prosperity in countries of the region. It therefore aims to improve the economic well-being and security of all citizens, to defend and strengthen democratic institutions, and to provide for social justice and stability.

As the Declaration notes:

As we enter a new century marked by rapid expansion and globalization of finance and investment, production and commerce, driven by revolutionary developments in technology, we acknowledge the need for a new era in our partnership. We note the increasing role of the human, technological and communication capacities required for operating in this new competitive international environment and the current reality in most Caribbean States and to accept the need for systematic, cooperative initiatives to strengthen the quality of their human resources and technological capacity.

Some of the key provisions of the Bridgetown Declaration can be categorized under institutional and policy support (see Box 1.1) and resources to the Caribbean (see Box 1.2).

Box 1.1: Institutional and Policy Support

The Caribbean region shares the common goal of achieving stable, sustainable economic development and widespread prosperity for all citizens in the region. To this end, the declaration affirms the region's strong commitment to

- internationally recognized labour standards and worker rights, especially freedom of association and collective bargaining;
- the empowerment of women to permit their participation in the political and economic spheres, through fair access to education, health care and credit while recognizing that addressing and preventing violence against women is an important step towards the goal of strengthening democracy;
- finding, at the earliest opportunity, a mechanism to facilitate rapid consultations on trade related issues;
- endorsing the recommendations of the Working Group on Smaller Economies to provide opportunities to facilitate the participation of the smaller economies during the negotiations and their effective integration in the FTAA, to make every effort to reduce the transnational costs and minimize dislocation to their economies during their implementation;
- encouraging the smaller economies in the Caribbean to consider the early implementation, to the extent possible, of internal adjustments which will enhance their ability to participate effectively in the FTAA; and
- finding institutional mechanisms, including Trade missions, to encourage dialogue between the Caribbean and U.S. private sectors.

Box 1.2: Resource Flows

The region welcomes the continuing commitment of the United States to assist Caribbean nations in their economic reforms by

- seeking to support measures, including technical assistance, in support of programs that promote internal structural adjustment;
- providing technical assistance to Caribbean countries to support their economic diversification and in particular, to assist the OECS countries in pooling their resources in order to enhance the competitiveness of their products;
- facilitating the Caribbean's implementation of its Uruguay Round commitments. In so doing, the United States will initiate a three-year grant agreement with Caribbean countries to provide technical assistance for trade liberalization and labour relations;
- the need for technical assistance to strengthen Caribbean human, institutional and infrastructural development necessary to assist in the adjustment process and to enable them to participate meaningfully. In this regard, we urge Caribbean countries to analyse their particular circumstances and identify their specific technical assistance needs;
- exploring ways by which current bilateral and multilateral debt management programs can support adjustment efforts in highly indebted countries; and
- joining in the call to the IDB to meet its eighth replenishment, to target 35 per cent of Bank lending to smaller economies, including those in the Caribbean.

With respect to trade matters, the Bridgetown Declaration pledges to enhance the Caribbean–US trade relationship by working jointly towards the further reduction of trade barriers between the United States and the Caribbean countries and endeavouring to refrain from introducing new import restrictions, consistent with WTO rules. There has been a shift in US trade policy, which now focuses less on Caribbean membership than on building transition space through the CBI parity mechanism prior to the eventual establishment of FTAA. Many Caribbean countries that therefore had hopes of membership in NAFTA should remove that from their agenda based on the summit declaration. US interests will dominate over the Caribbean's interests outside the United States.

With respect to resource flows, the communiqué calls for an increase in technical cooperation and for the Inter-American Development Bank to honour its eighth replenishment commitment to channel more funds to smaller economies, including the Caribbean. In this respect, the summit did not provide the confidence that there will be additional resource flows to the region. It merely underlines the existing resource situation, with the promise of some technical assistance. The Bridgetown Declaration would not alter in any fundamental way the economic relations between the Caribbean and the United States; instead it opts for incremental change that will come about at the current pace of movement.

Green Paper on Relations between EU and ACP Countries[29]

In November 1996, the European Commission issued a long-awaited "Green Paper on Relations between the European Union and the ACP [African, Caribbean, and Pacific] Countries on the Eve of the Twenty-First Century: Challenges and Options for a New Partnership."[30] The commission presented its green paper as a "discussion tool" whose aim is "to provide food for thought, trigger wide-ranging debate and pave the way for dialogue between those concerned by the expiry of the Lomé Convention. It does not frame any formal proposals and the options put forward in no way predetermine the proposals that the Commission may table in due course."

According to George Huggins, the core of the European Union's position and the basis of the policy, and hence of negotiations, appears to revolve around a number of tenets derived both from the main trends of political globalization and from the experience of Europe itself. These include the following:

- an expanded role for the private sector vis-a-vis that of the state, with the state acting as a catalyst for development and the private sector taking leadership for development;
- institutional reform for improved public-sector management and progress in private-sector-led growth among a clear line of democratic participation as a precondition for earning partnership;
- transparency and efficiency in the use of resources by ACP countries: both to ensure accountability to the European donor public and to promote development discipline; and
- a shift towards a duality, at least, and certainly a stratification of ACP members: those likely to make it into the inner ranks of partnership through reforms and successful private promotion and

those that have severe difficulties in doing so. The EU proposes for the later a heavy helping hand, assuming direct responsibility for carrying them along.

The first area of cooperation, the social and economic dimension, has two intertwined aspects: economic development and poverty alleviation. The main vehicle for economic development has been identified as the private sector. Indeed, a persistent reality of many ACP countries is the relatively low state of development of their private sector. However, private-sector-led development may not be sufficient to bring about social redistribution and may therefore inhibit the quest for equality in development.

The second area of cooperation, the institutional and public-sector dimension, is an essential element for the development of the ACP countries and regional organizations. This area of cooperation should be the first priority, as it conditions both the development of ACP countries and the efficiency of aid. However, it is how the institutional reform is carried out that will determine its success.

According to independent comments on the Green Paper of the European Commission on Partnership 2000,[31] three broad areas of recognition may be called for:

- the political will for sustainable development, with particular reference to the profound internal cultural, social, institutional, and policy issues and with all the implications for internal restructuring and external space of the entire society;
- sustained moral, political, financial, and other forms of support for the long process of poverty reduction, with equal access by all sectors to resources and services; and
- a genuinely open democratic context of cooperation and participation.

The ACP response to these measures remains somewhat blurred. One of the key issues emerging in the deal so far is whether the ACP should be kept as a combined forum or should be broken down to its constituents: pan-African, Caribbean, and Pacific. Caribbean countries appear to support the continuation of the ACP forum, but are yet to work towards common cooperation goals that need to be achieved on a wider global basis. A second issue facing this debate is the continuation of the preference arrangements and its compatibility with the new world trading discipline reflected in the WTO. Recent decisions of the WTO in support of the argument against Caribbean bananas are an adequate illustration of this incipient conflict.

Other issues that emerged in this debate relate to the question of political conditionalities working through issues such as human rights, environment, and labour standards. When the Lomé Protocol was established, the signatories of the protocol derived their motivation from the need to establish an equal union between the European and ACP countries. Now, it would appear that the continuation of these protocols is predicated on a combined European foreign policy towards the Caribbean, Africa, and the Pacific countries. In this sense, the new arrangements are more likely to be fitted to a European vision of its global presence than they are to add new life to an old partnership, notwithstanding the green paper's call for a new partnership in the "Global 2000."

Changing Roles in a Changing World

Today, as trade matters in the Caribbean are faced with a built-in agenda, the region has to identify its vital economic interests in the various concentric circles surrounding it. Apart from the WTO, FTAA, EU-ACP trade relations, the Caribbean has to contend with the Latin American options, including Mercosur and, more recently, the Association of Caribbean States (ACS). The ACS, with a clear mandate of increasing trade and investment among its members, has not been able to get an emerging consensus on how. CARICOM's call for a free-trade area in the ACS is still some distance away from the expectation of other ACS members, adding new concentric circles as CARICOM attempts to expand its geographical base. The waters are indeed murky. The question that must be brought to the fore at all times is whether the waves echo the past or signal a future.

These changing roles have led the region into a "stand-alone" position. Alan Henrikson speaks of Clinton's Caribbean policy as "altering in nature but not in depth"; this is what President Clinton told Caribbean leaders at a meeting at the White House. President Castro's quick response to his exclusion from the Miami Summit was: "we are not going to negotiate the normalization of our relations on the basis of concessions." Henrikson encapsulates the issue: "without Cuba, the Caribbean cannot be regionally integrated … yet with Cuba still under Fidel Castro's leadership, the Caribbean countries cannot acceptably negotiate as a region with the United States.[32] The Caribbean's diplomatic charge is to resist "protest diplomacy" and adopt a more affirmative foreign policy stand where vital interests are negotiated in the world councils.

Clearly, in this changing world there are changing roles. Development financing institutions are also being challenged to a changing role.

Is development banking in the Caribbean sensitive to the agonizing choices and anguishing changes that are being advocated for Caribbean development? I raise the question with great temerity, but also with an instinct that this question may soon arise. Already, development banks are being forced into the commercial arena in national economies. Central bankers are facing new challenges in the era of floating exchange rates, a possible return to currency boards, and the emergence of digital currency. In the post-liberalization world, commercial banks have begun to restructure as changes in the financial markets are the result of global practices. Long-term development finance is likely to be more accessible in the international private capital market.

The debate on "conditionalities" has now shifted from the broad economic platform to micromanagement and political concerns through the search for good governance. The effectiveness of development finance is now being questioned, particularly as the gap between delivery and expectations widens. The growing gap in the Caribbean between expectations and performance, and the rising tension between intention and reality, have widened the space between the art of politics and the discharge of governance. This is the politics of illusion, where yesterday's hopes remain unfulfilled, and new hopes emerge with little expectation that they will be realized.

Poverty and social capital concerns and the working of the political system are now at the top of the political economy agenda in today's Caribbean. So too is the choice of international road maps. Caribbean economist Anthony Gonzales has stated that a free trade area between the European Union and the Caribbean "may be a superior instrument to most favoured nation treatment (MFN), Generalized System of Preferences (GSP) and the Lomé Convention." In addition, he argues for "a common Caribbean external trade policy towards the EU that takes into account the needs of the region in the future as well as the evolving trends in the EU, the Western Hemisphere and internationally."[33] At around the same time Trinidad and Tobago's then-foreign minister announced his government's intention to remain a part of MERCOSUR while maintaining its berth in NAFTA.

CARICOM, although it may have reached its limits and, in economic terms, "come to a dead-end," may be widened beyond Suriname to include the Dominican Republic and Haiti. The ACS, like a "medicine in search of a disease," is looking for its own platform; the process for the construction of the Free Trade Area of the Americas has commenced. There are now many road maps, and although these are still in outline stages, they may inspire the mapping of possible blueprints. The growing divergence between our political and economic boundaries must be addressed, for groups of nations rather than the nation state will now be the main actors in the conduct of international politics. The stage is perhaps set for the emergence of a different notion of the regional state as a vehicle for creating political and negotiating space in the international arena. Perhaps, Keohane's distinction between "operational" and "formal" sovereignty may now be incorporated in the new theoretical construct for institutional behaviour in the Caribbean region. A clear political statement that is credible and effective may now be required so as to place the region's agenda in the global dialogue. It is in this context that we may look at a different notion of the regional state as the vehicle to achieve this goal.

In the post–Cold War era, the geostrategic role of the Caribbean has now been reduced and US interest in the region is based on specific concerns that fit into the US domestic political agenda. A recent Canadian foreign policy review has placed the Caribbean in a Latin American framework, and gone is the term "special relationship," which at one time was used to describe the (British) Caribbean-Canada links. With the formation of the single market in Europe, as well as the enlargement of EU membership to include near and far Europe, and the strategic importance of the Mediterranean countries to the European Union, the Caribbean now has a lower priority in the European foreign policy agenda. The link between the English-speaking countries of the Caribbean and the Commonwealth of Nations is now much weaker, as common interests now diverge.

Today, the agenda before us has widened considerably, covering the old issues of democracy, development, and integration but at the same time responding to the new issues of sustainable development, good governance, and a new integration paradigm for the region. Perhaps now more than before our resilience is being tested, and the sense of our own Caribbean identity is quickly changing. Our response must therefore be to build an enduring commitment to confidence in the Caribbean future that will at the same time retain a sense of Caribbean nationhood.

2 Caribbean Policy Analysis: Shaping the Issues*

The Caribbean is a complex, even enigmatic region, characterized by great disparities in size, population, geography, history, language, religion, race, and politics. Notwithstanding these important differences, the economic parameters of the countries in the region are largely symmetrical: they are primarily small economies with narrow resource bases and high trade-to-output ratios, whose GDP is largely related to the export of primary resource and agricultural commodities. Despite persistent efforts, most Caribbean nations still depend on preferential export markets, among other factors. Compared with other developing countries, the standard of living is relatively high, though this is due more to periodic windfalls and protected markets than to the region's productivity or international competitiveness.

The platforms defining Caribbean economic and political space over the last forty years include the triangular trade of the pre-independence period, the era of multinational corporations and US hegemony, and the more recent IMF-World Bank structural adjustment programs. Out of this framework came theories of exploitation, neocolonialism, and marginalization and the export of protest diplomacy. There followed heavy moral and political overtures for protection, special consideration, aid, trade, and investment support from the developed world. Given their history of colonialism, the mandates of nation-building, and conditions at the time of independence, Caribbean nations pursued inward paths towards development that included a high degree of state involvement in the economy.

---

* The text in this chapter was adapted from Winston Dookeran, "Crosscurrents in Caribbean Policy Analysis," in *Choices and Change: Reflections on the Caribbean*, edited by Winston Dookeran, 1–13 (Washington, DC: Inter-American Development Bank, 1996).

This approach may have been feasible in the 1960s and 1970s, given the state of thought about development and the geopolitical structure of the world economy in that period, but it is no longer sustainable. For decades, the plantation economy of the hinterland has adjusted only to a persistent low-level equilibrium, resulting in lower incomes. Although the region's resource-based industries were integrated into the global economy, this resulted in economic enclaves within the domestic economy, without sufficient development benefits. Caribbean countries remain highly sensitive to exogenous forces, such as shocks, exchange-rate manipulation, and crises, all of which can adversely affect their critical foreign exchange, their largely export-derived public revenues, and their competitiveness.

The liberalization of the global economic system and other conditions are now eroding the preferential terms of trade on which the Caribbean standard of living is built. Faced with adverse terms of trade, the need for technological advancement, stresses in the political system, and changing political and economic ties with the rest of the world, the Caribbean is confronting its most severe challenges since many of its nations became independent a generation ago.

Political and Economic Imperatives

The premise of any future economic strategy for the Caribbean must be the creation of a dynamic export sector that is sustainable without trade preferences. While push-started by negotiated treaties, this sustainability must be founded on market forces. Yet what meaningful steps have been taken to address this crisis and to create a new generation of exports? How will these new exports relate to the region's domestic capacity, to the unit cost of production, and to technology requirements, and how will this transformation be financed? How will the region respond to the worldwide liberalization of financial markets, so as not to place its entire foreign exchange in jeopardy?[1] What new policy framework will meet the looming crisis faced by the region's smaller islands in particular, many of which are almost totally dependent on the exchange they receive from their sugar, bananas, citrus, cocoa, and coffee? Furthermore, are the steps now being taken sufficient to lauch the economy into an integrated world economy, so that it can gain a more equitable share of world commerce?

For these questions there have been only partial answers. Despite a great deal of rhetoric and debate, the region has not yet found ways to change its industrial structure, so that transnational Caribbean enterprises can perform on a more competitive basis in the world economy. Over time, the Caribbean economy has declined in productivity, negatively affecting their competitive position in the world economy. At the same time the population's expectations of benefiting from the results of development have increased enormously. This dichotomy has now opened up a creative space for the interplay of the art of politics and the discharge of governance. It sets the stage for a growing gap between economic performance and the aspirations of the electorate on the platform and calls into question the non-realization of social goals in the development paradigm.[2]

In the face of seriously deteriorating conditions and the abandonment of many social goals, the sense that the Caribbean is not preparing for the future is a deep source of anguish for its people. Not only has this resulted in a deep disillusionment with institutions and politicians, but the role of the state and its ability to govern have come into question.

The Caribbean must determine its capacity for entering the mainstream of income-generating activities and reposition itself in world markets by expanding the range of its economy. Accomplishing this task will require new theoretical models to address the practical issues of policy, implementation, and international relations; outward-looking – and forward-looking – strategies to design paradigms for development; new approaches to the region's persistent problems; and a plan for integration based on contemporary realities that will increase the region's political space.[3]

To be effective, any new integration paradigm for the Caribbean must go beyond matters of trade and respond to the international situation. This paradigm should link productive structures, promote interaction between the private sectors of different countries, and create technological advances that will reduce the costs of doing business, increase institutional flexibility, and promote social capital among the peoples of the region. The alternative is further economic marginalization and political peripheralization. But what the specific targets and methods will be, and how development will be secured by new integration paradigms, remain uncertain.

Sovereignty and Regionalism

The quest for a regional state in the Caribbean has been an underlying theme of attempts at integration and the search for economic space. At the core, the issue of sovereignty emerges as a major hurdle, both within the region and regarding the region's strategic value to the major powers in world politics. The early collapse of the West Indian Federation was partly a reflection of nationalist sentiments and tensions in sharing power in newly independent nations. Knight and Persaud argue that a basic principle in the reconstruction of social order in a community is the devolution of power and authority, where "devolution ... also means a sharing or, perhaps more accurately, a diffusion of power, as well as a distribution of the burdens of governance."[4] They maintain that the Caribbean will benefit from a regional governance structure through a subsidiarity framework that embodies the core elements of inclusiveness, transparency, burden sharing, recursivity (democratic participation), and a regional security regime.

Caribbean sovereignty in an interconnected world was the subject of a major publication[5] in which the paradox of functional sovereignty was raised in the context of international cooperation and coordination of global policies that affect countries in the region. The Association of Caribbean States was set up partly to further this goal, but also to expand the diplomatic space for the region in the conduct of diplomacy. Adaptability has become the key attribute in the global practice of diplomacy for countries in the Caribbean. Galbraith's "new dialectics"[6] – the view that political systems undergoing stress may not be able to make the necessary adjustments to cope with the forces in the integration process – will test the endurance of regional models of integration.

Regionalism, apart from trade creation and diversion processes, also places stress on issues of national identity and the workings of the models of sovereignty. In the first round of regionalism, the lowering of trade barriers worldwide extended the new integrationist agenda far beyond matters of security, trade, and markets, towards convergence on such matters as common regulatory systems, environmental and labour standards, and reform of institutions. This leads to a type of interdependency that creates a change in the financial geography; with cross-border trading and capital flows, it becomes increasingly difficult to separate international banks from domestic ones. Furthermore, the removal of capital flows in many countries has encouraged financial integration, global safety nets for international trading, external policy coordination, and common fiscal and monetary policies.

The second point to consider is that regionalism need not be a stumbling block towards a multilateral trading system. The European Community, for instance, furthered the GATT negotiations, and it may very well be that the Western hemispheric, European, and Asian trading blocs will be better able to carry out negotiations leading to global free trade than the 120-odd nations that are signatories under the GATT.[7] The danger, of course, is that this will not happen and that, by turning inward, they will fracture the global system. Regardless of the outcome, however, governments and other actors can no longer define their interests primarily in terms of their geopolitical boundaries, but must increasingly do so in regional and even global terms.

Regional integration is a necessary step for solving the Caribbean's problems, but its countries resist taking the next step, that of building institutional and private-sector linkages. The goal has been to reduce tariffs and to maximize internal trade – but without establishing external linkages that would increase the Caribbean's international and regional trade. The result has been integration with no convergence, whose premises are outdated, and institutions that may be efficient, but in terms of achieving the real goals of integration are certainly ineffective. This is due, at least in part, to the region's insularity: divisiveness remains a prominent, even an institutionalized feature of the domestic political scene. The cultural basis for a new integration process must address matters of Caribbean identity and social capital, so that the process will be more durable and be premised on the integration of peoples, not just policies. In this, integration should also be less anxious about trade, investment, and the creation of human and physical capital, and place greater emphasis on what Robert Putnam terms "social capital," a vital ingredient in the mix for economic development.[8]

This psychology also extends to the construct of sovereignty in the context of the region's nations that are still engaged in the task of nation-building. Sovereignty is often confused with notions of size and unilateralism, but its essence – the capacity to make effective, intelligent, and timely decisions that promote a nation's welfare and autonomy – is altogether different.

In Keohane's analysis, sovereignty is twofold: formal and operational. In terms of formal sovereignty, "a state has a legal supremacy over all other authorities within a given territory, and is legally independent ... except where it has accepted obligations under international law."[9] In this, all legally recognized states, regardless of size, are "egaux en droit."[10] Nations sacrifice some operational sovereignty, or "legal freedom of action,"[11] when they enter into international agreements, but they do so in return for reciprocal limits on other states.

In practice, such agreements must be able increase economic well-being at home and at the same time meet the external obligations required to satisfy global/regional common interest. When delicately done, they need not limit the state's power, but rather expand the reach of the state in inserting the national economy into a wider economic space. In our digital age, this shift from territorial to functional sovereignty will accelerate quickly, to allow digital competition to flourish while protecting the benefits to citizens and the values of the society. This challenge is already creating tensions among nations, and small nations will increasingly look to the multilateral process as a safeguard of its interest.

Building Negotiating Space

Historically, the US attitude towards the Caribbean has been conditioned by the geopolitical significance of the region's proximity, and this is still true, despite the end of the Cold War. The regional agenda has decisively widened, however, and there is now a convergence of interests on such issues as drug trafficking, money laundering, immigration, the management of common resources, environmental degradation, and the strengthening of democracy. The Caribbean must seek to establish a new relationship with Washington in the light of these circumstances, and since resources and attention have shifted from the region, it will be taken seriously only if it negotiates as a unified entity.

Furthermore, if the Caribbean is to strengthen its negotiating position at a time when both the United States and the European Union are preoccupied with matters unrelated to Caribbean development, it must speak with a greater voice. The Caribbean and its neighbours in South and Central America need to work together in greater harmony, if not always in total agreement. Regionalism is an inescapable feature of the landscape, and the asymmetrical integration of the Caribbean nations with its larger neighbours does not, as many fear, present a bona fide threat to Caribbean identity. On the contrary, it will enable the Caribbean to distinguish what is uniquely its own, while at the same time facilitating the emergence of a trans-Caribbean identity that encompasses the Caribbean littoral.

The Association of Caribbean States, created soon after the West Indian Commission report had recommended that CARICOM achieve greater cooperation and economic integration within the Caribbean Basin, was an effort to respond to global conditions.[12] But without an explicit agenda or clearly identified targets, the precise function of ACS is unclear, and it is in danger of becoming an expansion of outdated and ineffective structures that cannot deal with the present crisis.[13]

Is There Scope for a "Non-sovereign" Regional State?

The best model that the Caribbean can consider at this juncture is a form of open regionalism, which encompasses a number of the above issues and trends.[14] In a time of great uncertainty regarding the eventual outcome of the multilateral and minilateral trading systems, open regionalism encourages nations to form sub-regional trading blocs in ways that facilitate linkages with others, thus synthesizing the globalization and regionalization trends. While an open regionalism includes some preferential elements, import barriers are low and it allows for the open-ended participation of its members in other trade agreements and regional schemes, so that these various groupings will function as building blocks towards global accords and an open and more transparent international economy.

The first round of regionalism led to a form of integration that widened the production base, erected trade fortresses, and began to build on policy convergences. This cycle is now over, and the integration process being pursued by CARICOM, despite the recent inclusion of Suriname, is in need of a different design. The current round of regionalism, however, which combines the integration of production with open markets, is representative of an intermediate position in a global move towards a more open multilateral trading system.

The hurdles – historical and contemporary – facing a regional state in the Caribbean are huge, which has led to the establishment of surrogate bodies and associations to provide platforms for diplomatic leverage. The Association of Caribbean States is one such creation, providing an expanded platform to include all countries bordering and within the geography of the Caribbean Sea.[15] Shifting from the orthodox protest diplomacy towards a more affirmative stance allows for greater cooperation in building resilience and a stronger voice in world affairs.

The Nordic countries – Denmark, Norway, Sweden, Finland, Greenland, Iceland, and the Aland and Faroe Islands – with strong historical, cultural, and linguistic ties, are the world's oldest regional partnership. The Nordic prime ministers in August 2019 stated that the Nordic region will become the most sustainable and integrated region in the world by 2030.[16] This model of cooperation has been extended in the global stage, in regional cooperation, in the funding policies of international financial institutions, and in cooperation in the United Nations. The actions of the Nordic states dovetail nicely with the notion of a non-sovereign regional state.

Could Structural Adjustment Policies Work?

Since the oil crisis of the 1970s, the path towards development in many of the world's poorer countries has been hindered by deteriorating terms of trade for export commodities and inappropriate development policies. These difficulties culminated in the debt crisis of the 1980s, following which many developing countries had to restructure their economies along the lines of structural adjustment policies. These programs consist of both short- and medium-term measures for improving the overall economic situation by such means as cuts in public spending, contraction of the money supply, changes in import restrictions, devaluation of the currency, and privatization of state enterprises. In general, this new orthodoxy views the market as the major instrument of reform, while the state is seen as the key obstacle to development.[17]

The structural adjustment policy debate in the Caribbean has centred on the sequencing of measures and a time period for these policies to work, when its focus should be on the results on development. After a decade of adjustment, development still remains an elusive goal. This is largely a static model, based on two-dimensional premises that cannot be supported. The neoclassical policy prescriptions for "getting the prices right," such as reducing costs, getting the right technology, flexible exchange rates, and removing price controls and subsidies, are all well and good in themselves, but competition is a complex, dynamic phenomenon in which price is only a single element. Moreover, while strict fiscal and monetary measures may promote stabilization, they will not unleash the internal forces for change that will result in growth; and while the divestiture of state enterprises, for instance, may be necessary to balance the books, unless privatization takes place within a post-structural adjustment framework for development, it will not result in a new platform from which output, income, and well-being can be increased. Furthermore, such a framework must engender the dynamics for endogenous growth, so that the industrial structure of production may be transformed, creating new vehicles for the empowerment of peoples that will yield a high-level equilibrium and momentum for sustainable development.

Similarly, the measures for "getting the state out of the way" ignore the need for an enhanced state role in building meaningful regional institutions that will create and promote an environment of growth. The state is needed to enforce regulations, formulate and implement policy, build international linkages, forge collective public- and private-sector initiatives, and promote human resource development that will bring the disadvantaged into the development process. The world that we now inhabit will likely call for constant economic adjustment; but if the foundations of social life are not to be further eroded, this process must be countered with a "high-energy politics ... capable of repeated basic reform," involving intensified public participation and democracy.[18] Correcting economic accounts regardless of social costs can only destroy any basis for future growth.

The state must be redesigned, but not eliminated. Callaghy points out that "contrary to free-market mythology, the state has always played a central role in economic development ... [and] economic adjustment in the Third World today requires a balanced tension ... between state and market forces."[19] While the international financial institutions are slowly coming around to this view, this is the formula in the developed world: interventionist strategies, such as incentives and subsidies, are at the core of East Asian development. Furthermore, while the structural adjustment process depends on externally propelled growth, these movements are cyclical, as W. Arthur Lewis has pointed out, and there is nothing inevitable about the process.[20]

The Quest for Justice

At the core of political economy are the prospects of economic growth, the concentration of wealth, and the forces that generate inequality. Thomas Piketty examined these issues in an extraordinary and original work that argues that while modern economic growth has avoided inequalities of an apocalyptic scale, we have not modified the deep structures of capital and inequality that today threaten "to generate extreme inequalities that stir discontent and undermine democratic values."[21]

In the Caribbean setting, the data in other chapters of this book may add validity to this broad assertion. The demand for equality and justice is a legitimate matter of public policy, which has often been expressed as the alleviation of poverty. Of particular interest here is Amartya Sen's conceptualization of development – and thereby the alleviation of poverty – as an expansion of freedom. S.R. Osmani has commented, "Sen defines poverty in the space of capabilities – a person is said to be poor when the resources available to her do not permit her to achieve minimally acceptable levels of some basic capabilities."[22]

In political economy terms, Piketty's "undermining democratic values" and Sen's notion that "development is freedom" mesh under the rubric of "justice." The fight for democracy has historically been viewed as a battle for justice, and it is freedom that permits societies to pursue the cause of justice. Amartya Sen, speaking on the theme of "identity and justice," had this to say: "the world in which we live contains very many different groups of people, whose identities differ, and whose interactions with each other influence the way they think about themselves and about others. Furthermore, each person frequently has various distinct identities connected with the diversity of the groups to which that individual may belong. And it is these complexities from which the foundational ideas of justice are often abstracted."[23] Linking the reach of the idea of identity to the demands of social justice is one such complexity.

In the discourse on political economy in Caribbean societies, and in the practice of politics, the cause of social justice is central, and is permeated with the recurring quest for human justice. In Box 2.1, I provide a public statement that reflects that aspiration.

Box 2.1: Constitutional Justice – Human Justice in Our Land

What "human justice" can do is solve, or attempt to solve, concrete problems of individual and societal life: to enact and enforce norms, to create institutions, to design processes, all with that one goal in mind – to solve actual problems. But human problems continuously change, and so do norms, processes, and institutions. Human justice is changing justice – whether or not there is, at a final point, an all-encompassing permanence, an Absolute which gives pause, and meaning, and light to all this moving and striving and passing which is human life. I am honored to join you today in paying a tribute of respect and gratitude to Pope John XXIII.[24]

Thus the eminent scholar Mauro Cappelletti opened his contribution on legal justice and the pursuit of political freedom. In this defining article, Cappelletti listed among "the challenging life-problems of our epoch" the problems of human freedom and dignity. The solutions to these problems should "unite all men of goodwill, whatever their race, nationality, and faith … and give us a basis for designing a philosophy of life for individuals and nations of our epoch."

The anguish and the outrage that erupted in my homeland in the aftermath of the brutal murder of Andrea Bharatt, so soon after another equally heinous murder of Ashanti Riley, two of our young women, has left our society naked, shaken to the core, and exposed to "whatever-it-takes" solutions to regain human freedom and dignity. Leaders have been left speechless, and those whose duty it is to uphold the constitutional order of the country are clearly stunned, and confused. Adhering to the norms of the justice process cannot explain the outcome of that process, and it would be a colossal abdication of public responsibility to simply move on until the next episode occurs.

We must use these tragedies as a basis for adhering to a philosophy of life for individuals in which public value and private action mesh in a community spiritual accord. As such, constitutional justice, not only in terms of politics but also morality – must be placed at the forefront of our undertakings. Human justice must be at the center of all measures to solve concrete problems. The law, and effecting it, have a morality of its own, and it is now an obstacle in the pursuit of human freedom and dignity. Leaders in high places are missing a genuine sense of compassion, institutions are conflicted between procedures and purpose, and society is unable to distinguish between outrage and outcome. Individuals are in perpetual anguish, and according to a psychological analyst, the collective state of mind is one of despair.

Now, men of goodwill must rise in a form of inspiration, to embrace "an all-encompassing permanence, an Absolute, which gives pause, and meaning, and light to all this moving and striving and passing, which is human life," so aptly put by Professor Cappelletti, and so fitting and timely to the challenge today of human justice in our land.

Human justice is enmeshed in the study of political economy in the Caribbean civilization. A society is largely defined by citizens who possess a common notion of their identity and a common loyalty to shared ideals. As we move into the next millennium, Caribbean society must create a sense of civic identity, anchored in its desire for human justice, where people feel free to express themselves, speak their own languages, practice their cultural traditions, and transmit these to their children, as they embrace, at the same time, common goals with the larger society.

Source: Statement by Winston Dookeran, 14 February 2021.

3 Caribbean Catalogue: Recasting the Strategies[*]

As we enter the twenty-first century, it seems an appropriate point for Caribbean countries[1] to reflect on their past performance, not only to assess their economic successes and failures, but more importantly to use these to assess their future prospects and to address some of the important challenges that lie ahead. Introspection of this kind is difficult at the best of times, but often necessary. It requires a level of maturity to acknowledge past mistakes and to summon the strength, courage, and determination to put matters right. On the basis of a rigorous assessment of the lessons of the immediate past and the distinctive prospects and challenges of the future, we in the Caribbean must also be prepared to construct a dynamic leading to a fresh approach that could improve the living condition of the peoples of this region.

This chapter provides a public arena in which we can assess the past and look forward to the future with realistic answers to the global challenges with which the Caribbean community is faced. Today, I want to share with you my thoughts on some of these challenges for both the English- and non-English-speaking countries that are seeking to secure for themselves a level of growth and development within an increasingly competitive global economy. I cannot, within one chapter, comprehensively examine all the important issues, but will attempt to focus the discussion on a core set of issues that I believe will have a significant bearing on the economic fortunes of the Caribbean in the coming years, and to suggest some possible approaches. But first, let me provide some background that will form the context for the rest of my discussion.

---

[*] The text in this chapter was adapted from Winston Dookeran, "The Caribbean: A Catalogue of Open Issues," in *Uncertainty, Stability and Challenges*, 154–70 (San Juan: Central Bank of Trinidad and Tobago/Lexicon Trinidad, 2006).

The countries of the Caribbean do not comprise a homogeneous group in any sense. Indeed, these countries differ significantly in terms of size, resource endowment, economic structure and performance, language, ethnic composition, and culture. Hence, while a broad-based approach may be essential to mitigate some of the developmental challenges facing the region, a successful regional developmental strategy must be tailored to suit each country's particular set of circumstances.

Notwithstanding this, Caribbean countries have many common characteristics. These countries meet most of the criteria that define small states, such as limited size of market, openness, and limited diversity in production, among other things. Most Caribbean countries have also attained a high level of political stability and social development. Although more effort must be directed to encouraging greater participation in the governance process, especially during the years between elections, multiparty democracy has taken root in most of these islands, with elections largely rated as fair and regular.

According to the United Nations Human Development Report 1997, human development indicators for the Caribbean, except Haiti, are reasonably high, falling somewhere between the high and medium human development categories established by the study (see Table 3.1). Adult literacy rates in many of these countries exceed 80 per cent, and although AIDS and some curable diseases present significant health challenges for the region, life expectancy in most of these countries is over seventy years, with the quality of the environment contributing in a significant way to the quality of life.

While most social development indicators are reasonably high, the Caribbean has significant pockets of poverty, varying in severity among countries. Measures of per capita income levels and growth for several Caribbean countries suggest that they have performed fairly well, but for the region as a whole, growth was far below what is needed to reduce poverty. At the regional level, output growth was disappointing in the 1980s and improved only slightly in the 1990s. This performance can be blamed partly on unfavourable commodity prices and instability in the international financial system, but economic mismanagement, delayed and inadequate reforms, and natural disasters have also been important factors. With the weak performance of the last two decades, the unemployment situation has improved only in those countries where tourism and free-trade zones are major employers and where ample amounts of foreign direct investment inflows have occurred.

Table 3.1. Basic social indicators for Caribbean countries

	Poverty, % of population, 1986–98	Life expectancy, years, 1998	Infant mortality per 1,000 births, 1998	Access to clean water, % of population, 1998	Literacy, % of adult population, 1998
Antigua/Barbuda	12	75	17	95	89
Bahamas	5	74	17	94	95
Barbados	1.3	76	14	100	97
Belize	3.3	75	28	83	93
Cuba	n.a.	76	7	93	96
Dominica	28	76	15	92	94
Dominican Republic	21	71	40	73	83
Grenada	31	72	14	85	96
Guyana	43	64	57	83	98
Haiti	65	54	71	39	48
Jamaica	16	75	21	93	86
St. Kitts/Nevis	15	72	21	100	90
St. Lucia	25	70	17	99	82
St. Vincent	38	73	22	99	82
Suriname	39	70	28	89	93
Trinidad and Tobago	21	73	16	96	93

Source: ECLAC, *Reconceptualizing Social Indicators in the Caribbean: A Review and Discussion*. October 2000, https://repositorio.cepal.org/bitstream/handle/11362/27469/1 /LCcarG612_en.pdf.

The fundamental challenge facing Caribbean nations is to create the political, social, and economic conditions conducive to the enhanced well-being of a population that is projected to grow at an average annual rate of 1 per cent, from 34.2 million in 2000 to 41.8 million in 2020. This has to be achieved while coping with a changing international environment, pressures on the fragile physical environment, a high risk of natural disasters, and the disadvantages of small size and underdeveloped physical and institutional infrastructures. Can Caribbean countries successfully confront these challenges? In the following sections I examine four of the significant issues that are likely to weigh heavily on the region's economic fortune. First, however, I provide context via tables 3.1, 3.2, and 3.2 and figure 3.1, which supply a data profile of social indicators for the Caribbean, with updates for Trinidad and Tobago. Updated data on the Human Development Index (HDI) are also given, including a figure depicting trends of the HDI Composite indices 1990–2019 for Trinidad and Tobago.

Table 3.2. Social indicators for Trinidad and Tobago, updated

	2010	2015	2020
Population growth rate (average annual %)	0.5	0.6	0.4
Urban population (% of total population)	54.0	53.3	53.2
Urban population growth rate (average annual %)	0.1	0.2	...
Fertility rate, total (live births per woman)	1.8	1.8	1.7
Life expectancy at birth (females/males, years)	74.2/68.6	75.2/69.8	76.0/70.7
Population age distribution (1–14/60+ years old, %)	20.7/12.4	20.7/14.5	20.1/16.9
International migrant stock (000/% of total population)	48.2/3.6	50.0/3.7	59.2/4.2
Refugees and others of concern to UNHCR (000)	0.1	0.2	43.0
Infant mortality rate (per 1,000 live births)	28.5	26.1	22.0
Health: Current expenditure (% of GDP)	5.1	6.0	7.0
Health: Physicians (per 1,000 population)	1.8	2.6	4.2
Education: Primary gross enrolment ratio (f/m per 100 population)	104.4/108.0	.../...	.../...
Intentional homicide rate (per 100,000 population)	35.6	30.6	...
Seats held by women in national parliaments (%)	26.6	28.6	31.0

Source: UN data, https://data.un.org/en/iso/tt.html.

Table 3.3. Trinidad and Tobago's HDI trends based on consistent time series data and new goal posts

	Life expectancy at birth	Expected years of schooling	Mean years of schooling	GNI per capita (2017 PPP$)	HDI value
1990	68.1	11.2	7.9	10,445	0.668
1995	68.6	11.2	8.5	10,748	0.681
2000	69.4	11.9	9.2	15,565	0.717
2005	70.7	11.4	10.0	23,162	0.748
2010	71.9	12.7	10.8	27,344	0.784
2015	72.9	12.6	10.9	28,744	0.792
2016	73.1	12.8	11.0	26,678	0.792
2017	73.2	13.0	11.0	26,503	0.795
2018	73.4	13.0	11.0	26,328	0.795
2019	73.5	13.0	11.0	26,231	0.796

Source: Briefing Note for Trinidad and Tobago, Human Development Report 2020, 3.

Small States and Global Competition

The Joint Commonwealth Secretariat/World Bank Task Force on Small States recognizes that small states face special challenges and constraints, which hinder the international competitiveness of these

Figure 3.1. Trends in Trinidad and Tobago's HDI component indices, 1990–2019

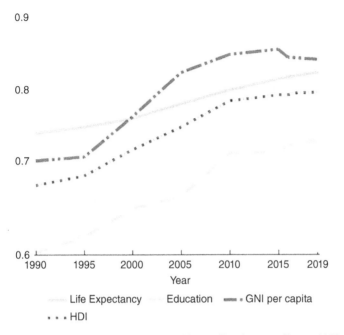

Life Expectancy   Education   GNI per capita
HDI

Source: Briefing Note for Trinidad and Tobago, Human Development Report 2020, 3.

economies. All Caribbean countries fall within this working definition of small states. In recent years, these countries have been attempting to adjust to the new era of rules-based trade regimes under the auspices of the World Trade Organization, where principles of differential and preferential treatment are set to be phased out over time. Not only is this regulatory regime increasingly embracing new sectors of trade – an example of which is trade in financial services – but also Caribbean countries are voiceless in this process and largely unprepared for this new trade environment.

Small states, especially those in the Caribbean, are defined by a range of distinctive vulnerabilities, not only those that relate to their geographical position but also those that relate to the functioning of their economies and that pose special developmental challenges. Such vulnerabilities imply exposure to disruptive external shocks and events against which these countries have little capacity to insulate themselves. The Commonwealth Secretariat/World Bank report rightly notes that small states "are especially vulnerable to external events, including natural disasters, that cause high volatility in national incomes; many of them are currently facing an uncertain and difficult economic transition to a changing world trade regime; and they suffer from limited capacity in the public and private sectors."[2] In more specific terms, remoteness and isolation, openness, limited diversification, and income volatility have all been identified as severely constraining factors.

Even so, only a few international organizations and advanced countries recognize the exceptional problems of small island states. The Commonwealth, the UN, and the European Union, for example, have put in place specifically targeted programs to deal with this group of developing countries. And in its relatively recent association, in an ongoing collaborative enterprise with the Commonwealth Secretariat on the small-state issue, the World Bank appears to be moving in this direction. Despite being the Caribbean's biggest trading partner, the United States has been slower in coming to this recognition.

In fact, the Caribbean Basin Initiative (CBI), some contend, may have been of more benefit to the United States than the Caribbean economies it purported to assist. US exports to the Caribbean Basin more than tripled since 1984 when that agreement was signed. Moreover, the implementation of the North American Free Trade Agreement (NAFTA) saw many of the trade advantages included in the CBI superseded by the NAFTA parity granted to Mexico. However, the new Caribbean Basin Trade Partnership Agreement (CBTPA), a revised CBI arrangement, not only substantially increases market access for apparel and increases the number of products incorporated under the regime, but also upgrades beneficiary countries up to NAFTA parity status. This development augurs well for the evolving of a wider consensus in this connection. In other words, small states are increasingly being perceived as facing certain peculiarities of circumstances and conditions that deserve consideration for unique treatment.

The much-maligned principle of special and differential treatment does not necessarily mean a timeless and indiscriminate extension of privileges and deviations from the general rules of global economic intercourse. What it does mean is, first, the concession of special treatment and, second, the design of the appropriate operational mechanisms to give practical and meaningful effect to a differentiated condition. Such an approach is consistent with the ethos of globalization with a human face that seeks to ensure not only efficient outcomes in the functioning of the global economy, but also equitable outcomes. It also assures that these countries are provided with an appropriate period of transition in which they can equip themselves to function effectively in the global economy.

While the burdens of adjusting to the new international trading regime are real and Caribbean governments understandably try to negotiate a slow phasing in of the WTO's rules, these should not be allowed to delay the necessary adjustments for improving the international competitiveness of these economies. Given that the adjustment costs to the new global trading system are ultimately unavoidable, Caribbean economies must continuously strive to create the capacity to successfully exploit this new environment as they work to achieve their developmental objectives. While governments might successfully negotiate for and capture some of the benefits of delayed application of the WTO rules, these benefits should be passed on to businesses if, and only if, in the interim they serve as incentives for businesses to gain international competitive strength.

Competition should not be viewed negatively; it is perhaps the best possible incentive for businesses to improve and to become more productive. Competitive markets at home can help provide a springboard for global success. It is obviously not enough just to strengthen competition in the domestic market; Caribbean businesses also need to compete effectively in international markets. In this respect, Caribbean businesses should view CARICOM as an opportunity to test competitive strength against regional companies of similar strength, while positioning themselves to take on larger competitors in the global market.

To move to this point, however, the region must develop a strong forward-looking industrial policy that encourages innovation and contributes to building the types of enterprises that are suitable for a globally competitive knowledge-driven economy. Industrial policy formulation in the present era means meeting the requirements of the knowledge-driven economy. Promoting open competitive markets provides the sharpest spur to innovation and is perhaps one of the best ways of rewarding risk-taking. But governments need not do this alone; business leaders throughout the Caribbean should be part of the process of shaping policies on competition as well as monitoring and reviewing progress made.

The alternative to open markets and competition is, of course, protectionism and regulation. But as past experience shows, excessive and poorly conceived regulation only limits choice and increases costs, especially to small businesses. Smaller businesses bear the brunt of these regulations mainly because they have fewer resources to meet these costs. Policymakers therefore need to ensure that markets are fair and accessible to all firms, including small ones. In the long haul, Caribbean economies will gain more through productivity growth when governments work to reduce bureaucracy and lessen the burdens of unnecessary regulation. In adapting to the global economy, the Caribbean needs also to reduce its reliance on price factors in adjustment strategies and focus instead on non-price factors. By the price factor, I mean variables such as exchange rates and interest rates. In the past, in the typical adjustment program, too much emphasis has been placed on these price factors. The rationale for this shift is that in the real world, markets are imperfect and resource transfers emanating from changes in the price factor can turn out to be negative. This has been the case in the Caribbean, which has seen a net outflow of resources to multilateral institutions. The challenge of building a competitive economy cannot rely as heavily as it has in the past on price adjustments; rather, a better mix of price and non-price factors need to be worked into the adjustment matrix.

Building a Knowledge-Driven Economy

In the face of a rapidly changing business environment, Caribbean governments also face the challenge of modernizing their economies to close the performance gap between their enterprises and well-established firms from other, leading economies. While the world has become more open, with larger markets offering greater opportunities, it has also become far more competitive. With the removal of trade barriers, low-quality goods are produced by efficient enterprises in all parts of the world for sale in the global marketplace. To achieve sustained growth and increased profits, all businesses need to continually improve their processes and to develop new and better-designed products and services. Knowledge, which drives this change, is derived from research and development, from learning from competitors, and from investing in technology.

In a highly integrated and competitive marketplace, Caribbean economies can find their niche by identifying and exploiting their distinctive capabilities. For many modern economies, these distinctive assets are increasingly the knowledge, skills, and creativity of their people rather than traditional factors such as land and natural resources. Most successful modern economies are built on the ability of their people, who are at the heart of a knowledge-driven economy. Indeed, the small size of most Caribbean economies and their relatively limited endowment of raw materials suggest that their only competitive advantages are likely to be with their people. But the skills needed for a knowledge-based economy are in very limited supply and could impose severe constraints on the region's development. To compete in the global market, the region must place greater emphasis on developing an adequate amount of skilled labour and managerial talent.

Part of the process of accomplishing this transformation is that government, business, and each individual need to take on the challenge of upgrading skills. To successfully compete with foreign companies, Caribbean businesses must combine modem technology, which involves the effective use of digital technology (the nerve centre of the knowledge-driven economy) with information, knowledge, skills, and the creativity of their workforces to raise productivity levels and improve their products and services.

The Caribbean private sector needs to strengthen its capacity for innovation and risk-taking. Entrepreneurship is the lifeblood of a knowledge-driven economy. With the pace of innovation in global markets, any competitive advantage gained has to be constantly refreshed; successful businesses are likely to be those that can continuously turn new ideas into winning products and processes. This has to become the common objective of both large and small enterprises in our region. Although it takes time to bring about shifts in culture and business attitudes, this should not prevent us from acting. The aim must be to create an environment in which the entrepreneurial spirit of people of all ages is nurtured.

Caribbean businesses also need to have better access to investment financing. Too many small businesses with good ideas have had problems raising the credit they need to invest and grow. In a knowledge-driven environment, commercial banks cannot afford to be as risk averse as they have been in the past. In the new economy, banks and other financiers would be required to be almost as enterprising as entrepreneurs themselves. As the main source of financing for Caribbean enterprises, banks therefore need to become more proactive. They must not only embrace but also search out innovative small businesses. This does not mean that banks must throw caution to the wind. What is needed is an attitude shift that is complemented by a better assessment of business risk, which enables banks to identify those non-traditional business ideas that are deserving of financial support.

Off-shore financing is a crucial industry in some Caribbean countries, where off-shore financial centres are established. They provide tax incentives to high-value clients, and a safe depository of foreign currency, acting as a hedge for investors. At the same time, major regulatory concerns have been raised, and the OECD in particular has been on the forefront of advocating global practices that are transparent and accountable. This has created high risks for many countries who rely on this as a major source of income. In order to address the issues of financial access – due diligence requirements, arbitrary closure of bank accounts, and security concerns – "de-risking" activities have been introduced by financial institutions. The IMF, in developing an approach to mitigate these risks, has brought the de-risking issue to the forefront of public finance. Small countries face major negative externalities, by jurisdictions completely outside their control or influence. This loss of control initially manifested itself via regulatory measures, but has now extended to the issue of governance of the global regulatory system.

Regional financial institutions like the Caribbean Development Bank (CDB) also have an important role to play in project financing. In the new dispensation, the CDB needs to undergo a paradigm shift with regard to its view of the role of the state and of the private sector in development. There is both theoretical and empirical support for the view that social welfare will be greater when governments and public concerns undertake to provide only those services that are considered public goods as well as those concerns in which the private sector has little incentive to invest.

The CDB therefore needs to place far greater emphasis on private-sector financing and helping to position the private sector as the engine of growth in the region's economies. The CDB must also continue its pioneering work of supporting the development of regional capital markets, which should provide private-sector firms with an opportunity to shift their capital structure away from over-reliance on loan financing and towards the use of less risky equity capital.

The link between business, education, and research in a knowledge-driven economy is critical. Part of the drive to create a knowledge-based economy must of necessity involve strengthening the science base and promoting the exploitation of knowledge. Investment in and the drive for excellence in research and development are essential in providing businesses with a competitive edge. This requires closer collaboration and greater funding for regional educational and research institutions. The curricula of these institutions must, however, be geared towards developing the work-related and entrepreneurial skills that are appropriate to the region's development plan. The objective must be to create a highly educated and skilled labour force that is well resourced and capable of delivering sophisticated goods and services.

Very little will be accomplished if research and industry remain out of sync with each other. Scientific and technological knowledge needs to be combined with other forms of expertise to create innovative products and services. The most dynamic economies have strong universities that develop creative partnerships with industry. Stronger links between the University of the West Indies and industry could also lead to greater commercial exploitation of research. While governments in the region have been supporting this research effort, universities can become more effective if creative ways can be found for private-public partnership funding. The private sector need not feel a loser in this partnership arrangement, since the next logical step must be to translate research work into better processes and to commercialize new products developed.

To exploit our capabilities in people and technologies to the fullest, businesses must also collaborate across sectors and throughout the region. Few companies have all the skills and know-how to make technologically complex products. Successful businesses tend to be those that continually adapt their ideas and techniques outside of the business and promote cooperation within the business. With a shared vision of creating knowledge-based economies, governments within the region should encourage business collaboration and teamwork at local and regional levels. Sectoral partnerships, networking, and clusters can play a critical role in sharing knowledge and upgrading skills among complementary businesses.

While success in creating this kind of knowledge-driven economy depends on the extent to which the private sector embraces these ideas, governments and regional institutions can facilitate the process. Governments can help by maintaining a stable macroeconomic framework, which would underpin business confidence and help promote long-term planning and investment. In addition, every effort should be made to modernize the public service and to remove regulations and bureaucratic red tape, which retard productivity and impose unwarranted costs on businesses.

Expanding the Region's Economic Space

Other important challenges to the Caribbean involve expanding and increasing its economic space. Understanding the linkages in our economic system is central to the design of appropriate policies to accomplish this. The situation has become even more complex, as we now operate in a world where our environment extends beyond our local borders and, as the contagion from the Asian financial crisis shows, external conditions in faraway places can have far-reaching consequences for the domestic economy. Notwithstanding these new risks, the new global economy also creates many new opportunities for trade and investment. These are the opportunities that Caribbean economies must exploit in their pursuit of a wider economic space.

Real GDP growth for the region was disappointing during the 1980s, and while it increased during the most of the 1990s, it slipped again towards the end of the decade. During the 1980s, real output in the region expanded by a mere 1.2 per cent. Guyana, Haiti, and Trinidad and Tobago had negative rates of growth. In the second half of the decade, Cuba also stagnated.

In the 1990s, economic restructuring in many of these countries led to an improvement in regional growth rates. Although the average growth in GDP per capita is rising slightly over the 1990s, the rate of expansion has been far below what is required to make significant inroads in reducing unemployment and poverty (see Tables 3.4 and 3.5). To the extent that the Caribbean becomes more competitive, productive activities and sectors should expand to contribute to the required GDP growth and employment creation. There are perhaps two basic approaches to raising the level of growth and employment. As discussed above, one approach is to radically reorient the productive capacities of the economies by creating a knowledge-driven economy that can take advantage of the new opportunities being created by the process of globalization. This essentially relies on the exploitation of new technology to help extend the region's capacity to produce beyond the limits of its natural endowment. This strategy can be pursued alongside measures to improve the efficiency of traditional lines of production.

Naturally, the more diversified the economy and the larger the contribution from traditional sectors, the less likely it is that new opportunities will have to be sought in entirely new lines of production. Recent trends in technology growth may in fact be offering small economies greater room for manoeuvre in designing efficient supply-side policies. A new trend in technological innovation that allows for low costs even without massive production volumes seems to favour small economies, or at least, makes the playing field more level vis-à-vis larger economies. E-commerce also offers new prospects for geographically isolated small economies. However, higher levels of investment in human capital, which have been key to the success of the small, developed economies in Europe, will be crucial to the implementation of such strategies.

Future strategies to enhance efficiency and to expand economic space for these economies must therefore be linked to promoting innovations, developing synergies and strategic complementarities, and expanding the network of production centres. Although some of the problems that have retarded growth to date stem from conventional defects in factor markets, efforts must be made to explore these factors further. Particular attention should be paid to the "re-engineering" of the public and private sectors, with a view to encouraging the emergence of new economic activities and to motivating economic agents to think in new ways.

Table 3.4. Growth in GDP per capita

	1986	1994	1997	1999
Antigua/Barbuda	3.92	2.69	3.9	3.0
Bahamas	1.43	2.69	3.0	5.8
Barbados	1.35	3.88	4.8	2.9
Belize	6.03	2.65	1.5	6.2
Dominica	3.20	2.55	3.5	0.0
Dominican Republic	4.51	6.84	7.3	8.3
Grenada	3.38	3.52	4.8	8.2
Guyana	3.10	4.34	−1.5	1.8
Haiti	−0.72	2.91	3.1	2.2
Jamaica	1.89	−1.11	−0.7	0.4
St. Kitts/Nevis	5.19	4.61	1.6	2.0
St. Lucia	3.75	2.62	2.9	3.1
St. Vincent	4.26	4.57	5.2	4.0
Suriname	3.50	5.42	3.9	−1.0
Trinidad and Tobago	0.78	3.65	4.1	4.2

Table 3.5. Labour force growth and required GDP growth and tentative targets

	Labour force growth (average % per annum)	Required growth (minimum average %)
Bahamas	1.5	3.5
Barbados	0.4	2.4
Belize	2.9	4.9
Cuba	0.9	2.9
Dominican Republic	1.8	3.8
Guyana	0.6	2.6
Haiti	3.5	5.5
Jamaica	1.5	3.5
OECS	0.9	2.9
Suriname	1.4	3.4
Trinidad and Tobago	0.9	2.9
Total	1.8	3.8
Total (excluding Cuba)	2.1	4.1

Increasingly, the public sector's task is to provide an environment that is suited to overall growth and development. On the other hand, the private sector must become the engine of growth. There are several prerequisites for this engine to work, one of which is that the private sector must be given the freedom to conduct business without undue interference by the state. For the private sector to allocate its resources efficiently, market distortions must be at a minimum. The prices of input and output must reflect their productivity and relative scarcity. In other words, labour markets must be made flexible and protective subsidies and quotas must be minimized.

Expansion of economic space places other demands on these economies. Given the savings-investment-growth nexus, an important challenge to the region in the future will be raising its savings rates. High savings rates mean relatively high rates of investment. This is particularly important since only a few countries can maintain the current account deficits implied by reliance on high rates of foreign savings. Indeed, when domestic investment is heavily financed by foreign savings, restoring external equilibrium can lead to sharp fluctuations in investment and growth, which ultimately affect the average level of investment throughout the business cycle.

To summarize, in their drive to expand the economic space for their economies, Caribbean governments must recognize that enterprises, not countries, compete internationally. To achieve the desired level of productivity growth and economic development, it is important that attention be paid to the following:

- A suitable strategy for improving efficiency in both private- and public-sector enterprises must be found.
- Effort must be made to make the region more attractive for private domestic and foreign capital to play a major role in the expansion.
- Domestic savings must be increased so that financing requirements can be met despite reduced aid inflows.
- Education and skill development must be given priority, since one of the most important constraints on the development of Caribbean economies is their limited supply of skilled labour and managerial talent.
- Prices for inputs and output should be subjected to competition in the domestic economy, especially to rein in relatively high public utility prices. All unnecessary regulations and bureaucratic obstacles to private economic activity must be removed or substantially reduced.
- Diaspora bonds should be used to tap into an overseas market, and allow for remittances to be increased by offering returns to an investment, where the risks are shared.

Resetting Macroeconomic Planning

Leaders in the Caribbean have been calling for reform of the architecture of global trade and finance to make it more sensitive to the diverse levels of members' development in the design of globalization and liberalization. Many of these calls have been aimed at the International Monetary Fund and the World Bank – in the wake of the recent financial crisis around the world – but even more directly at the trading regime administered by the WTO. Many have pointed to the real burden imposed on small states, which hitherto have received preferential treatment because of their size, but whose enterprises must now compete on even terms with well-established enterprises from advanced countries. The end of the European Union's banana regime, in particular, will impose significant adjustment costs on producers in small Caribbean economies if it is dismantled in as short a time as is being demanded. In contrast, it is quite ironic that the dismantling, negotiated at the Uruguay Round, of the Multi-Fibre Arrangement (MFA) involves a ten-year, back-loaded phase-out that will provide ample time for the industrialized countries involved to adjust.

Of course, issues of equity are behind many of these calls for an interim transitional arrangement for smaller states. What is not readily understood and appreciated is that in the new trading regime there will be winners and losers. It is assumed that the benefits to gainers will be large enough to compensate losers, but so far, no mechanisms for such sharing have been developed. Indeed, any such sharing arrangement is unlikely. International trading regimes are essentially a matter of the political economy: they are in place at least as much to protect nations from their own interest groups as to protect nations from each other.

In this sense, the process of change and adaptation can best be analysed within a framework of political economy in which there are "winners" and "losers." Since the change process is normally associated with the altering of national expenditure, from one set of expenditures that emerges out of the current structure and behaviour of the economy to another set of expenditures that will usher in a new matrix of investment and consumption, the critical issue is how to affect that shift. "Losers" are easily identified, for they represent the participants in the current structure of the economy and normally are represented in the political system. They are organized to make appropriate noises. On the other hand, "winners" perhaps belong to the next generation or to opportunities not yet realized and therefore cannot be easily identified or mobilized. In such a framework, the process of change is challenged by finding a workable compensation mechanism that would allow "losers" to become part of the constituency of "winners." Adaptation by small states to the new trading environment before us can best take place if the framework for the political economy of change can be designed and an appropriate strategy spelled out. Benefits and costs are not static, and some of today's losers can become tomorrow's winners – depending on how they adjust and are compensated.

Even at the international level, where nations protect each other from other nations, strategic policies have become part of that framework. We are well aware of strategic policies implied in the "social clause" on environmental and labour issues, which have been viewed as being against exporters from developing countries. So too is the "Super 301" clause in the US Trade Act, which from time to time has been used.

The strategic approach, therefore, in the context of adaptation to the new trading environment by small countries, must become part of a deliberate strategy. Such strategic policies will tend to alter the pace, the timing, and the scope envisaged in the change process.

Another aspect of the political economy of change deals with the core-periphery dynamics of the new economic geography. Market forces must work together with new economic geographical arrangements. In this sense, there are two distinct and related processes that seem to be taking place:

- the relocation of industries and services in regions that are favoured with an attractive and richly endowed environment; and
- the specialization of economies that favour regions with a head start in production and attract industries away from those with lesser initial conditions.

New knowledge of and insight into these three aspects of the political economy of change – winners and losers, strategic policies, economic geography dynamics – can form part of a scholarship agenda as small states adapt to the new trading environment.

Development in the Caribbean entails a comprehensive political economy of change, including the development of endogenous growth capacity to drive the economy. Only then can the region benefit from the new and flexible world economy in which ends and means are readily adjusted to changing opportunities in different countries. This will require an integration model that transcends trade and converges at the institutional level, and facilitates backward and forward, macro- and micro-economic linkages.

SECTION 2

The Missing Link in Thinking

4 Policy Response to the Pandemic

The agenda before scholars and policy-makers is extensive, but we can neither succumb to the forces of history nor surrender to the new vulnerabilities that will surface in the path ahead. In declaring the COVID-19 a pandemic, the director general of the World Health Organization politely cautioned, "We have rung the alarm bells loud and clear. This is not just a public health crisis. It is a crisis that will touch every sector – so every sector and every individual must be involved in the fight."[1] What is the nature of the economic shock that will face the Caribbean? And how can economic policy respond?

I have argued[2] that the region is facing a "loop-type" cycle of shock, where demand and purchasing power will fall in tandem with disruptions in the supply chain and reduction in wages and production. Buffers and shock absorbers are weak in the Caribbean economy, and adjustments take place mainly through austerity measures. In this pandemic, to avoid a pending collapse, the level of fiscal injection must be at least equivalent to the expected fall in the gross domestic product. This is a tall order, and shifts in policy analysis and design are mandatory. Figures 4.1, 4.2, and 4.3 depict those shifts in the growth model, the framework for designing a solution, and policy proposals for action to restore purchasing power, increase capital flows and foreign exchange, source new funding, catalyse growth, rebuild buffers, and protect a livable basic income.

At the Dawn of the Modern Era

At the dawn of the modern era, in 1597, Francis Bacon's spoke his famous words "knowledge is power," observing that "without knowledge no nation can govern its economy, manage its environment, sustain its public health, produce goods or services, understand its own history, or enable its citizens to understand the circumstances in which

Figure 4.1. Framing the context for recovery

"LOOP-TYPE" CYCLES OF SHOCK

The COVID-19 crisis has induced a supply shock, which in turn fuels a demand shock and a fall in purchasing power.

SUPPLY SHOCK
REDUCES WAGES & PRODUCTION

LOOP-TYPE
CYCLE OF SHOCKS

DEMAND SHOCK
FALL IN PURCHASING POWER

AFTER-SHOCK

This is coupled with an after-shock in the energy market, a key pillar of the economy.

RIPPLES

This would be followed by future ripples, given a steep and sudden decline in global aggregate demand.

The size, speed, and depth of these "hits" have contracted our economic base by an estimated 20–25%, which will be reflected steeply in income, employment, and poverty levels.

Source: From "Reflections on the COVID-19 Pandemic and the Caribbean," by Winston Dookeran, EUCLID Global Health, 1 April 2020.

Figure 4.2. Designing the solution

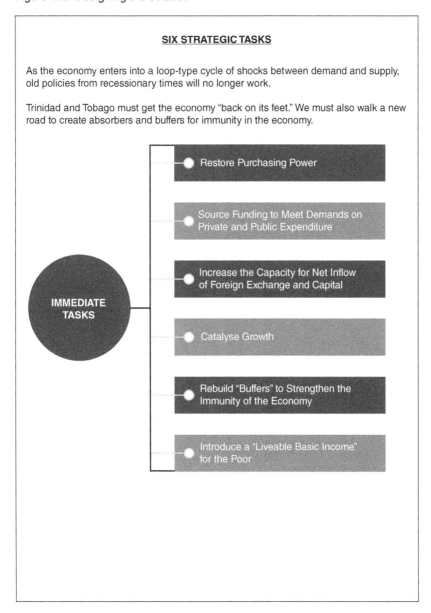

SIX STRATEGIC TASKS

As the economy enters into a loop-type cycle of shocks between demand and supply, old policies from recessionary times will no longer work.

Trinidad and Tobago must get the economy "back on its feet." We must also walk a new road to create absorbers and buffers for immunity in the economy.

IMMEDIATE TASKS

- Restore Purchasing Power
- Source Funding to Meet Demands on Private and Public Expenditure
- Increase the Capacity for Net Inflow of Foreign Exchange and Capital
- Catalyse Growth
- Rebuild "Buffers" to Strengthen the Immunity of the Economy
- Introduce a "Liveable Basic Income" for the Poor

Figure 4.3. Proposals for action: Roadmap to recovery

BUILDING AN IMMUNE ECONOMY

Restore Purchasing Power

- Central Bank to engage in quantitative easing as a supplement to discount rate management
- Central Bank should immediately negotiate better terms of borrowing for small and micro enterprises
- Government should meet all its obligations to small business's suppliers forthwith to urgently increase aggregate demand

Source Funding

- Financing through modern monetary theory measures (direct government, private bond, and equity purchases) to create new sources of funding for government use
- An expert technical team should be established to examine this proposal and the conditions that must be put in place to apply this form of "quantitative easing" in an unprecedented period
- Place CLICO on the market as a going concern for equity investors (with the right safeguards)

Increase the Capacity for Net Inflow of Foreign Exchange and Capital

- Take a diplomatic initiative to apply for currency swap under FIMA arrangement with the Federal Reserve Bank
- Open negotiations with the IMF to access the Rapid Financing Instrument for funding

Catalyse Growth

- Design process to provide catalytic equity finance to ventures in private and public sectors to support growth-boosting technology, engineering, or marketing interventions
- Set up a single catalytic funding window through diplomatic and other channels, with sources including private-sector affiliates of institutions, government bodies, international organizations, banks, and other organizations
- Establish a COVID-19 Corporate Financing Facility to provide financing for the public and private sector funded by issuing reserves, with government sharing the risks

Rebuild Buffers to Strengthen Immunity

- Replenish the Heritage and Stabilization Fund with the proceeds of a tax on import of "final" goods from outside CARICOM

Liveable Basic Income – Beginning of Social Transformation

- Extend the remit of the National Insurance Board to include the self-employed in the first instance
- Develop the capacity to provide a liveable basic income for those outside the catchment are of existing support programs

---

Source: Based on the author's presentation (2020) to the Roadmap for Recovery Committee of the Government of Trinidad and Tobago.

they live." Today's pandemic is a crisis;[3] nations have pressed the pause button and are looking for a reset.

"Pandenomics" as cleverly defined by Mark Cliffe[4] is the yearning to get back to normal despite the biggest economic downturn of the postwar period. Policy-makers face a transformed landscape where "economic policy will have to be reshaped around a fundamental review of objectives, instruments and institutions." As such, "our previous preoccupation with growth, mobility and optimization will likely give way to a new emphasis on equality, sustainability and agility."

Resetting the Parameters for Policy Action

The Role of the State

The time has come for a resetting of the roles of the state and the market in the development process. There is no doubt that the state has been pivotal in directing the progress of development towards equity and egalitarian public values. Yet the obstacles to the growth process lie in undue reliance on the state and its outdated controls and systems.

Major economic costs have been incurred. Market forces by themselves will not suffice to protect the public good. As such, a new role for the state, neither controlling nor facilitating, must make change happen. We now need a "catalytic" role for the state – a role that results in change at the dawn of the modern era.

It is worth remembering the words of Martin Wolf, *Financial Times* lead economic writer and author of *The Shifts and the Shocks*: "a microbe has overthrown our arrogance and sent global output into a tailspin."[5] The COVID-19 epidemic has morphed from a health crisis into a full-blown economic crisis that has triggered unprecedented repercussions in the global, regional, and domestic economies.

Mario Draghi, former president of the European Central Bank, when asked how much we can do regarding the pandemic, answered "whatever it takes" to protect lives and livelihoods. The choice between lives and livelihood is already a harsh reality for the world at large, and equally so for those of us in the Caribbean.

Regarding the structural impact of the pandemic on the Caribbean, I have written: "The coronavirus crisis has induced a supply shock – reducing wages and production – which in turn has fueled a demand shockfall in purchasing power. This becomes a 'loop type' cycle of shocks; in growth models shock absorbers mitigate the adverse effects on growth. But buffers and shock absorbers are weak in the Caribbean economy. Shocks are absorbed through adjustments in labor and austerity. That may work in normal times, but given the magnitude of the shocks it will not work even in 'normal' times."[6]

Tests for Policy-Makers

In discussing the tests faced by Canadian policy-makers, Michael Sabia of the *Globe and Mail*[7] asked, "Is there a public roadmap to build confidence in the public that, should the situation deteriorate, government action is locked and ready to go?" The primary question is "Is it safe?" – a question better answered by the health management experts and policy-makers. Another writer warns that "stimulus packages" are not "confidence tricks" played on the people.[8]

But as policy-makers look to restart the economy, Sabia pointed out, and I fully agree, that we must reset some of our basic thinking on macroeconomic dogma. We must set aside our traditional thinking about fiscal deficits. It is generally argued that to prevent an immediate collapse, the size of the fiscal injection must be at least equivalent to the fall in the GDP. But fiscal stability must be measured not in static measures but in a moving trajectory. Mark Cliffe writes that it is time to abandon the futile debate about "normalization." Growth models must abandon linear assumptions and accept that the growth process is a non-linear one. This pandemic is a fitting example of the non-linear logic of the growth process. There is a call for analytical leadership to understand this non-linearity in the growth process. Inertia, defined in physics as "a property of matter by which it continues in its existing state of rest or uniform motion in a straight line, unless that state is changed by an external force" (encyclopedia.com) is a tendency to do nothing or to remain unchanged.

A group of young professionals – Adam Raffoul, Pearce Robinson, Jason Maule, Ibrahim Adbullah, Eric Hopkins II, Quweina Roberts, and Nneka Matthews – have captured the moment in a dramatic presentation, "Resetting T&T's Economy: A Sustainable Response to the COVID-19 Crisis," with a doable set of initiatives to confront "the two-fold challenges, the health and safety fallout causing mass unemployment and many businesses to shutter." They recommend "a whole government approach ... with a focus on individuals and small business hardest hit by the current crisis."[9] These young professionals deserve high commendation, not only for their specific recommendations but for unleashing the energy needed to start the reset necessary to emerge from the COVID-19 pandemic. The whole-of-government approach has been endorsed by ECLAC and advocated by Kay Floyd, director of William and Mary University's Whole Government Center of Excellence, as a basis for inter-agency cooperation during the pandemic. It provides a playbook for instituting parallel and coordinating systems in response to COVID-19.[10]

Building an Immune Economy

At the start of the pandemic, Trinidad and Tobago introduced appropriate health protocols to mitigate the health risks that faced us and the global community. This health crisis has seen great valour among our health professionals and others and positioned public health as key to our well-being. But the economic fallout of this historic effort is telling, as many livelihoods are at stake, and the uncertainty of the duration of this pandemic has left many nations on the edge of a precipice.

As the economy enters a "loop" cycle of demand and supply shocks, old policy prescriptions for recessionary times will no longer work.

The coronavirus crisis, as explained, has induced a supply shock – reducing wages and production, which in turn fuels a demand shock – and a fall in purchasing power: resulting in a loop cycle of shock. This is coupled with an after-shock in the energy market, a key pillar of the economy, with future ripples to come from dramatically falling growth rates in the world economy. The size, speed, and depth of these hits have contracted Trinidad and Tobago's economic base by an estimated 20 to 25 per cent,[11] which will be reflected as steep declines in income and employment and increased poverty levels. The OECD evaluation suggest that "the shutdowns could be a decline in the level out output of being one-fifth to one quarter in many economies, with consumers' expenditure potentially dropping by around one third."[12] The task now is to get the economy back on its feet – to snap back into activity – and walk a new road where there will be absorbers and buffers for immunity in the economy.

The Awakening of a New World Order?

There was at one point a strong sense that once a vaccine was discovered and accessible, the old economic order would return to normalcy and the pathway to prosperity would once again be clear. A noted editor, Khuloud Al Omian, disagreed: "of course not, everything will be different."

Her predictions are as follows:[13]

- There will be a shift in the balance of power, where the scale will tip more towards China, and the Asian countries will recover before the United States.
- A highly automated production infrastructure will save energy by lowering costs and improving quality.

- There will be increased confidence in technology shown in consumer behaviour and digital transactions in medicine and payments.
- The emergence of video conferencing will decrease business travel.
- Governments will introduce e-services in courts, immigration, passport, and other institutions that may not be easily reversible.
- More investment will take place in healthcare systems and products and national hygiene applications.
- Several institutions will transform by "doing" – central banks, philanthropy, and companies (such as with a reduction in carbon dioxide emissions).
- The educational system – from higher learning to primary schools – will adjust to new economic circumstances, learning innovations, and home-schooling initiatives. The crucial question is, will the poor and powerless be better off or will inequality deepen?

Globalization Will Take Another Hit

On the wider front, globalization will take another hit as countries search for safety, not as much through efficiency as through resiliency, nearer home or within national boundaries. As influential economic thinker Mohamed El-Erian says in a recent Munk dialogue, "This is by far the biggest hit to the US economy and the global economy that we have seen since the great depression … It will be different and we must have an open mind in navigating the differences."[14] This is another blow to globalization as the forces of inequality, trade tensions, and weakening of multilateralism press forward. The implication is that regionalism will make a comeback and that resilience will be a higher priority than efficiency in trade matters. In the Caribbean, integration has reached its limits, and a "new regionalism" will gain attention. Caribbean convergence may return to the agenda for Caribbean integration.

No Comfort for "Upper Deck" People in Kenya

Eminent Kenyan economist David Ndii, in an article on the pandemic in Kenya, spared no comfort for "upper deck" people: "in another month, a quarter of the Nairobi metropolitan area population – about 1.5 million people – may not have a penny to their name." Ndii saw the coronavirus "as a negative permanent technology shock with a long-term productivity slowdown – a great leap backwards if you like."[15] The state-society relationship will be up for critical examination, and the national political class will abandon the people – resulting in a mindless obsession with power. And though these points concern Kenya, we must not discount the wider applicability of the social forces at work and the nonlinear social consequences. Ndii's critical observation is that the business sector is key to reigniting economic activities and a supportive environment is the best guarantee of social stability.

Grand Strategy and Incrementalism

In the May/June 2020 issue of *Foreign Affairs*, a thoughtful analysis of the "end of grand strategy" was provided in the context of US and global politics.[16] The premises of the argument are applicable in a smaller context. Defining a grand strategy as "a road map on how to match means and ends" the authors write that it works best on predictable terrain – where there is a clear understanding of the distribution of power, a solid domestic consensus about national goals and identity, and stable political and national security institutions."

In an unpredictable terrain, there will be a fractured national narrative, which may lead to chaos when the equilibrium is shattered. The economic equilibrium in Trinidad and Tobago has been disrupted, having been hit by the shock of COVID-19 – a loop-type shock – the collapse of the global oil market, and a sudden return to global recession. In such conditions, global strategic thinking cannot be linear, as forces today are complex and interactive, so the most direct path between two points is not a straight line. Grand strategies are elusive and must give way to incrementalism that adds up to a coherent whole, where "actors must constantly change their strategies."[17]

Level 1 Strategies

In the prevailing circumstances, the most critical level 1 strategies are to

- restore purchasing power;
- source funding to meet demands on private and public expenditure;
- increase the capacity for net inflow of foreign exchange and capital;
- catalyse forces for growth;
- introduce a livable basic income for the poor; and
- rebuild buffers to strengthen the immunity of the economy.

These tasks as outlined above are the most critical ones to be carried out.

Level 2 Strategies

Level 1 strategies must be done in tandem with the level 2 strategies outlined below, which are key for resilience:

- Re-opening: Establish enforceable health-related protocols for the opening of schools and emergency financial support for upgrading the health sector and improving access to medicine
- Regulatory roll-back: Take steps to remove unnecessary and ineffective regulatory controls that are inhibiting performance of the commercial sector
- Business: Revise framework for bankruptcy practices
- Foreign exchange: Explore other instruments, like currency swaps, export credit, and service expansion
- Infrastructure: Fill gaps to ensure continuous supply of water, electricity, sanitation, and other public goods
- State roll-back: Begin institutional rationalization of public bodies and create new instruments to encourage public share ownership of public enterprises
- Food: Enhance the food sector, including fisheries and the food-processing sector, to ensure removal of any supply-side bottlenecks; invest in cold-storage capacity and equitable access to food
- Social welfare: Create an employer's wage fund, where employers and workers match savings

Level 3 Strategies – Analysis to Start Now

Level 3 outlines the strategies that must be analysed now:

- Review the existing macro fundamentals – current ratios and projected – for GDP, debt, employment, consumption, investment, exports, imports, per capita income, and scope of fiscal space
- Review current expenditure of public- and public-enterprise sectors to switch to new directions for transformation
- Model the size of the funding required to put the economy back on its feet and walk a new road; identify the scope for domestic mobilization in the short term
- Develop a strategy for external support in quickly disbursing facilities, from all international sources
- Encourage the private sector to invest in incremental additions to their capital stock in areas consistent with new directions for transformation

These tasks must aim to satisfy triple synergy – the immediate, the recovery, and sustainability. The first step must seamlessly lead to the recovery, and then the process must sustain itself. It is like the old adage "Give a man a fish and you feed him for a day, teach a man to fish and you feed him for a lifetime," and if I may add, "He earns a cornerstone for his fish house and the whole village gets a feast." This circularity thinking is at the core of the non-linear approach to development. Complexity is at the core of development,[18] so for the situation today I will focus initially on two aspects of this complexity: monetary finance and income support for the poor. In the pandemic experience, technology may well become a positive externality that permeates the entire development matrix.

These are extraordinary times, with high degrees of uncertainty. The pathways ahead will adjust as we go. It is a time for flexibility and agility, but also a time for steady progress, with renewed public values and the analytics to take bold measures. Indeed, it is a time where knowledge is power.

Restore Purchasing Power

Development banks and rating agencies are wedded to static measures of fiscal stability and other macroeconomic fundamentals. In a period of sustained uncertainty, shut down, loop-type shocks, and other shocks and ripples, is "whatever it takes" enough to put the economy on its feet and start walking the correct path? Already analysts, in looking at measures of economic health, are saying that the new normal is not the old normal. How can we be in unprecedented times but rely on the old measures to assess our fitness?

Central banks have often used monetary financing through programs of quantitative easing by buying and selling long-term government bonds, as well as reserve and liquidity rations for commercial banks. This is a good initial step. But is it enough, in these circumstances? An intense dialogue has started on monetary financing – between money creation and reserve allocation – with the suggestion that central banks must facilitate long-term government liabilities through reserve allocation at zero rates of interest. This is not to undermine the price stability objective of the central bank but rather to support the wider fiscal and monetary stability of the economy. Adair Turner, in a comprehensive analysis on monetary financing of fiscal deficits, concluded that "there is no doubt that monetary finance is technically feasible and that wise fiscal and monetary authorities could choose just the 'right' amount."[19] There is room to unleash a new, "non-inflationary" tranche of support to public liabilities, but it is essentially a political issue to determine the "emergency" circumstances and limits.

Balance of payments account will be under extreme stress. Inward flows of funds to finance adjustment and transformation paths of the economy will be required. Foreign borrowing, investment, and net foreign exchange earnings must fill the gap and reduce the stress. No doubt, a new generation of infrastructure will be necessary. Retooling the health care system and refinancing of micro, small, and medium-sized enterprises as well as digital innovations, public hygiene, food and medicine security, and safety in international travel are clearly areas of priority spending. This must fit into changes in the global system. Khuloud Al Omian[20] sets that frame for investment decisions with her ten predictions of how the restructuring of the global system will take place.

Funding to Meet Expenditure Demands

The flow of funds into the economy from the banking and energy sectors is a traditional anchor of the financial stability of Trinidad and Tobago. Both sectors are critical to the amount of net capital available for domestic production and consumption. This may no longer be the case, at least during recovery from the pandemic. Yet a careful assessment of the "gas" sector is critical to determining the financial gaps ahead.

What is the financing gap to get the economy back on its feet and on a new path? Using some back-of-the-envelope calculations, we can estimate that restoring the level of economic activity to the pre-pandemic level may require between 20 and 25 per cent of GDP. Restoring purchasing power to pre-COVID-19 level, meeting the budgetary deficits resulting from the stoppage and fall in growth rates, and stimulus packages to ignite a growth process are the main components of public-sector funding requirements. The timeline is indeterminate, as time is elastic and the impact feeds upon itself.

Table 4.1 gives an updated status from several sources of the size of the fiscal challenge facing Trinidad and Tobago.

It is critically important to build public confidence that the government is ready to act if the situation deteriorates, as volatility can be expected and policy leaders will have to be agile. Building confidence is not only about arithmetic and will be the defining challenge in our path to recover.

MODERN MONETARY THEORY AND QUANTITATIVE EASING[21]

After much debate amongst the world's senior economists and heads of G7 central banks, modern monetary theory (MMT) has become the tool of choice of the Federal Reserve, Bank of England, and Bank of Japan. The concern that Trinidad and Tobago's currency is not an international

Table 4.1. Measuring the fiscal challenge facing Trinidad and Tobago

	2019	2020	2021	2022	Unit of Measure	Source
GDP growth projection	0	−5.3	2.5	1.9	%	*The Economist* Intelligence Unit
GDP growth projection	–	−4.5	2.6	–	%	IMF World Economic Oulook April 2020 data
GDP growth projection	−0.2	−2.7	0.7	0.9	%	S&P Rating: Trinidad and Tobago March 2020
GDP growth projection	–	−4.3	3.0	–	%	Moody's changes the outlook on Trinidad and Tobago's ratings May 2020
Private consumption	2	−4	3	–	% GDP	*The Economist* Intelligence Unit
Government consumption	4	5.7	−3.2	–	% GDP	*The Economist* Intelligence Unit
Revenue	42.6223	34.6329766	40.5513067	–	Billions local currency	IMF World Economic Oulook April 2020 data
Expense	48.6173	51.5880772	52.6088414	–	Billions local currency	IMF World Economic Oulook April 2020 data
Deficit	−5.995	−16.955101	−12.057535	–	–	IMF World Economic Oulook April 2020 data
Exports of goods and services, current prices	63.8703908	43.9665076	51.232173	–	Billions local currency	IMF World Economic Oulook April 2020 data
Export growth	−4	−29.7	15	–	%	S&P Rating: Trinidad and Tobago March 2020
Debt to GDP	73.4	85.8	87.6	89.5	%	S&P Rating: Trinidad and Tobago March 2020
Total domestic demand	148.217502	145.709148	150.440294	–	Billions local currency	IMF World Economic Outlook April 2020 data

Sources: The data in this table were gathered from: https://www.imf.org/en/Publications/WEO/weo-database/2020/April/weo-report?c=369,&s
=NGDP_RPCH,PPPGDP,NGDPRPPPPCPCH,PCPIPCH,PCPIEPCH,LUR,GGXCNL_NGDP,BCA_NGDPD,&sy=2000&ey=2000&ssm=0&scsm
=1&scc=0&ssd=1&ssc=0&sort=country&ds=.&br=1; Moody's Investors Service, "Rating Action: Moody's Changes the Outlook on Trinidad
and Tobago's Ratings to Negative, Affirms Ba1 Ratings," 22 May 2020; S&P Global Ratings, "Research Update: Trinidad and Tobago Sovereign
Rating Lowered to 'BBB-' From 'BBB' on Lower Hydrocarbon Price Assumptions," 26 March 2020; The Economist Intelligence Unit, 2020,
unpublished data tables.

one and the use of such a tool may create instability in foreign exchange market can be addressed by the structuring of a long-term bond backed by a self-liquidating US instrument. The foreign exchange leakage can be mitigated by guiding where the money is spent – where the marginal propensity to consume foreign exchange for every dollar spent is compared against the marginal export growth generated. For example, a capital infrastructure project like housing should be compared against loans to the private sector to initiate expansion for export. In 2012 when the government of Trinidad and Tobago issued TT$5 billion in zero coupon bonds, it did not see a corresponding surge in foreign exchange demand.

In order to deal with the current downside risk of a steep decline in aggregate decline – during which deferrals turn into defaults – stress tests of the liquidity situation on a preemptive basis will be prudent and inform monetary action. As a further anticipatory move, the government should seek expert opinion on the issuance of long-term government bonds to the central bank via quantitative easing. This borrowing from the central bank should be structured as a sinking fund that is self-liquidating and not reliant on future taxes or the recovery of the economy.

Central banks all over the world have been acting swiftly to maintain financial stability through a variety of tools, including asset purchase[22] programs and lending facilities. An Expert Opinion Committee should be established to assess the macro-implications of COVID-19 and propose targeted time-bound financing structures to contain and mitigate the negative impact on monetary and financial stability. The terms of reference of this committee should include:

- Assessing the likely implications of the crisis for the balance sheets of major financial institutions, the corporate sector (including small and medium-sized enterprises) and the household sector.
- Identifying potential sources of liquidity (including the introduction of specialized credit facilities to various components of the financial sector) to support financial sectors[23] that are likely to be negatively impacted by the ongoing crisis. This should include measures to maintain an adequate supply of liquidity to firms and households and to support the functioning of the payments system. Some options might include special credit facilities for commercial paper, money market liquidity, and corporate credit.
- Identifying regulatory actions that can be taken to support business continuity without compromising financial-sector soundness and transparency. These might include loan restructuring arrangements

in the form of renegotiated terms (maturity, interest rates, and fees), moratorium policies, and grace periods.

INTEREST RATES AND LIQUIDITY

The Trinidad and Tobago Central Bank has taken steps to increase liquidity and lower interest rates in the system. There is scope for the bank to go further and inject more liquidity with lower rates to improve the purchasing power of the economy. Quantitative easing – purchases and sales of long-term securities – is another instrument that can be skilfully employed to reduce rates. The current stoppage in the economy makes it necessary to further reduce interest costs and lengthen deferral periods, to provide breathing space for small enterprises to catch up. Some have strongly suggested that the "reverse mortgage" instrument be assessed for introduction in Trinidad and Tobago. Interest in diaspora bonds could be revived as an active source of new funds – once the risk-reward ratios are plausible. The contribution to the Inter-American Development Bank blog "Caribbean DEV Trends" explores the potential and mechanism for such bonds.[24]

The Bank of England has introduced a COVID-19 Corporate Financing Facility to provide financing for the private sector, in the event there is tightening of financial conditions. Purchases of commercial paper by corporate entities are funded by issuing reserves with the government assuming all the risks via an indemnity. Similar arrangements are being introduced by the European Central Bank, and may be explored for their applicability to the financial market in Trinidad and Tobago.

Recently the Federal Reserve Bank of the US (the Fed) agreed to sign on a new repo facility called FIMA (Foreign and International Monetary Authorities). The Fed is offering dollars to central banks in currency swap arrangements. Recently, Mexico and Brazil signed up for Fed swap deals to increase the supply of US dollars available to those countries. FIMA account holders consist of most central banks and other monetary authorities with accounts at the Federal Reserve Bank of New York, who are eligible to apply to use the facility. Such applications must be approved by the Federal Reserve. Although the practice has not been extended to small countries, as in so many instances, the right entrepreneurial diplomacy will yield high dividends.

The Catalytic Role in Development

Turning around an economy often requires a shift from the step-by-step process of conventional models towards new approaches based on capturing strategic options. The conditions for such a shift are more likely to emerge during a crisis – such as riots, natural disasters, and pandemics. The role of the state in economic development has been a central question for leaders, as they always seek a balance between ideology and strategy. It has always been about a political equilibrium, although at times through the lens of economic development.

In the pursuit of that balance in Trinidad and Tobago, the early focus on the "commanding heights" – sugar and oil – saw the involvement of state ownership. Structural adjustment policies gave prominence to the market forces and a robust regulatory system. A mix between state control and market power was how the ideology and strategy issues traded off, in pursuit of performance. The governance goals are also, and rightly, to create socially equitable, environmentally sustainable, and healthier places to live and work. But when times are no longer normal, as in 2007–2009 and in today's pandemic, policy leaders are called upon to change the strategies for development.

Models of state-centric governance, as opposed to state control, have often worked in tandem with the free market system. A dichotomy in the management of private- and public-sector enterprises emerged, between risks and performance. The new incarnation of this dichotomy is the private-public partnership. How must we shift gears at this time?

The obstacles to the growth process lie in undue reliance on the state and its outdated controls and systems. Major economic costs are incurred. But market forces by themselves will not suffice to protect the public good. We must embrace a catalytic role for the state – a role that causes change. This notion is strategic and was previously employed by Singapore's Prime Minister Lee Kuan Yew to promote state investments in global ventures in shipping, finance, and air and sea travel. The circumstances are different today, but the logic of a catalytic role of the state can change the calculus of state economic activities. The case for a developmental state was articulated by Dillion Alleyne and Nikolaos Karagiannis; their work brings into focus the proactive role of the state in building a competitive economy in the Caribbean.[25]

This can be applied to the transformation of the state enterprise sector, with a new assessment of the basis for restructuring. This is a potentially multi-billion-dollar-earning project and can create a new profitability in a high-growth zone. There will be no one model – public offerings, private-public partnerships, clustering synergies, and supply chain prospects – but the common goal is to be thrust into a high growth zone.

This new focus of the state can also be applied to "ease of doing business," as it radically switches the rules of control to those of performance through a single legislative act.

Catalytic "shares" – similar to the old "golden share" concept – can be strategically used to enhance productivity, production, and marketing in key "take-off" ventures like food processing, maritime dry-docking services, and others that meet high-growth-zone expectations. Such catalytic shares could aim at technological refitting or enhancing market demand or such factors that place the venture in a high-growth zone. The introduction of a finance house to support catalytic investment in small ventures may be valuable addition to existing financing windows. This facility exists in the United States and Canada and is taking root in countries like India. To capture these and other opportunities, rapid economic growth must be the main driving objective of a catalytic equity instrument. If it catches on, we can learn by doing, testing new waters rather than swimming in already travelled lanes. And if the global economy moves into a V-shaped recovery, Trinidad and Tobago will be well positioned for the next round.

A Blueprint for the State Enterprise System

The strategic value of government assets has informed the state's ownership of enterprises. This is a proposition of merit. However, where such value is not strategic, we must be prudent in selecting the right blueprint. There is much at risk in relying on intuition or populist appeals.

Even the OECD benchmark,[26] aimed at improving how state ownership can add value to society – efficiency, transparency, level playing field, best practices and governance – falls short in framing new blueprints. This raises the questions: what are the labour capital ratios and factor productivity in state-owned enterprises,[27] and how do they work against restructuring? The Inter-American Development Bank's publication *Fixing State-Owned Enterprises: New Policy Solutions to Old Problems* provides some practical ways to finance and issue bonds, reduce "political risks," and explicitly conduct sensitivity analyses on the impact of macroeconomic shocks on state enterprises.[28]

In quick time, an assessment framework for decision-making and retooling for expansion should be designed, amid the prevailing conditions of a shrinking fiscal space. Daniel Berkowitz and others have designed a model for the restructuring of state-owned enterprises, showing how in China they became more profitable in an environment of political pressures and high elasticities in capital-labour ratios. This model provides useful insights for a state enterprise restructuring system.[29]

Yet there is now the need to support government financing for the recovery process. The Trinidad and Tobago government has invested heavily in the Colonial Life Insurance Company (CLICO) rescue effort (which at one time placed between 10 and 18 per cent of CARICOM countries' GDP at risk). Today CLICO is a viable enterprise from which the government can redeem its remaining obligations and secure a good surplus in a transparently negotiated transaction. The timing of such decisions will of course be subject to market conditions.

With TT$3 billion in preferred shares and a 49.9 per cent shareholding in CLICO valued at book at just over TT$1 billion, selling the securities position as a going concern is more advantageous than an attempt to strip its assets and liabilities. Apart from legal complexities and impediments, a simple exit strategy that brings cash to the government with speed must be facilitated by packaging the prospectus of CLICO as a going concern. The transaction must satisfy the rules of transparency. There are distinct economic advantages in such a prospectus. The company as a whole has emerged as a valuable asset to the government and is likely to attract equity investors in the marketplace. In promoting this prospectus, a development component of the proceeds may be included, given the heritage value of this enterprise.

Funding in Response to COVID-19

Sourcing funding from international financial institutions has always faced obstacles of conditionalities, timeliness, and development effectiveness. Now is the moment to change that around, not only because of the gravity of the current financial dilemma but also because these institutions need to change several practices to which they have become wedded. As such, a new negotiation strategy – networking diplomacy, a microlateral approach to global issues – will see borrowing countries exacting greater leeway and negotiating space, and will help shape their future policies. This opportunity should be grasped, and current emergency windows established by these bodies should be accessed.

In the post-COVID-19 pandemic, the IMF is providing emergency financial assistance Trinidad and Tobago is eligible for emergency financing, which allows for 100 per cent of its IMF quota amounting to US$ 641.18 million designed for rapid responses to the crisis. Several countries in the Caribbean and Central America have already accessed funds from the IMF's Rapid Financing Instrument (RFI). Funds provided through the RFI are "in the form of outright purchases without the need for a full-fledged program or reviews."[30] In the event of exogeneous shocks, repeated use of the RFI is possible. A carefully articulated negotiating strategy must be the pillar of this approach.

The approach should include the International Monetary Fund, which has always been the "policy leader" among international financial institutions.

Support for the United Nations Conference on Trade and Development's initiative to expand the use of special drawing rights of the IMF should be solidly backed by active collective diplomacy in the Caribbean. Indeed, such diplomatic actions have borne fruit, as the IMF announced increases in the SDRs as of 23 August 2021. ECLAC's executive secretary, Alicia Bárcena, has been at the forefront of this advocacy, urging the IMF to act with urgency on this proposal and to include small countries like those in the Caribbean with excess SDRs.[31] The Caribbean should immediately take steps to resume the G20 Development Working Group with Caribbean countries that was inaugurated during Turkey's 2015 presidency. G20 Commonwealth countries, the UK, Canada, Australia, South Africa, and India may be approached to support this initiative, in time for the next summit of the G20, at which time it is expected that G20 support for developing countries will be discussed.[32]

In accepting a second term as UN secretary-general, António Guterres called for a new era of "solidarity and equality," saying of the world that "we are truly at a crossroads, with consequential choices before us, paradigms are shifting, old orthodoxies are being flipped."[33] This era is manifested the UN reform changes to concrete structures and activities of the UN resident coordinator.

Catalysing Forces for Growth

WIDEN THE SPACE FOR EXPANSION OF COMMERCIAL ACTIVITIES

We must design an open process to select ventures in the private and public sectors that may require catalytic equity finance for technological, engineering, or marketing interventions that place the enterprise on a "fast" growth track. The Caribbean region should take diplomatic steps to set up a funding mechanism with the private-sector affiliates of the international financial institutions, national government bodies, international organizations, and local banks and organizations and to operationalize the funding window along the lines of an initiative on catalytic financing.[34]

NEW BLUEPRINTS FOR PRIVATE AND STATE ENTERPRISES

In the post-COVID-19 period, business enterprises may find it necessary to create new blueprints. Supply chain mapping, risk exposure models, and logistics capacities may have to be reset in the circumstances, while flexible plans will be needed to determine time to start and recover. Interest rate support and deferral plans will significantly affect the program. I suggest that all local and national chambers of commerce embark on a program to advocate the determination of these blueprints. Steps should be taken to equip enterprises with expansion and productivity capacity.

PRIVATE-SECTOR RISK EXPOSURE MODEL

In the Caribbean micro, small, and medium-sized enterprises are the backbone of income and employment creation. The shut-down of the economy dealt a major blow to this sector, and its survival is linked to curtailment of its cash flow and the uncertainty of the time horizons ahead. In addition, disruptions in the supply chain abroad and maintaining employment levels add further burdens to planning. As such, the sector's blueprint requires flexibility amid cost-cutting measures if we are to manage through production shortages for consumers. In designing a recovery process, a risk exposure model must inform the channelling of fiscal support: identifying time to recovery and performance impact of the shocks, particularly on firms' operations and profitability.

As such, each subsector needs to measure its risks in a risk exposure model. The COVID-19 credit line referred to above must be accessible by addressing the key risk factors with no ex-ante conditionalities but with ex-post accountability. The performance and profitability ratios of these new blueprints will inform the kind and level of bank lending necessary to walk the new road with confidence.

Rebuilding Buffers for Immunity

Trinidad and Tobago's Heritage and Stabilization Fund is a key anchor of the country's credit rating and a strategic buffer in the country's balance sheet. In this crisis, it provided some support. That said, the optimal level is still years away from being realized. With the extreme uncertainty expected in the energy market, it would be prudent to replenish the fund on an ongoing basis as a buffer against future shocks. At the same time, it is an opportune moment to introduce a tax on the importation of "final" goods from outside the CARICOM region, in order to, amongst other things, balance the trade account. The term "final" implies that this measure excludes intermediate imports for domestic production. This will provide an incentive for local exports, while the timing means that the impact of such a tax on prices during this deflationary period will be minimal.

Towards a Universal Basic Income

In spite of some current actuarial concerns, the National Insurance Board (NIB) is the most reliable institution for promoting social security. The proposal to extend its coverage to the self-employed should recommence, and extending it further to each citizen should not be beyond our reach. In the current climate, we have an opportunity to implement a "livable basic income" for those now out of any of the catchment areas of existing support programs. Focusing on the "new vulnerable," there is need for urgent income support that could be translated to a permanent livable income through contributions over time, which can be funded by the state. Beneficiaries would receive grants and saving deposits for a pre-agreed time to be applied as contributions to the NIS. This can be considered social investment rather than an additional public expenditure. The arithmetic for this start in social transformation can be worked out in the analytical stage of the development of the idea.

In a philosophical sense this sort of measure is consistent with the "rights-based approach" to development – shaping a "new normal" that gets at the core of sustainability. Such a program should be designed to be included in a universal social security program. Indeed, the setting-up cost of the program can be negotiated into the transaction from the proceeds of the CLICO proposal, referred to earlier.

Geopolitics: Is the Pandemic a Turning Point?

The *Economist*, in the May 2020 issue on the geopolitics of the pandemics, suggests that there are three important ways to watch for change:

- It will bring to the surface less-acknowledged trends like China's growing sphere of influence.
- It will accelerate existing geopolitical trends – particularly the growing rivalry between China and the United States and the shift in balance of power from West to East.
- It will be a catalyst for change in the future of Europe and relations between China and the developing world.

The *Economist* predicts that a disinformation war to determine who is responsible for the spread of the virus will continue; the global balance of power will shift from West to East, and that China will emerge as a bigger global player. It asks whether US global leadership will diminish, affirms that the EU will emerge weakened, and asserts that emerging powers will seek to capitalize on the crisis.

Whatever the analysis of the geopolitics of the pandemic, the diplomatic agenda for the Caribbean could end up in no-man's land. Sir Ronald Sanders summed up the dilemma this way: "One certainty in any new global dispensation is that, if [countries] fail to act together, they will remain in the backwater of human development. That is particularly true for CARICOM countries."[35] Perhaps, this time offers the Caribbean a geo-political opportunity to define its regional state, refrain from a sterile focus on the "implementing deficit" in CARICOM, and capture the new architectural design fitting for the geo-politics of Caribbean history and geography.[36] (In this regard the CARICOM Commission on the Economy made some useful suggestions.)[37] Geopolitical cooperation of the region in international affairs is inescapable and, in the context of COVID-19, of utmost urgency.

Policy Choices for Action

Policy choices are determined by the policy space open at the time. This is a central premise of this analysis. At a time when Trinidad and Tobago is facing shocks, aftershocks, and ripples, limits of policy space in navigating the road ahead will constrain us. Rising above those limits – and orthodoxy in thinking – is the challenge to policy action. The limits to policy action are depicted as "a fragile path to recovery."[38]

To attempt to go beyond those limits, I have raised the issues of the catalytic role of the state in development, the adoption of an active monetary policy in sourcing funds and lowering interest costs, the building of purchasing power and immunity in the economy, the search for defining technical negotiations with the IFI's, a new focus on business expansion, restructuring and catalytic capital, exploring of new frontiers in policy analysis with in-depth analysis to preserve macro-stability, and initiation of concrete social transformation by introducing a sustainable basic livable income for the poor.

The COVID-19 pandemic, in a real twist, has provided an opportunity – to adjust to the new hit on globalization, to awaken to a turning point in everyday use of technology, and to place public health and the environment at the centre of development. All this is amidst a rocky global political order, with fractured societies everywhere and a converging fiscal space at home. The roadmap will only be drawn from the experiences of the journey itself.

5 The Politics of Development[*]

The Growth Report (2008), commissioned by the World Bank,[1] and the papers presented at the UNU-WIDER Conference on Country Role Models[2] provide extensive accounts of development experiences of several countries. These accounts bring new insights into the theories of growth and development. In all these studies, the politics of development remained missing, although the importance of the issue was evident in the analysis. The work of the political institutions, the political economy approach, and the politics of the future are difficult subjects to integrate into a development agenda. Yet these are essential to explain the complete process of development.

In addition, the recent literature on the great transformation of governance and democracy all point to politics as a key ingredient in the search for answers in development thinking and practice. Rekindling a strategic conversation on the link between development and politics is the aim of this chapter.

Politics and Development

As we enter the twenty-first century, development has come face to face with politics, one of the key factors in the advancement of growth and development. Previous attention to this link focused on politics in policymaking, and the conferring of benefits to parts of a society that will enhance the whole society's well-being and national interest. Specifying national interest is the work of the political process that is

* The text in this chapter was adapted from Winston Dookeran, "Politics and Development: A Strategic Conversation on the Missing Politics in Development," in *Leadership and Governance in Small States*, ed. Winston Dookeran and Akhil Malaki, 22–34 (Düsseldorf: VDM Verlag, 2008).

usually conducted in a competitive democratic system. This brings out large differences in the choice of the national interest, differences that at times may manifest in competing ideologies. Today, the debate has shifted towards the "right policies that will yield the right outcomes."

The polity of a society strives to work out the "best balance" in the equilibrium between political and economic goals (i.e., reconciling political and economic logics), while reflecting the national values of the society. Often, this equilibrium is unstable and constrained by the powers of the institutions in the society and the state. The application of a matrix of political economy allows the society to find the "right balance" that will promote sustained growth and development. Politics is about the distribution of power in a society, while political economy is about compensation to the "winners" and "losers" in any given distribution of power. Development is about closing the gaps in social equity and growth potential of the society. How to acquire and consolidate power depends on the nature and outcome of the mechanisms of the political system. How to compensate the losers is part of the process of reshaping the society's social welfare. How to bring about development is about all of these questions (and more).

The politics of development is often viewed in narrow terms of the distribution of income and opportunities. Looking at inequality and injustice in our global economy, Nancy Birdsall argues for higher weights to these goals in the policy paradigm of development.[3] Her argument is that globalization is dis-equalizing for three reasons: (1) the market works by rewarding countries and individuals with the most productive assets; (2) the market fails by generating negative externalities for the vulnerable and increasing the risks faced by the weak; (3) the market has power – rules and regimes – to systematically favour already rich countries and people.

To address these inequities, Birdsall advocates a global social contract to deal with unequal endowments and to build sound institutions that will

- link global transfers to the supply of global public goods;
- construct global regulations to address market failures; and
- provide better representation of developing countries in world bodies.

These elements in the global social contract raise critical issues of politics, which cannot be overlooked. The idea of policy conditionality has taken up many pages in the documents on policy dialogue. Currently, processing conditionality as "making it happen" is a crucial methodological challenge in policy design. The argument will shift in a generic sense from "what" to "how," opening up a whole plethora of political matters.

Politics in development is likely to get deeper, as each political choice will have different development outcomes. As such, analysis of the political choices becomes an essential part of the data requirements for good decision-making. This poses a tremendous challenge to leaders in development, politics, policymaking, and management alike. Apart from the undertaking to build models of politics and development, there will be the need to secure the population's assent to this trade-off, as they are critical in making political choices. Let us briefly examine the challenge of history in economic thinking.

Is there a "great transformation" in development economics ahead of us? Frances Stewart boldly and articulately raises this question.[4] Stewart first traces Polanyi's arguments about Europe, where the harsh consequences of the unregulated market led to a countermovement to regulate and humanize the market, so that society controlled the market rather than vice versa, which she refers to as a "great transformation." She then considers developing countries, where the harsh consequences of the market make a great new transformation desirable but the possibilities of change are severely constrained by global forces and democratic politics. Admitting that her search for a great transformation in our times does not represent a finished product, Stewart calls for an ambitious research program to understand the strength of movements for political change in particular countries around the world.

The First Wave of Reforms

The World Bank's *The Growth Report* traces the development experience of "successful" developing countries. The analysis for the most part excludes the incentive structure that informs political behaviour and omits how political logic will support strategies for growth and development. What is astonishingly missing in this far-reaching work is an analysis of the politics of development. In the last twenty-five years, some developing countries have been on the "catch-up" trajectory in the development cycle. Many have persistently attained high growth rates over the period. The report identifies thirteen such economies with a sustained growth rate of 7 per cent over a quarter century. Is there a formula? What is the underlying growth strategy? How is the framework built to sustain high growth rates over a long period? Clearly, domestic policies, important as they are, worked in an open integrated world economy. Increasing global demand together with abundant labour supply enables catch-up growth in the early stages of development.

For small economies, this is a special challenge. High growth rates are possible through sustained transformation of the society and economy. Such dynamics unleash a new energy of microeconomic undergrowth, sometimes referred to as "creative destruction" – creating new frontiers while protecting the people adversely affected by this change.

The report's preface states that growth is not an end in itself, but it is a necessary, if not sufficient, condition for "broader development." Could broader development take place without high growth rates? The report is silent on this issue, albeit regarding inclusive development as a critical objective. This implies that the nature of development must focus on inequality and poverty. Such challenges remain the key focal points of development, which can be pursued effectively even by societies without high growth rates. This raises the question: what is the natural rate of growth of a specific economy? How could inclusive development take place in any growth scenario? After all, inclusive development may well have a higher priority in the social welfare of the population. If not, the democratic outcome may alter the social welfare function through the workings of the political process.

The report calls for a long-term commitment by political leaders operating with patience, perseverance and pragmatism. Do the incentives facing political leaders support that nature of the commitment? How can continuity in growth strategy be attained in a competitive political market where the very disruption of that continuity creates a new political opportunity? Why would the development agenda take precedence over the political agendas of political entities vying for office? Understanding the link between politics and development is crucial and is an important ingredient in constructing a rapid-growth formula. A credible and strong political leadership must be able to emerge from the workings of the democratic system, which itself must have in-built incentive structures if this has to occur. Merely identifying deficits in the political economy is not enough. Rather, we must ask whether the democratic rules and behaviour by which leaders operate allow for a development outcome.

Such outcomes should create a greater demand for good governance. Unless such a demand exists, there is less possibility for the emergence of a supply of good governance. Here, the interaction between policy, institutions, and the market becomes a critical ingredient in the growth strategy, a lesson learned from the experiences of the reform process. The first wave of reform policies concentrated on issues of macroeconomic stability, of putting the house in order. The main measures of macroeconomic stability were opening up the economy to become competitive, removal of persistent budget and non-budget deficits, control over liquidity and inflationary excesses, and altering the supply structure of private and public goods.

The Second Wave of Reforms

The second wave, that "institutions matter," came to the forefront as issues of effective regulatory systems. More market-based initiatives and new institutions to promote inclusive development became central to the new reform. The right governance now acquires a special meaning to influence market behaviour so that the public interest is paramount. Sustained high growth rates and inclusive development like equality of opportunity, giving everyone a fair chance to enjoy the fruits of growth, are the anchors of the new legitimacy of right governance. Honest and transparent processes in both the public and private sectors add to that legitimacy.

Small states face a special challenge because of the high per capita cost of public services, limited scope for production diversification, and increasing risks to economic shocks. The *Growth Report*'s analysis of small states is rather limited, although in numbers these states comprise a significant portion of sovereign nations. Its prescription for small states is this: embrace the world economy, form regional clubs, and outsource some government functions. In small states, short-term cyclical capital inflows cannot mitigate the risk factors of emerging fiscal deficits, loss of competitive advantage, and secular decline in productivity. In defining the current challenge of Caribbean small states, a recent report by the Foundation for Politics and Leadership has this to say: "Caribbean societies are caught in a profound wave of change, as they respond to a different globalized order and to an emerging crisis within the borders of their own politics. The political and economic paradigms of yesterday have lost their legitimacy to promote workable solutions for a generation that is impatient and has high expectations."[5] The realization of these expectations cuts across social and generational space, unleashing the inherent conflict with politics and creating new obstacles to advancing development.

The new obstacles may also surface in the strategy for high growth if countries are unable to navigate through global challenges ahead. As the world faces up to the prospects of global warming and climate change, efforts to satisfy the criteria of efficiency and fairness as a global solution have reached an impasse. The global search for solutions in balancing growth, income equality, and environment has also been stalled on critical financial issues. Changes in global relative prices may affect a country's choice of sectors in its development strategy, and have a fiscal and balance-of-payments impact. Demographic changes and policy co-ordination in multilateral systems will add to the challenges of assessing global risks, uncertainties, and opportunities. In particular, changes in the world's currency reserve system may provide a new impetus for shifting power in the governance of financial institutions to reduce the risks faced by developing countries and improve the efficiency of the global system. One imminent risk is the rise of protectionism in the face of the World Trade Organization's commitment to a flexible multilateral trading system.

The report identifies the "adding-up" problem: if many individual countries simultaneously pursue export-led growth, will aggregate exports increase for individual countries? The idea is dismissed as a fallacy of composition, as there is little evidence in the pattern of trade that early entrants block late arrivals. Countries graduate to higher levels of labour intensity in their exports, thus keeping the door open to lower levels for new entrants. This may well be a fallacy, as the very composition of trade may change with the demands of an information era, making it non-competitive to tread the old path. In any event, high growth rates are sustainable by structural changes in an economy that is at the same time competitive. It is unlikely that old paths will remain competitive, an essential ingredient in a strategy of sustained growth.

True enough, there is no generic formula for countries to emulate, as each country has specific characteristics and historical experiences that must be reflected in the growth strategy. Do the experiences of these countries help in understanding the general theory of development? Do we need to design a new vintage of embodied and disembodied growth models that will explain the present reality in development? These are questions open to scholars of model-building in the economics of development. The success stories of even China and India do not deny that development remains the central global problem of our times. It would be a mistake to call a victory too early, as the *Growth Report* is tempted to do.

Development Policy Experiences: What Is at Stake?

The UNU-WIDER Conference on Country Role Models carefully examines the issues of macroeconomic stability, reform of institutions, and the politics of development as the model countries look ahead to economic and political challenges. There is a lot of normative analysis on this theme, and each group of countries exhibits special features that allow for some generalization. A key focus is on the third wave of the reform process, the "next step." Success stories of some economies are presented, which provide insights and may have shed new light on the performance of different strategies for economic development. What emerges from the conference are propositions that may guide thinking to reflect on the current reality, hurdles, and pathways.

The Nordic and European Experience

The Nordic experience suggests that the key is to organize the society for consensus, being adaptable to innovative change and strengthening effective institutions to counter the adversities of the resource curse. With little political room, Finland was able to achieve a political compromise that was deemed legitimate, preserving democratic institutions and basic freedoms and allowing for necessary capital accumulation, wage moderation, and welfare reforms.

In the non-Nordic developed economies of Europe, the focus was on changing the economic structure to sustain employment and reduce demand for the welfare state. The key strengths lie in the competitiveness of the economy and the contestability in the political system. A special case of having devised the right political institutions was Switzerland, starting from the Swiss confederation in 1848 to the current "direct democracy" model that paved the way for sustained economic growth of a consensus nature.[6]

The East Asian and Pacific Economies

The argument shifts to process and the microeconomic foundations of capabilities in the presentations of the East Asian and Pacific economies. Economic development results from domestic capital accumulation and enhancing the capabilities of the population in this emerging pan of the world economy. The Asian giants face the challenge of sustainable economic growth translating into economic development. The key factor of these successes lies in dynamic learning and flexible institution-building as components of a strategic approach to development. The ideas raised in *The Growth Report* are consistent with this approach, focusing on development as a process with strong microeconomic foundations embedded in the people themselves.

The Transition Economies

The transition economies confused critics in their ability to cope with the politics of changing the system as they work the new institutions of a market economy. Here, shock therapy could not bring results, as the initial conditions did not prevail and private accumulation of wealth raised a new dichotomy between the roles of the state and the market. The key lesson for development is not to discard the existing strengths in the economy. Hungary offers an example of a neo-institutionalist political economy approach to development where coalitions were in-built in a reform strategy shaping the new waves.[7]

The African Experience

When the issue of development is applied to sub-Saharan Africa, the main missing ingredient to success is getting the political-economic model right. Where the state is regarded as an agent of development, the political dynamics swing between taking control of the state and state failure. Augustin K. Fosu's work on the anti-growth syndrome traces the political and economic context of development in African countries from independence to the end of the last century. It is an extraordinary account where he succinctly shows the persistent conflict between the workings of political forces and institutions for economic growth.[8]

The conservative policy framework gives way to more soft and hard state interventions, a phenomenon that appears to occur in all the African case studies. This approach emphasizes the challenges of macroeconomic management in a post-colonial Africa. Fosu argues that a common thread emerges where the institutional framework displayed an anti-growth bias, retarding economic development. This experience illuminates the importance of the institutional constraint in macroeconomic performance and the emergence of democracy and development models as a key learning requirement to understand change in Africa.

Latin American and the Caribbean

Latin American and Caribbean economies faced the development challenge of stability in fragility, as the reform process was fractured and incomplete. Here, more than anywhere else, the issue of theory vs. real change emerges, as good macroeconomic indicators do not necessarily imply a fall in inequality and poverty levels and improvements in other development indicators. The dichotomy between growth and development is stark, as the entropy index (measure of diversification) suggests that the development cycle may recur. There is much uncertainty since development discontent may find expression in political populism.

The Middle East and North Africa

The process of economic behaviour re-emerges in discussion of Middle Eastern and North African economies. Development here is seen as correcting mistakes on the road map to higher levels of development. These economies exhibit "uniqueness," and their concern is how to use the "Dutch disease" phenomenon to change direction and broaden the development process from fragility to sustainability. Stable leadership rooted in their history and culture currently provides the right politics for growth, if not development and democracy.

Getting the Politics Right

An overriding theme in the Conference on Country Role Models is the role of leadership and governance in economic development. Such leadership and governance must be rooted in the "right politics," reconciling economic outcomes with political democracy. A clear distinction between policies and institutions needs articulation, as policies do change when right institutions evolve. A key premise in formulating development strategy is to recognize the initial conditions and the successes of the past, as this becomes the departure point from the old paradigms.

There has been significant progress in development performance over the last fifty years, yet the path ahead is still treacherous, given uncertainties in the direction of global adjustment and global market failures, especially in the context of the current financial crisis and global recession. Misalignment of currencies and upward inflationary pressures, due partly to new aggregate demand, are drawing the attention of world leaders. Rising food and fuel prices are a reflection of the stress in the fundamentals of the world economy. Adjustment to this current global macro imbalance is unclear and itself poses new risks to developed and developing countries alike. It may lead to a shift in political power and a reaction, as evident in the current postures of G8 and G5 countries. Political leadership in today's world is the new development challenge of tomorrow.

A Synthesis of Ideas from the Experience of Development

The current phase of globalization has deepened considerably. There are benefits of globalization even for developing countries, as the Nobel laureate Joseph Stiglitz observes. Globalization has reduced the sense of isolation of developing countries and "has given many people in the developing world access to knowledge well beyond the reach of even the wealthiest in any country a century ago."[9] Nevertheless, as Birdsall points out, income inequality has risen in most regions over the last two decades, and consumption data from groups of developing countries reveal the striking inequality that exists between the richest and the poorest in populations across different regions. Globalization is gathering momentum.

The importance of sovereign governments should not be overlooked, as they still have the power to erect significant obstacles to globalization, ranging from tariffs to immigration restrictions to military hostilities, and the world is still made up of nation states and a global marketplace. George Mavrotas and Anthony Shorrocks raise the bar in the search for "big ideas" in development.[10] They admit to the scarcity of theory today, as development thinking since the 1980s has gone back to the basics to understand the expanded general concept of development. Previously, the promise of the new political economy of the development approach did not go further than the role of institutions, making a strong case that development depends on institutional quality. Here, the nexus between growth, inequality, and poverty is seen as an indivisible process yet to be properly understood in development theory.

Louis Emmerij states that the fork before us is whether there is one theory (development) and one practice for the entire world, or whether there should be many theories in order to tailor development policies to the culture and habits of countries.[11] This opens up the question of the definition of development. It is here that Nobel laureate Amartya Sen's insights throw new light on the nature of development – development is about creating a set of "capabilities," and development is about "freedom." The scope is now widened, as Sen's interest shifts from the pure theory of social choice to a more practical approach that sees individual advantage not merely as opulence or utility, but primarily in terms of the lives people manage to live and the freedom they have to choose the kind of life they have reason to value.[12]

Sen's emphasis on freedom of choice naturally leads him to democracy as a preferred political system where a country does not have to be deemed fit for democracy; rather, it has to become fit through democracy. The focus has now moved to democracy and good governance as a critical requirement of development. However, there is still the search for a consensus on the precise indicators of democracy and good governance. What is clear is that the conduct of politics will greatly influence the measurement of these indicators.

In the search for these indicators of good governance, the notions of political tolerance and pluralism can differ remarkably depending on whether one views government from a Western liberal perspective or from the perspective of development outcomes. The World Bank, with a Western liberal eye, considers the six components of good governance to be voice and accountability, political instability and violence, government effectiveness, regulatory burden, rule of law, and control of corruption. These are important indicators, but may miss issues like economic inequality, poverty, employment, technology, liberty and rights, capabilities, and well-being. In several developing countries, the institutional framework may not be mature, yet the outcomes of governance may be high when measured by indices like human development and gross happiness. Therefore, a consensus on a set of good governance indicators must capture the dynamics of development that takes place in an ever-changing institutional framework.

The World Bank has measured a "development dividend" of good governance. This dividend is a difficult proposition to isolate and to measure, but there is no doubt that good governance can deliver significant improvements to people, particularly if the demand for good governance grows among the population in a steady manner. Here, the dynamics of the political culture becomes important, as good governance will thrive if the demand for it increases. Often, this is a matter of political choice and the conduct of politics in any given situation. In spite of a growing proliferation of good governance initiatives, much work is needed on the issues of the nature, measurement, and supply of good governance.

An evolutionary view of the major waves of development is presented by Mannermaa in her work for the Finnish parliament.[13] Mannermaa states that the agrarian era (ca. 6000 BC–AD 1750) attended to issues of community interest within the village context. The industrial era followed for the next 250 years, driven by new means of production where models of representative democracy emerged as a governmental form. Today, the information era is upon us, creating an information society that is yet to mature, characterized by innovations in communication technology. Networks, rapid changes, and flexible thinking will now inform the political process, creating a democracy of "minorities" that will undermine the "majority" notion in representative democracy.

How will the conduct of politics be affected by this new wave of development? According to the Committee for the Future in the Finnish parliament, the notion of "instantism" (the expectation that things have to happen immediately) may cause a shift towards electronic voting and an increase in "non-representative" civil society's influence in the political process. Consequently, the welfare function that reflects the developmental needs of the society may be at risk, adding new challenges to development and democracy.

In a path-breaking study two decades ago, Robert Scalapino identified the key link between politics and development in Asia at that time.[14] A large part of the "success" of Asian development over three decades can be attributed to the management of tensions and politics in these countries. To a Western mind, the kind of political system may not fit the indicators of the democracy matrix, thus bringing into focus the link between political systems and economic development.

Yao bases his explanation for China's record of economic growth on the notion of "disinterested government."[15] He defines a disinterested government as one that does not have differentiated interests among the segments of the society and is more likely to foster overall economic growth of the country instead of advancing the interest of certain segments that it represents or forms an alliance with. This is because reform is seen as a historical evolution reaffirmed by the belief that the pursuit of egalitarian policies and an equal society is the trusted prerogative of the political elite that cannot be comprised by alliances with any segment of the society. Yao dismisses the claim that the one-party system is anti-democratic, as there are democratic elements in China's political structure allowing for "voice and accountability," and indeed other components of indicators of good governance.

Politics and economics have been central to the analysis of development, and the Western academic tradition has kept it apart partly for pedagogical reasons. However, in the study of development such a separation may conceal the dynamic interconnections between economic and political factors. This chapter is an attempt to rekindle a strategic conversation on the subject. Could it lead to a synergy between economic and political logic in the study of development?

6 Political Economy and Strategy[*]

Questions in the Economic Debate

In the history of political economy, there are always departure points and shifts in the prevailing economic paradigm putting the economy on a different path. One such departure point in the Western hemisphere and the Caribbean region occurred in the 1980s. In Trinidad and To-bago, we shifted from a "commanding heights" economy to a market-driven economic process. We embraced the economic strategy of the Washington Consensus and began to answer the following questions:

- What macroeconomic measures are required to stabilize the economy?
- How do we liberalize our markets to exploit opportunities abroad?
- Why do we need a better relationship between the private and public sectors?

The answers to these questions came to be called the first-generation reforms, a challenge of structural adjustment. The political process was intense, culminating in a failed coup attempt in 1990 that threatened to derail the new direction. The first-generation reforms were soon seen to be insufficient, giving scope for a second generation of reforms focusing on building institutions. Suddenly, it became evident that institutions matter, and major policy changes were required:

- a change in the exchange rate regime;
- a new regulatory model in telecommunication and technology;

---

* The text in this chapter was adapted from Winston Dookeran, "Political Economy of Development: The Search for New Thinking," in Crisis and Promise in the Caribbean, 49–60 (London: Ashgate, 2015).

- meeting of international banking standards; and
- creation of new delivery systems for public goods like water, electricity, postal services, roads, bridges, education, and health.

Changing institutions became much more difficult than imagined, as it also meant a change in the power structure controlling these institutions. Many talked about change, but few were prepared to give up power and privileges for the common good. Once again the development results were disappointing, and populist discontent emerged as poverty levels rose, prices soared beyond the reach of large segments of the population, and violence led to lawlessness. In the meantime, the integrity of the political process was questioned as bribery and corruption drew the national attention. This is the context of our development path since the turning point of the 1980s as the country embraced a reform agenda, similar to what was taking place in the Caribbean and Latin American region.

Is the Magic from Macroeconomics Over?[1]

What are those movements of political change? Looking ahead – very far ahead, maybe up to 2050 – we are likely to see some fundamental reordering of and a new configuration of global power, for a number of reasons.

The first is that demographic dividends are likely to accelerate economic growth due to a decline in fertility and mortality rates that impacts the age structure of the population and thus the economics of the future. The second aspect is that the process of capital accumulation to which we have been accustomed is, too, in a period of variation. Many of the incentives and behaviours for capital accumulation were based on premises that are now being revised in the dynamics of a more complex growth process. Third, the sources of productivity in the economy are likely to alter in the future and certainly so in this digital age. These factors and others will lead to a change in the pattern of global demand and supply.

Underlying these changes, and with the economic and political shifts happening today, the structures of global governance will shake, placing global institutions under stress for reform and radical change in the next many years. What are we likely to see as the outcome of that change? The world's largest economies of the future will not necessarily be the richest, and the spending pattern in the global population will alter significantly. Recent studies[2] have suggested that that pattern of spending will affect the dynamics of political power which in turn will impact on the practice and process of governance that are now in place. What is the relevance of these developments for today' situation?

State strategies in the global political economy must respond to the global shifts affecting the macro reset of policies in economics, finance, trade, shocks, survival, and sustainability. What are the global shifts affecting the Caribbean, and how will they define the strategic focus of the region's development?

The World Economic Forum's January 2021 summit set the theme of the Great Reset – "the COVID-19 crisis could reverse global human development – measured in terms of education, health and living standards. Small island developing states are particularly vulnerable … and will have an inordinate amount of difficulty of recovering, without sufficient finance."

The policy choices coming out of the "great reset" will face tense political stress and acute testing of the new policy frames. The global setting will also be redefined by answers to the following questions:

- What are the global forces that underlie the geostrategic shifts?
- Is the world political order of the Bretton Woods vintage now on its knees?
- How will these trends affect global cooperation?
- Will the Caribbean region be ready for the geostrategic shifts?

Answers to these questions are addressed in other chapters in this book. In this chapter, we open a conversation on the changing strategic focus of the global political economy, in the areas of global governance, integration and convergence, financing of development, changing diplomacy, survival and sustainability, and the alignment of politics.

Changing Strategic Focus of Shifts in Global Political Economy

We now introduce some agenda ideas on these issues that will require a macro reset of strategies and policies in the frontiers of Caribbean analysis.

Global Governance

The issue of institutions of global governance, whether at the United Nations or the Bretton Woods Institutions, will now be a matter that attracts intense scrutiny. In 2014 the Sixty-Ninth Session of the UN General Assembly, at a conference on the theme of global governance in today's world, came up with a number of recommendations for defining the situation before us, among which the most pronounced was inclusive dialogue.[3]

Global governance and the international financial system have both been based on the framework of the liberal project that promotes global cooperation on security, trade, and monetary policy. Today, both "inclusive dialogue" and the "liberal project" are facing major political stress scrutiny, generating a redesign in the practice of diplomacy and pathways for development.

Integration and Convergence

Integration movements in the world are in many cases at a point of inflection. The crisis in the Eurozone, which was once seen as emanating from the failure of the market in the financial sector, soon turned into one of sovereignty, later into a crisis of politics and now with a focus on strategic autonomy. But integration movements are not only being tested in Europe; in many parts of Latin America and certainly in the Caribbean region such movements are under great stress.

The Caribbean region has not been able to achieve the equilibrium between growth and equity in its integration efforts that it was once expected to balance. Not that that goal was wrong; indeed, it was and is appropriate – a necessary but not sufficient objective. But the time has come for us to ask whether the integration movement is in need of a new architecture that will broaden the frontiers of integration to give it a competitive reach into the global economy.

It has become essential to build economic space beyond one's borders. This is no longer a matter for rhetoric, and the models of integration for doing so have perhaps reached their limits. To extend those limits, the integration process should move beyond to embrace a wider model of convergence.

In that process, one big issue is whether capital accumulation or equity is going to be the driver for development; for too long we have believed that capital accumulation is the source of growth. Several reports from the World Bank, IDB, and ECLAC examine this issue of equity and growth and question the dialectical process between growth and equity.[4] The analytics of that arrangement point to a fresh appraisal.

Economic convergence, thus, is bringing the traditional private sector to the forefront in creating opportunities for growth and development. Financing of development requires a strong synergy between the private sector and the public sector, as the development of each reinforces the other in a national frame. Projects that support regional convergence and extend our economic space may need innovative financing mechanisms. As such, developing financing for convergence may add to the integration efforts, thus redefining its role and institutional structure from what exits. Is it time to introduce a financing model for Caribbean convergence?

Financing of Development

The small economies of the Caribbean are at times described as frag ile and vulnerable, always subject to what has been called external shocks. The reality is that there are some new challenges emerging, and the first of these has to do with finance. The Caribbean has a robust financial sector; the recent World Bank report on the region wrote that the financial sector in the Caribbean is 350 per cent of gross domes tic product. That report revealed that the financial sector, which has been dominated by the banks but not exclusively so, has been strong in many different ways; yet the region itself is in major deficit on public financing.[5]

How do we convert the strength of the financial flows in the region to deal with the financial deficits in the public sector, and how do we at the same time ensure that confidence in this process is enhanced? Too often the Caribbean has searched for solutions that require external support – and indeed external support will always be necessary – but, regardless of the source of finance, development "cannot be imported."

Development is about how you channel the flow of funds within your own economy in order to support the development thrust. There is no doubt that the financial sector has operated in an enclave, responding to the incentives of the global system but less so with respect to the development impetus of the region – another major alignment issue. But external support is necessary. International financial institutions often err in measuring sustainability on arithmetical ratio – debt to GDP, reserve to export, fiscal balance – focusing on arithmetical ratios rather than moving averages in a loop cycle.

Changing Diplomacy

The issues that have emerged in global relations stem from the old paradigm of the centre-periphery in the orthodox definition of the relationship. Events in some countries in the periphery, like Cyprus recently, and before that Greece and others, have shown a new realignment between the centre and the periphery, where developments in the periphery can directly affect the core interest of the centre. As such, the old pattern of political power between the centre and the periphery will see a new mapping.

This will happen not because there is a need to include many small countries in this operation but because in the interconnected world in which we live, in the spillover world in which we will be living, and in the new patterns of spending that will emerge over the next many years, the periphery is going to become more of a partner in this process. The basics in small-states diplomacy will open new options and prospects in the conduct of international relations.

Survival and Sustainability

Public measures aimed at survival of small economies often are not done in a framework of sustainability. This is a big challenge, given the frequency of natural calamities, the emergency nature of the situation, and the missing institutions that are not in place.

The truth is that the way to measure sustainability is itself in need of change: sustainability must be measured in terms of its ability to cope, in our capacity to adjust, and in institutions that build buffers for the future. The international financial institutions may wish to reassess how sustainability is measured in a Caribbean context, and adopt a more dynamic framework that can support actions that increase flexibility in coping with external shocks, by building buffers both locally and externally.

Why? Shocks have been viewed as a temporary phenomenon, but in the Caribbean they have been a permanent feature of the policy landscape. Indeed, the history of management of the economy of the Caribbean is one of managing shocks. International institutions tend to analyse shocks as short-term phenomenon to be dealt with in the context of the exigencies of the time. In the Caribbean, the buffers to deal with shocks must be sustainable in the long term – international buffers must be supported by local buffers. This calls for a full appraisal of measures of sustainability beyond the global concerns of environment and climate action.

Alignment of the Politics

Finally, in terms of the region, this entire process is a political process; whether in terms of change of governance in the world or governance in the region itself, it is a political process. And therefore, the alignment between the logic of politics and the logic of economics must now be reviewed and realigned. For too long politics has been the obstacle to development; there is need for a new alignment, and that alignment requires a new diplomacy in the relationship between economics and politics.

In the region we are neither isolated nor insulated, and therefore we have to adopt a strategy that is consistent with the dictates of world development, which will have an impact on us whether we like it or not. We must look ahead, anticipate shifts in the global political economy, and calibrate the framework responses required by the Caribbean nations. In that vein, the structures for delivering a common Caribbean foreign policy are missing, and the processes are in need of radical coordination and coherence.

Questions about Inclusive Development

In their widely acclaimed book *Why Nations Fail: The Origins of Power, Prosperity, and Poverty*,[6] Daron Acemoglu and James A. Robinson argue extensively that inclusiveness, particularly of institutions, is a requirement of economic development. More importantly, Acemoglu and Robinson maintain that inclusive development has the power to make or break a nation – they give compelling evidence of this by juxtaposing poverty-prone and economically stable communities, attributing the contrast to the former's exclusiveness. The book, which also gives a historical overview of world politics and economic strategies, has generated numerous debates. Business giant Bill Gates critiqued the explanations as being simplistic, arguing that "most examples of economic growth in the last 50 years – the Asian miracles of Hong Kong, Korea, Taiwan, Singapore – took place when their politics tended more toward exclusiveness."[7]

However, as Acemoglu and Robinson's insights show, inclusive development depends on the economic forces and flow of funds within and from outside the economy. Focus on the following leverage points may target inclusive development.

- Foreign exchange management must be a central economic instrument in the economic policy package.
- Economic policies must deliberately seek to link the growth process with distribution targets.
- Regional developments must be encouraged via effective fiscal and other measures.
- The distribution system that is the basis upon which the production structure is built and the consumption pattern formed must be at centre stage in any multisectoral plan.
- Technology forecasting must be an ongoing process so as to ensure flexibility in the entire economic structure and the performance of that structure.
- High-skilled, human-based industries must be part of our longer-term program.

A Strategic Focus on Leadership and Sustainable Growth

A clear distinction between policies and institutions needs articulation, as policies do change when the right institutions evolve. A key premise in formulating development strategy is to recognize the initial conditions and the successes of the past, since these becomes a departure point from the old paradigms.

There have been significant strides in development performance over the last fifty years, yet the path ahead is still treacherous given uncertainties in the direction of global adjustment and global market failures, especially in the context of the current financial crisis and global recession. Misalignment of currencies and upward inflationary pressures due partly to new aggregate demand are drawing the attention of world leaders. Rising food and fuel prices are a reflection of stress in the fundamentals of the world economy. The adjustment to this current global macro imbalance is unclear and poses new risks to developed and the developing countries alike. It may lead to a shift in political power and a reaction, as evident in the current postures of G8 (7+1) and G5 (BRICS) countries. Political leadership in today's world is the new development challenge of tomorrow.

While growth is at the core of national development, sustainable growth is hard to achieve; hence long-term national development is at risk. However, a key feature of developing countries is that the growth process lacks persistence. Periods of rapid growth are punctuated by collapses and even long periods of stagnation. The goal therefore is to achieve sustainable growth or at least prolong the duration of growth. What determines the length of the growth spell? While external shocks, initial income, institutional quality, openness to trade, and macroeconomic stability are critical determinants of growth, income inequalities must be taken into account.

Is there a formula? What is the underlying growth strategy? How is the framework built to sustain high growth rates over a long period? In the long term the relationship between income inequality and economic growth matters. Kuznets's hypothesis that as an economy develops inequality first increases and then decreases has not stood the empirical test of time. So, the focus moved to growth spells and inequality. Berg and Ostry[8] assert that longer growth spells are robustly associated with more equality in income distribution.[9]

Clearly domestic policies, important as they are, worked in an open, integrated world economy. Increasing global demand together with abundant labour supply enables "catch-up" growth in the early stages of development. While neoliberalism frameworks in tackling income distribution and poverty are important, national agency also plays a significant part in poor performance on equality. This is especially so when funding for the national agency depends on the fiscal cycle of boom-and-bust economies, which is often the case. The impact is transient, not only because of the effectiveness of such programs but also because the funding is not sustainable. Funding mechanisms that are self-financing, based on actuarial-derived data, allow the national agency to be more sustaining in promoting equality and reducing poverty on a structural basis. National insurance schemes are good institutions that can be designed in a creative and innovative way to widen the coverage in the population that will also include vulnerable groups in society, and to do so in an actuarially sound basis. This requires visionary and analytical leadership and will have a sustained impact on the growth of the economy with sustained equity for the society as a whole.

7 Political Logic and Economic Logic[*]

The Missing Politics of Development

Several attempts at restructuring the economy and pursuing high-level economic policy measures in the Caribbean fell short, partly due to design issues and often to shortcomings in the implementation process. In Trinidad and Tobago, the "imperatives of adjustment" and "restructuring for economic independence"[1] are two outstanding examples of highly acclaimed economic policy reports that were tested and failed to realize expected outcomes. What was missing in the arithmetic of the development strategy?

The failure to explicitly incorporate the politics of development into the matrix of analysis has been cited as the missing part of the conversation. It is a truism to say that economics alone will not define the national interest, but to add political analysis into the economic equation is a tricky matter, although an important one. The logic of the economic equation is often at odds with the logic of the political equation. Synchronizing these logics is the art of good governance.

Getting the right balance and policies is a major challenge in political economy. It is about the politics of the distribution of power in a society, the political sociology of sustaining stability, and the right economic formula for compensation between winners and losers with any given policy. Closing the gap in social equity and realizing the growth

---

* The first two sections of this chapter were adapted from Winston Dookeran, "Synchronizing the Logic of Politics and Economics: Fiscal Management and Job Creation," in *Crisis and Promise in the Caribbean*, 61–78 (London: Ashgate, 2015). The third section is based on Dookeran, "A New Frontier for Caribbean Conversion," *Caribbean Journal of International Relations and Diplomacy* 1, no. 2 (2013): 5–20 and on a presentation at the 4th ITO Global Conference, New Delhi, 7–9 December 2011.

potential of the economy generate tensions that could derail well-structured plans for development. A strategic conversation that misses the politics of development may keep a country at a standstill or move it forward to higher levels of attainment. The application of the calculus of political economy allows the society to find the right balance that will promote sustained growth and development.

Managing the Economy

If politics and economics are inseparable, politics without economics is disastrous. Political decisions over time have created the current distorted and mismanaged economy in Trinidad and Tobago, and must be set right. A mismanaged economy has

- no sustainable national development policy;
- misdirected priorities placing development of buildings before people;
- misallocated national resources; and/or
- mismanagement in the massive transfer payments from the energy sector into mostly unproductive activities.

Therefore, government must address not only the mismanaged economy but also the distortions that affect our society. The mismanaged economy has over time distorted the culture and behaviour of the entire society. It has had a corrupting influence on all economic, social, and political activities, which allows for democracy to be replaced by a creeping dictatorship when critical national resources and economic activities are redirected to unproductive use. This creates a shift in focus from hard work, productivity, wealth creation, and long-term sustainable development to short-term measures for the sake of political advantage.

Short-term measures destabilize the society and its major institutions. The purpose of the huge transfer payments from the energy sector has been to sustain political power. While the rich have been getting richer, more people are now ranked as working poor, and the numbers of those dependent on the state for employment have also increased.

Past administrations with misplaced economic priorities have not dealt with the increased threat to our safety and security from the powerful illicit drug economy. Drug transfer payments have been flowing into this country, causing not only violence but major economic distortions, affecting all aspects and levels of our society.

The time has come, therefore, for leadership to search for a new development paradigm, one that will identify political logic and economic logic. This logic will construct new measures for financial sustainability and design a strategy for basic development that puts equity at the centre. This requires us to drill deeper into development. Why? For the simple reason that unless economic logic and political logic are synchronized, we cannot move towards any particular solution.

Growth and Inequality

One issue[2] is the sources of growth and of inequality. Are they really meshing? How can we have added equity along with added growth? But more important, is growth now seen as the search for new economic space within a country – whether geographically or by bringing new people into an economic space that was not there before through what is sometimes referred to as the inclusion concept? It is in this context that inequality restricts growth. In that context, equality is the best way to enhance growth potential.

Given the outlook for its energy sector, and the dependence of its non-energy sector on the government as its primary market and source of significant transfers, Trinidad and Tobago faces the significant development challenge of transitioning its economy into a post-hydrocarbon model while continuing to improve its standard of living. This transition will require that a number of reforms and investments be undertaken so as to foster an environment in which non-traditional economic activities can flourish independently. Public-sector spending will have to become more efficient and effective, and the multitude of subsidies and transfers feeding patronage systems and distorting incentives for private-sector activities will have to be rationalized and targeted to create incentives for the transition to the post-hydrocarbon economy.

There is a clear mandate to transform the country by channelling it towards a new path that moves away from an entitlement model fueled by transfers to one that is competitive and sustainable without such heavy reliance on the energy sector. We have to work towards creating different conditions for achieving more sustainable growth, which requires a fundamental reorientation of our outdated policies, and putting in place new and more modern governance and institutional structures. Without this, investment will never achieve the expected results.

Tax Efficiency, Fiscal Effectiveness, and Jobs

The debate must then be put in the perspective of synchronization between the economic and the political logics. Unless there is synchronization between economic logic and political logic, it is hardly likely that we can progress towards a particular solution. What are the issues that emerge out of that framing of the solution matrix?

First, I will identify how I frame the issue: it is an issue of tax efficiency on one side and of fiscal effectiveness on the other. By "tax efficiency" I merely mean the framework for economic activity, and by "fiscal effectiveness" I mean how fiscal policy will add value to growth, to equity, and in the final analysis to jobs – for it is now well recognized that the bottom line in this whole equation is jobs. As minister of finance, I summarized the issue as follows: "We believe our energy resources are finite. We need to ensure that those resources are efficiently and wisely monetised, to provide us with the capital to build an economy that can provide a sustainable future when oil and gas are depleted. We believe that the natural and mineral resources of this country belong to every citizen. Every citizen must be able to legitimately expect to partake in the opportunities those resources can provide. We believe that the best indicator of national development is a fairer distribution of income that ensures that no one is left behind."[3]

Tax Efficiency: The Framework for Economic Activity

One issue, as I note above, is the sources of growth and the sources of inequality. Are they really meshing, and how can they mesh together? How can we have added growth and added equality? That is one of the fundamental issues that must be resolved.

The other issue is the political economy within which decisions are made. It has less to do with the technical aspects of tax administration, whether in terms of the mix or level of taxes, than with who are the winners and who the losers, and what is the best equilibrium that will be sustainable politically between winners and losers in this game of taxation and fiscal effectiveness.

Growth, Equity, and Taxation

In order to deal with these issues, clearly we must find the right theoretical framework. What is before us, really, is a choice between thinking that may be outdated and new thinking that has emerged in the theoretical literature on the issues of growth, equity, and taxation.

We all remember in our early days the study of economics; most of us are familiar with Kuznets curves and the view that savings will enhance capital accumulation. Capital accumulation will in turn generate growth, and savings are likely to be more effective in distributions that are unequal rather than equal. That was the view many of us were taught as students.

Today there is a growing consensus that perhaps this is not quite correct. Andrew G. Berg and Jonathan D. Ostry's studies have now identified that there are in fact positive attributes to growth as a result of equality.[4] Three basic observations emerged in the theoretical literature.

One observation is that increasing the length of growth spells – and this introduces growth spells into the argument rather than just getting growth going as critical to achieving income gains over the long run – must introduce secular trends for sustainability. In other words, it is not so much increased growth but the duration of the growth period that enhances equality issues and income gains.

The second observation is that more equal income distribution tends to accompany significantly longer growth spells. Here we see the link between equality on the one hand and growth spells on the other hand. It is in this context that the new thinking – perhaps with respect to the links between tax and growth, and growth and equity – has now begun to take hold. Is equity the natural consequence of a deliberate strategy on the part of governments and expenditure policies; or to what extent is it really enforced by some form of revenue policy?

But more important than this is that growth is now seen as the search for new economic space within a country, whether geographical or created by bringing new people into the space – an economic space that was not there before. This, as we have seen, is referred to as the inclusion concept. Inequality does restrict the growth of economic space, and because it is important to look at growth from the perspective of creating more economic space, equalizing incomes is the surest path towards sustaining growth spells and space.

SECTION 3

Pathways in Analytical Leadership

8 The Imperative of Caribbean Convergence[*]

Defining the Inspirational Moment

The Forum on the Future of the Caribbean marked the start of an exciting new chapter in the development of the Caribbean. It was a moment of true possibility – one that we must grasp. It is incumbent upon those of us who attended and participated in the event to free ourselves from both the constraints of traditional thinking and the limits imposed by entrenched views that suggest "it's just not done that way."[1]

My inspiration to hold this forum was rooted in the changing global and economic landscape in which the Caribbean is strategically positioned, and the need for a forum to address the growing concerns among Caribbean nations. The opportunity to take a leadership role comes at a time when the Caribbean Community (CARICOM) is said to have stalled and perhaps run its course in addressing these issues, and now requires a different approach.

Fazal Karim, minister of tertiary education and skills training in Trinidad and Tobago, has aptly said that "leadership is about delivering results."[2] This forum is itself an act of assuming leadership responsibility to ensure the frontiers of future generations are as good as, or indeed better than, those of the present. Convergence plays a central role that requires a realignment of political and economic logic with the realities of the contemporary Caribbean economic *problématique*. I offer a full

---

[*] This chapter was adapted from Winston Dookeran, "Shifting the Frontiers: Defining the Imperative of Caribbean Convergence in the Twenty-First Century," in *Shifting the Frontiers: An Action Framework for the Future of the Caribbean*, edited by Winston Dookeran and Carlos Elias, 324–36 (Kingston: Ian Randle, 2016); and Dookeran, "A New Frontier for Caribbean Convergence," *Caribbean Journal of International Relations and Diplomacy* 1, no. 2 (2013): 5–20.

exposition of this in my book *Crisis and Promise in the Caribbean: Politics and Convergence.*

In the forty years since its birth, the Caribbean integration movement has achieved much but may have reached its limits.[3] Consequently, there is an urgent need to respond to the current realities and emerging global trends, which require greater engagement from the public, students, academics, and policymakers in moving CARICOM towards a new trajectory of Caribbean convergence. The immediate concern is to design ways to improve the convergence process among the Latin American and Caribbean countries. This convergence process must also be sensitive to the current and emerging global dynamics.

The emerging trade and economic structure is rapidly changing in both its dynamics and architecture. The articulations of global groups such as the BRICS economies (Brazil, Russia, India, China, and South Africa) and regional convergence as in the case of the Association of East Asian Nations (ASEAN) are some examples of alternative ways of dealing with global development. It is important to note that these emerging markets have become economic powerhouses in the current global economy. They have become the major consumers with increasing national savings and growing capital markets. It is interesting that south-south and north-south trade is overtaking the traditional north-north trade metrics. This emerging trade architecture is supported by a growth and expansion of multinationals from the emerging markets. In addition, emerging market economies hold almost three-quarters of sovereign wealth funds.[4]

The global financial architecture in the twenty-first century has also undergone dramatic changes. This emerging architecture is multipolar, with the yuan asserting its role alongside the dollar and the euro. Sovereign wealth funds from emerging markets are fueling outward foreign direct investments and growth in bilateral investment treaties. Furthermore, significant changes have occurred in the governance structure of the global financial system of the Basel III, where a number of rule-making institutions have extended membership to BRICS. In this way, all G20 countries were included as members in the Basel committee,[5] and Goldman Sachs's "Dreaming with BRICs: The Path to 2050" predicts that BRICS "could be larger than the G6 by 2039."[6]

Public-private partnerships provide necessary breathing room to countries with limited fiscal capacity to fund infrastructure and other investments in the region. The role of the private sector and private institutions in economic growth has become pivotal to the forging of convergence. It calls for innovative forms of partnerships between states and the private sector, and for global- and regional-development finance institutions in integrated production. In short, the emerging public-private partnership demonstrates the trend towards a more inclusive political economy.

The world has also moved from multilateral to multitrack diplomacy. We live in a different world today: the number of players has increased markedly, and the web of interests and influence has similarly become significantly more complex and interrelated. In Trinidad and Tobago, we have deliberately begun to search for a new method of reinforcing multilateralism, and we recognize that we must operate on a multitrack policy of diplomacy. But at this point in time, the choices are not clear. What is clear is that to protect our vital interests, we must be engaged in moving away from the diplomacy of protection to one of engagement. A multitrack diplomacy is really what we have been engaged in, whether it is at the United Nations, in our bilateral relationships with countries, or in our relationship with the emerging order globally; at all times, the fundamental objective is to ensure that we now move towards a diplomacy of engagement. Specifically, we have begun to open our doors to Latin American institutions. Trinidad and Tobago now enjoys full membership in the Latin American Development Bank (CAF), which is significant because we now see the integration of Latin America and the Caribbean being funded by sources and resources from Latin America and the Caribbean. This policy choice is a significant departure from our reliance on the traditional multilateral institutions such as the World Bank and the IDB.

Setting the Architectural Framework

For a new Caribbean economic space to become a reality, it must be based on new models of intervention that can position both CARICOM countries and the wider Caribbean to engage in this convergence in order to seize the opportunities that the global market provides. The international political economy has changed from what it was when CARICOM countries became independent nations, and thus requires a different approach to its economic development.

Sachs notes that convergence "occurs when the per capita income of the poorer regions rises more rapidly in percentage terms than the per capita income of the richer regions, so that the ratio of per capita incomes of the poorer regions to richer regions rises towards one, that is, the same standard of living."[7] Like other economists, Sachs believes this "catch-up effect" is taking place with the rise of the global middle class, bringing an unprecedented convergence of perceptions,

Figure 8.1. Convergence framework

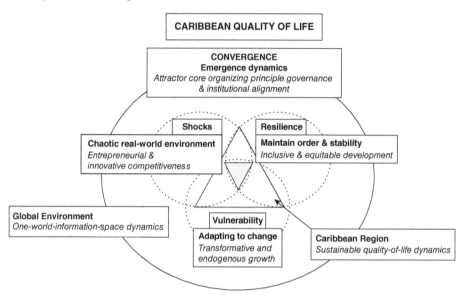

Source: Jantzen et al., "Caribbean Future Initiative."

ideas, and nuances signalling that a new global order has already arrived, and requiring the Caribbean region to create a new framework (going beyond the old inherited structural arrangements) that is better suited to its needs. With this convergence, relations can deepen to create the kinds of incisive institutions that can deal with today's challenges.

Dierdre McCloskey warns, correctly, that conditional convergence is not inevitable.[8] Countries must transform themselves to adapt to new conditions and to be prepared to take advantage of opportunities. As the history of Trinidad and Tobago shows, it is possible for real income per capita to be cut in half during an economic downturn, and then to rapidly double again during an economic boom. Why is volatility such a key characteristic of the Caribbean? In Trinidad and Tobago, and in other countries in the region, socioeconomic performance depends on many factors, among them appropriate or unsuitable policies, high or low prices of Caribbean exports, and good or bad luck. As the region moves forward, governments and stakeholders should be aware of these issues that transcend temporary political cycles. My thinking on the meaning of convergence is depicted in Figure 8.1.

Integration with Convergence

There are definite gains to be made by using convergence as a response to emerging global changes. Expanding the economic space provides scope for leverage in production and competitiveness. Caribbean convergence is the strategy to move the Caribbean integration process towards fuller and more complete integration within the Caribbean and beyond. The rationale behind the new "Caribbean integration" strategy is to strive towards a convergence of economies of scale with capital. The strategy draws upon the new convergence framework that transcends borders of integration both regionally and globally. Convergence of "economic spaces" is a response to the limitations of the CARICOM integration process and the opening of new spaces for confronting the development challenges ahead. Accordingly, convergence is a shift from a physically limited plane to an "open economic space."[9]

In the first instance, convergence is about the addition of new institutions that allow the Dominican Republic, the Dutch and French islands, and French Guiana to be engaged in the context of the Guiana Shield proposition. Convergence is not about creating something new, nor is it opposed to CARICOM integration. Rather, it is about bringing new political and economic dynamics to the process of Caribbean integration by reworking the existing frameworks in innovative and flexible ways (the logic of politics) to cope with changing global realities and redefining the modalities of execution.

What is innovative in this convergence framework is a new form of public-private partnership within an "economy of the Caribbean Sea" with a focus on production integration, distribution, and competitiveness (the logic of economics) as supporting trade and markets. Convergence is about adding future value to the workings of the integration process, and supporting the structures built over the last forty years. This is in line with the call for building regional capacity to address global challenges.[10]

Convergence strategies and partnership go together. Discussions on regional economic integration, Caribbean convergence, and competitiveness in the Caribbean Growth Forum launch event (2012) have, in a way, set the tone for action and change. Two important issues were recognized: the "political imperative of convergence" and the need for "appropriate correcting mechanisms" that align the needs of the local with the regional. It was also noted that the problem with Caribbean integration is in its "failure of implementation." The larger Caribbean space is heterogeneous with contrasting economic differences that are politically sensitive. The discussions concluded that the genesis for convergence (integration without borders) should first of all be political, requiring political will and advocacy. Creating the Caribbean Sea economy is first a politics-driven process.

The new structures must aim at production integration, competitiveness, and distribution across this economic space (the economic logic), in addition to trade and markets. It must allow for economies of scale and space. According to this economic logic, convergence is not just about enlargement of markets and trade – it is about making the region resilient and globally competitive to capture opportunities in the future. The partnership approach is a stakeholder approach that provides us with a practical way forward as we align national strategy with a regional one. Central to this regional space is aligning the logic of politics (e.g., inclusiveness, cooperation) with the logic of economics (e.g., production integration, competitiveness, distribution).

The idea of Caribbean convergence has already been discussed on various occasions over the last couple of years, with positive feedback. This feedback has provided the inputs for the framework developed here, which is an innovative approach to revive CARICOM in a different context to make it more relevant to capture "a new frontier of Caribbean convergence."[11]

ECLAC has recently raised some concerns the mechanisms of convergence and the modalities to engage the private sector in CARICOM. The framework addresses these concerns through the partnership approach, and more specifically through fostering public-private partnerships across the economy of the Caribbean Sea. The Trinidad and Tobago chapter of the Caribbean Growth Forum identified three themes (investment climate, logistics and connectivity, skills and productivity) to be achieved through public-private partnerships. These themes are reflected in the twelve-point action plan referred to in the Monos Island Chaguaramas Declaration of CARICOM foreign ministers.

The CARICOM institutional framework is under political stress, with many prominent leaders and scholars voicing this view. Sir Sridath Ramphal emphatically notes that leadership in the region has "put the gears of CARICOM Single Market in neutral and the gears of CARICOM Single Economy into reverse."[12] The countries in the region have been steadily drawing away from each other.[13] Although the CARICOM was a political concept from its inception, it has become an economic project.

The Caribbean institutions are "enslaved by the methods of the past" and "paralysis in thinking." They are no longer economically workable. The logic of economics that drove this project has been trade and markets.[14] However, the convergence argument here is that trade and markets should be buttressed by production, distribution, and competitiveness.

The former prime minister of Jamaica, P.J. Patterson, has commented that Caribbean integration has had pitfalls, and if it does not change, it will disappear.[15] In the current context, the forces of integration elsewhere in the world are shaken to the roots because integration is multitrack in nature – the forces of integration are local, regional, and international all at the same time.[16] Furthermore, the CARICOM as an economic project was mostly designed as integration of markets and expansion of trade, with negligible attention to the most important economic and market actor, the private sector.

The issue is not whether CARICOM integration has failed or is disappearing. Norman Girvan has aptly stated that economic integration in the Caribbean is still a work in progress, and what has been accomplished so far has not significantly affected regional economic development. The nature of the exercise of sovereignty has posed a constant challenge and therefore created the need to be innovative and flexible.

The issue, rather, is about fresh thinking and innovative ways of moving the process beyond CARICOM integration to Caribbean Sea convergence. This convergence process offers greater flexibility and benefits for the Caribbean Sea economies in responding to emerging global challenges to capture a new frontier space.

We know that the nature and characteristics of small Caribbean economies make them extremely sensitive to global trends. The success of these economies depends on how flexible they are: on their ability to adapt and adjust to the changing global conditions. We are getting some glimpses of the future in current discussions, from ECLAC[17] to the emerging post-2015 development framework.[18] There will be a greater role for public-private partnerships driven by non-state entities.[19] The effect of global financial rule-making on small and medium economies has already been noted.[20] Furthermore, the global economic and financial architecture has changed from G7 to now G20, which has its own implications for our region.[21] Even ACP-EU relations will undergo fundamental changes in the future, as a recent briefing paper notes a tacit understanding among Europeans that the ball is in the ACP's court in terms of defining their own future and their relationship to the EU.[22]

The Caribbean Sea as a special space has already been recognized by the Association of Caribbean States, which has even established a

Caribbean Sea Commission.[23] The Draft Declaration of Manos Island Chaguaramas endorses the initiative of the Republic of Trinidad and Tobago to promote economic advancement in the region through the creation of a Convergence Process structured on the facilitation of capital movement, the integration of capital markets, the development of transportation infrastructure and the reorientation of the policies of the International Financial Institutions to better equip regional economies to withstand exogenous shocks.[24]

ECLAC clearly calls for broader regional forums to foster cooperation that can unlock the synergies of different sub-regions and progress towards gradual convergence of regional economic space.[25] It is against the above background that the framework proposed here advocates the Caribbean Sea convergence as moving the process forward. The framework moves the Caribbean integration process in the direction of convergence. Put simply, there is another, better way to capture the future, through a new frontier for Caribbean convergence.

The convergence framework draws upon the practical convergence taking place in the world today, as opposed to integration. The focus is on converging economies regardless of structures, because structural integration is a problem everywhere, whether Latin America, the Caribbean, Europe, or elsewhere. Underlying this framework are the following pillars.

INCLUSIVE AND EQUITABLE DEVELOPMENT

Inclusiveness also implies enlargement of the Caribbean to bring in the other islands and widening of trade arrangements to include the Caribbean Sea economies, consisting of a market of forty million (inclusive of Cuba). Therefore, the proposal is to include the Dominican Republic as member of CARICOM and to incorporate the other French and Dutch islands and French Guiana into the CARICOM framework. Inclusive development also implies a new partnership approach to include in the process all actors and agencies, like the private sector and civil society, to improve quality of life for all stakeholders.

TRANSFORMATIVE AND ENDOGENOUS GROWTH

Endogenous growth must be based on regional space involving stakeholders at national and regional levels. The drivers of endogenous growth are growth in the capital sector, capacity to pool regional resources, and the restructuring of domestic and foreign investments/ finance. This implies a transformative approach by fostering a new public-private partnership. Endogenous growth should be predominantly private-sector driven.

A fast-track policymaking included in convergence will provide the stimulus for the private sector. Secondly, transformative endogenous growth means redefining the role of development finance and equity in the Caribbean Sea space. Thirdly, endogenous growth implies that production, distribution, and competition should be addressed at the same time.

INNOVATIVE AND ENTREPRENEURIAL COMPETITIVENESS

Building a competitive Caribbean Sea economic space is an absolute necessity for the new frontier of Caribbean convergence. In the current global context, information and communications technologies (ICTs) are central to efficiency and competitiveness. Competitiveness is driven by innovation in the areas of science and technology as well as entrepreneurship.

Improving labour productivity and skills in the Caribbean Sea space is also crucial. Access to finance, a supportive environment for business and innovation, and promotion of entrepreneurship and the private sector will enhance the region's potential of capturing a new frontier for Caribbean convergence. Competitiveness is also enhanced by expanding trade and markets across the Caribbean Sea space.

ADAPTIVE AND REALIGNED INSTITUTIONS

Institutions are key mechanisms for execution and sustainable convergence. If sustainability of actions is critical to convergence, then the roles of adaptive institutions become central. This means realigning existing regional institutions to achieve Caribbean Sea convergence in a sustainable way. It also implies a reorientation of policy imperative to align the regional institutions to the convergence outcome. There are a number of regional institutions that can become modalities of execution.

Critical Strategies for Caribbean Convergence

A careful review of the various ideas and solutions put forth so far identifies four broad convergence strategies to support the pillars of the Caribbean Sea economy: finance, clustering, infrastructure, and production. These strategies are mutually interdependent and therefore need to be addressed together. The entire convergence process rests on executing these strategies. While they may appear to be broad regional strategies, the specifics will be closely studied and spelled out by research and policy groups that are proposed in the policy imperatives outlined below.

Finance Strategy

The economic convergence process will have to confront political challenges and redesigning of the economic and financial architecture. Finance and liquidity are the lifeblood of any economic system, national, regional, or global. The task is to shore up sufficient regional finance to ensure there is enough liquidity to support convergence. There are four ways to achieve this financial strategy: buffers, capital mobility, regional stock market, and development finance.

The buffers are those that are internally generated and shored up as sovereign wealth funds and international reserves (as opposed to buffers that are externally supportive of small states and exist in terms of international institutions). These forms of regional and national buffers provide the necessary flexibility to adjust to a new frontier of Caribbean convergence. National buffers will also act to discipline the fiscal policy of Caribbean Sea economies. These economies will also need to look at engaging other Latin American countries and emerging markets in finding new buffers.[26]

Creation of a regional stock exchange is an added advantage in expanding regional production, trade, and equity markets. There must be a fully integrated capital market, free flow of capital, and open investment strategies, accompanied by a review of double taxation treaties.[27] We will need to review and harmonize rules that facilitate movement of capital in the economy of the Caribbean Sea. The financial sector in the Caribbean is 350 per cent of GDP and yet the region has a major deficit in public financing.[28] Therefore, convergence will also require redefining the role of development finance institutions that must respond to the need for a new convergence process.

Resource Clustering Strategy

Clustering is regional grouping of firms and institutions. Clusters include an array of collaborating and competing services and providers that create a specialized infrastructure supporting industries and businesses. Typically, clustering draws upon shared talent pool of specialized skills and/or resources. It represents a synergy and a dynamic relationship between companies, stakeholders, institutions, and economies in the region.[29] Clusters contribute to the development of regional networking through public-private partnerships.

Regional clusters have the ability to offer local goods and services, knowledge, and link-ups that cannot be matched by outside rivals. In this way clustering can contribute to innovative competitiveness and transformative endogenous growth. Clustering also encourages production integration that will enhance regional competitiveness and value-added manufacturing and services. It involves the clustering of regional resources to consolidate growth, innovation, and competitiveness; for instance, regional "branding" of products and multidestination tourism are ways of clustering.

Clustering also involves a regional strategy for capital mobility; foreign direct investment; facilitation of regional transfer of knowledge, skills, and technology; regionally based and owned investments for promoting innovation; and a regional strategy for ICTs and information exchange. There are also synergies in clustering universities and technical institutions in the region (e.g., partnering for innovation and competitiveness). Clustering is about complementarities in convergence in the Caribbean Sea economic space. Pooling of resources could precipitate faster and more sustained growth, which could then spill over to impact all other countries. It could also imply Caribbean convergence of capital with resource-rich countries driving the process.

Infrastructure Strategy

The infrastructure for the new frontier of Caribbean convergence includes terrestrial transport linkages, aerial linkages, and communications technology with cross-border capabilities, border management and security, and regulation of movement of people. Improved and low-cost regional transport (e.g., liberalize and encourage competition among regionally based/owned low-cost carriers) is critical to facilitate greater movement of goods and people within the region.

Endogenous growth is also needed to improve labour productivity, especially targeting youth, and to address goals of equality and equity that benefit all stakeholders. Improving infrastructure facilitates quicker and cheaper movement of goods, services, and people.

Regionally owned (private and/or public) low-cost air carriers operating in the economy of the Caribbean Sea will boost trade, production, and multiple tourist destinations. This in itself will promote entrepreneurship and business opportunities across the economic space – a kind of spread effect that will lock in the private sector. There is tremendous scope for public-private partnerships in developing the region's infrastructure (universities, R&D centres, hospitals, air and sea transportation networks, telecommunications network).

Industry and Production Strategy

A strategy of production integration is central to all the pillars of the economy of the Caribbean Sea.[30] The emphasis is on private-sector-led production integration. The important issue here is to design appropriate modalities to stimulate private-sector response. These modalities need to be incorporated in the partnership approach. Including the private sector as stakeholders in the new public-private partnership would invigorate the private sector.

The public-private partnership needs to be accompanied by a Caribbean Investment Program designed to foster production distribution and integration across the convergence space. This will stimulate subcontracting and outsourcing of manufacturing and services, which will in turn reinforce entrepreneurship and competitiveness across the Caribbean Sea economic space.

Production integration buttressed by capital mobility and regional equity markets will unleash a whole new regional economic dynamism in creating a new frontier of Caribbean convergence. It has been noted that encouraging regional value chains would link the internationalization decisions of the leading economic players with the convergence process.[31] The strategy should focus on reducing transaction costs and coordinating the supply of regional public goods and generating regional value chains.[32]

Institutional Drivers

Our framework includes "adaptive institutions" as a pillar of convergence. We will need to realign existing delivery instruments to adapt to the convergence process. In this section, we briefly examine existing institutions and organizations that can serve as modalities of execution towards a new frontier of Caribbean convergence.

- CARICOM Secretariat is the principle administrative organ of CARICOM. The new ambassador to CARICOM, Dr. Clarence Henry, has indicated there is need for CARICOM, through its secretariat, to "devise a Marshall-like strategic development plan to propel economic recovery."[33]
- The Revised Treaty of Chaguaramas (2001) led to the creation of a regional fund, the Caribbean Development Fund, to provide technical and financial assistance to address the issue of regional asymmetries among CARICOM members.

- Latin American and Caribbean Economic System (SELA), established in 1994, provides consultation and coordination for the adoption of common positions and strategies to foster cooperation and integration among countries in Latin America and the Caribbean.
- Association of Caribbean States (ACS) was established in 1994 to strengthen the regional cooperation and integration process in order to create an enhanced economic space in the region. Caribbean Sea Commission was established in 2008 under the auspices of ACS to share information, provide advice, and build consensus among partners in the wider Caribbean region over ocean governance.
- Economic Commission for Latin America and the Caribbean (ECLAC): The Caribbean was included in 1984. ECLAC is the central entity on issues of the region as a whole and for policy. The Council for Trade and Economic Development (COTED), under the auspices of CARICOM Secretariat, promotes trade and economic development in the region.
- Caribbean Growth Forum (CGF), launched in 2012, is an initiative to facilitate a platform for public-private dialogue around the growth challenge. It engages a broad group of stakeholders and critical players, including the private sector and civil society.

A Twelve-Point Action Proposal

It is now necessary to design and engineer catalytic drivers to propel structural and institutional changes. Restructuring of the CARICOM Secretariat alone is not enough; there is need for an additional catalyst on a more permanent basis that will keep driving the process/structure and include the private sector.

This framework of moving towards a new frontier of Caribbean convergence has generated some policy imperatives that require immediate attention and decision. The CARICOM foreign ministers therefore recommended, with immediate effect, adoption of the twelve-point proposal for action given in Box 8.1.

Getting the politics of development right requires solving the alignment gap between the logic of politics and the logic of economics. International, regional, and local politics may well be the most significant obstacles to development. Politics would also appear to be the single

Box 8.1: Manos Island Chaguaramas Declaration

1. Expanding the Political and Economic Space

Support and approve the expansion of CARICOM to the economy of the Caribbean Sea.

1 Recommend a fast-track decision to facilitate the entry of the Dominican Republic as a member of CARICOM.
2 Endorse the incorporation of the Dutch and French Caribbean islands and French Guiana into the CARICOM framework.

2. Developing a Caribbean Sea Commission–Integrated Transport Logistics

Reiterate that transport and logistics are critical to achieving transformative endogenous growth and competitiveness in the economy of the Caribbean Sea.

3 Propose a ministerial meeting to take place calling on all airlines operating in the region to look at how the logistics of transport could be rationalized and improved to provide better interconnection and networking.
4 Propose that this meeting look at low-cost air carriers involving the region's private sector, and/or public-private partnership to this end.
5 Establish a regional research group to look at sea transportation and make recommendations for providing a system of sea transportation within the economy of the Caribbean Sea.

3. Establishing a CSC Capital Mobility Policy

Endorse that finance and capital mobility is the backbone for sustaining the pillars of convergence of the economy of the Caribbean Sea. Reiterate that there must be a fully integrated capital market and free flow of capital.

6 Propose that a single capital market be established. Therefore, all stock exchanges in the region are mandated to meet and work out the modalities in a time frame.
7 Recommend that all members of the economy of the Caribbean Sea create national sovereign wealth funds and regional buffers as a measure to offset external shocks.

8 Set up a regional committee to review and harmonize mechanisms to facilitate intra-regional investments. Organize a regional meeting of all private-sector organizations to identify areas and strategies of production integration and public-private partnerships.

4. Developing CSC Energy and Food Security Policies

Reaffirm that energy and food security are essential for the convergence of the economy of the Caribbean Sea.

9 Set up a policy group to look at developing a common energy security plan to clearly define the rules for complementarities in the use and clustering of regional energy and natural resources for a new frontier of Caribbean convergence, in order to harness regional resources for strengthening production integration and competitiveness.

10 Set up a policy group to examine a common policy on self-sufficiency in food.

5. Implementing a CSC Finance Policy

Agree that development finance institutions are isolated and compartmentalized into public sector and private sector in their modus operandi.

11 Propose that all the development finance institutions in the region (COB, IDB, TAFF, CAE, and others) meet to redesign their lending paradigm in the region to deal with current problems and support the convergence process.

12 Bring together development finance institutions to redefine the role of development finance that is sensitive to and supportive of regional needs and the convergence process.

Source: Presented at the meeting of foreign ministers of CARICOM on 14–15 May 2013, under the chairmanship of Minister Winston Dookeran.

largest hurdle in finding solutions to the current global crisis. Getting the politics of development right requires cooperation and coordination of priorities, policies, and action at all levels.

A new leadership with a global mindset must engage the various communities of interest to find more durable solutions in a volatile global environment. This new international leadership must find the right mix of power, politics, and economics to achieve the necessary performance level for sustainable regional and global economic growth and ultimately development benefiting the citizens of all Caribbean nations.

The politics of this non-sovereign regional grouping is at an inflection point, and it is this generation, in the twenty-first century, that begins to turn the corner. We must not hold back growth and development; instead we must break the anti-growth coalition that has dominated Caribbean societies. The time has come for a new leadership to search for a new paradigm for development – one that will identify political and economic logic, construct new measures for financial sustainability, and design a strategy for basic development that puts enquiry at the centre.[34] We must do so within the framework of a democratic system functioning at its best.

This chapter provides what I hope will become the beginning of a new awakening for Caribbean development.

9 Capturing Space in the Power of Markets[*]

Financial markets and monetary instruments have an undue influence on world economies, as evidenced by recent crises. The International Monetary Fund and the World Bank seem destined to have a much smaller role. Financial liberalization and the growing use of electronic money, along with increasing financial sophistication, have stymied central banks.[1]

The system in Trinidad and Tobago must become more dynamic and less concentrated to spur growth whilst keeping regulations relevant and consistent for the whole Caribbean. Any Caribbean-wide strategy must acknowledge that the Caribbean community is in dire need of paradigm shifts, and more radical reforms are needed for economic integration. Currency unions in developing countries provide the right mix between flexibility and stability of exchange rates. Partnership may yet engender solutions for monetary stability. Inflation targeting – simple, transparent, and effective – seems the way forward for many developing countries. Strategic policies must be created to combat discriminatory tariffs, especially in light of an economic geography that creates economic blocks often with little regard for national boundaries. To build competitiveness, price and non-price monetary factors must find more common ground.

What is the central bank's role in development? Often, a recurring challenge for a governor of a central bank is the need to fix the gap between theory and practice. As the world economy staggers from crisis to crisis, financial markets that punish countries whose policies they judge inadequate, are blamed. Each new scene of financial turbulence

---

[*] This chapter was adapted from Winston Dookeran, "Finance and Development," in *Power, Politics and Performance: A Partnership Approach for Development*, 172–89 (Kingston: Ian Randle, 2012).

brings forth more demands for governments to subdue markets. Does this suggest that financial markets have become too powerful?

If so, then money does matter. The next questions are: How does it affect our lives? What must we do to steer economies in the right direction? The world of money today is filled with uncertainties; the toolkits available to us to tinker with and shape the economy are still being tested. Some of these uncertainties are derived from strong free-market behaviour that promotes a single global finance system. Rapid change and advances in information technology have made designing tools even more difficult.

This era of uncertainty has created new rigidities, "money illusions" and expectations that lie at the heart of the debate on money's impact. Effective monetary policy is nowadays primarily concerned with addressing short-run disequilibrium situations. The classical position is that relative prices are determined by real forces of demand and supply. The absolute price level is determined by the quantity of money and its velocity of circulation. This position has much less practical relevance than it once did and has little bearing on policy.

The shift of power from policymakers to financial markets has given rise to three main concerns. One is that the sheer size of foreign exchange and bond markets can overwhelm monetary and fiscal policy, wrestling influence over interest and exchange rates from the state. Daily turnover on the currency markets now exceeds the global stock of official foreign exchange reserves. Financial markets have become the oft-capricious and powerful judges of economic policymaking. Second, central banks and governments are accused of responding to financial markets rather than altering the market forces to benefit their countries. Their obsession with price stability, it is argued, could impose excessive deflation on economies. Finally, global financial liberalization and a vast array of new financial instruments may have dulled the effectiveness of monetary and fiscal tools, so that changes in interest rates or government borrowing have a smaller impact on an economy. There has been growing use of electronic money, which may further reduce central banks' control over the money supply, and an expansion in derivative activity, which allows firms to insulate themselves from changes in interest rates. Liberalization and innovation have made financial markets far more volatile and more vulnerable to financial meltdown, prompting increasing financial instability.[2]

As economies produce and grow, the spectre of inflation is rising once again. Inflation is not dead, and as risks remain asymmetrical concurrent with the admittedly encouraging global growth, inflation risks could intensify.

Apart from that inflationary risk, there are welcome signs of safety and stability in emerging markets. International investors appear increasingly willing to reward countries that show greater commitment to economic reform and transparency. More and more countries, including emerging market economies, have now subscribed to the IMF's Special Data Dissemination Standard. This standard, which promotes the availability of accurate and timely financial statistics, was established in April 1996 but assumed greater significance with the onset of the 1997–98 Asian crisis. Recognizing the greater transparency prompted by the Special Data Dissemination Standard and other measures fuelling the progress that emerging markets have been making in lowering risks, investors have rewarded them by improving their risk ratings.

The International Financial Architecture is reflective of the new political order. The countries of the G20 have assumed centre stage and have come to replace many of the institutions that previously wielded political power. There is clearly a shift in global economic and political power, and those in the Caribbean region must be very adaptive to that global political change. As minister of finance, I had proposed that in response to changing global politics, the G20 should be expanded to G21 to include a seat for Africa.

The Caribbean has in the past had to face some of the negative consequences of these architectural changes, and now they are once more on the national agenda. It is in this context that Trinidad and Tobago took the initiative to chair the Small States Forum at the World Bank, and began talks in that forum with both the IMF and the World Bank to find a voice in the G20. Small states cannot sit back and passively allow deliberations that affect people in their part of the world; they need to be an active party in those deliberations.

So, Trinidad and Tobago, representing small states, has made substantial diplomatic moves at IMF meetings to seek a voice for small economies and countries in the G20 deliberations. The response, at least from international financial institutions, has been encouraging. For instance, a G20 working group for the Caribbean was formally established. But there is much to be done, and the Caribbean countries must act collectively to secure that voice.

The Case for Small Economies

Some critical issues affecting small economies must be part of shaping the manifesto for the leadership of the IMF. In particular, there is concern that changes to the international architecture, in which the IMF and G20 sit, lend themselves to a potential contravention of natural justice where clubs of large countries develop rules for smaller states to follow without adequate consultation, consideration, and engagement.

Development of international financial regulation, supervision, risk management, and assessment of financial sectors does not support a level playing field between small and large states. Preferential treatment given to areas important in some large states, from mortgages and regional banks to hybrid capital – treatment that proved so dangerous in the 2008–9 global financial crisis – also penalizes institutions in small states beyond economic justification. Small, open economies such as St. Lucia and Tonga proved particularly vulnerable to this preferential treatment. For example, in the wake of the 2008 financial crisis, tourist-dependent St. Lucia's hotels were 80 per cent empty during its peak tourist period in late 2008 and early 2009, while remittances to Tonga dropped by 15 per cent from June 2008 to June 2009.[3] Additionally, Cambodia witnessed a 50 per cent decline in foreign direct investment in 2009. This has contributed to the loss of 102,527 jobs in the country since September 2009 (either permanently or temporarily) due to the closure of ninety-three garment and shoe factories in the first eleven months of that year. This is a significant development when one considers that the country's garment sector accounts for 83.2 per cent of its total exports.[4]

Furthermore, there is concern that, while small states particularly need help in financing infrastructure, the criteria of lending generated by multinational institutions is better suited to larger states with capital markets, credit ratings, and diversified private-sector players. The criteria used for long-term and short-term support pays too much attention to the level of GDP per capita, and does not sufficiently account for higher levels of fragility and vulnerability to natural and economic shocks. To address these issues, a new leadership position in the IMF focusing on the unique challenges of small economies may be required.

Liberalization of Financial Services

There is a trend towards the integration of banking and insurance services. If there are two industries that fit the requirements of the global market, these would be them. There is a new urgency in the world of financial services liberalization. Our immediate response in the Caribbean should be to establish a Caribbean-wide regulatory system as the first step in coping with the demands of liberalization. This proposal needs to be fast-tracked alongside the WTO process on the liberalization of financial services. Execution will require enormous professional effort and political determination.

One strand of economic literature argues that finance is unimportant; it is simply the handmaiden to real production. However, in recent years there has been increasing evidence that financial systems do play an essential role in economic development. Hence, the financial system must be linked to growth. As the effect of the global financial crisis shows, even relatively strong economies may collapse when the foundations underlying their financial systems are weak.

One of the important challenges of development in small states such as Trinidad and Tobago is to identify the best financial system that will promote fast yet sustainable economic growth. Evidence from richer countries has shown that as economies mature, capital markets become more effective at intermediation than banks. One simple truth was first expressed in what is called "Say's Identity":[5] regardless of the prices and interest with which they are confronted, individuals always prefer to use all of their proceeds from the sale of commodities and bonds to purchase other commodities and bonds. People sell goods only for the purpose of buying more. Supply creates its own demand. This basic identity has helped us to understand the workings of our foreign exchange market and suggests a need for a more diversified structure in financial intermediation.

What is the business of financial intermediaries? They lend at one level of interest rate and borrow at a lower level. They purchase primary securities from the market and substitute indirect securities and financial assets at higher prices. The margin between these prices is the intermediary's profit. Financial intermediation has grown significantly, globally and regionally. The banking sector, however, continues to dominate the financial landscape, accounting for as much as 80 per cent of all financial assets in some regional economies. Thus, financial sector diversification must push forward. Banking crises have been found to be far more devastating in countries where banking constitutes a relatively large share of the financial sector.

Trinidad and Tobago has a relatively modern and sophisticated financial structure, in both variety of institutions and range of financial instruments available. Its financial system today comprises a range of finance institutions, including commercial banks, merchant banks, trust companies, mortgage finance companies, thrift institutions, development banks, mutual funds, credit unions, insurance firms, and other institutions. Today, more than ever, the system needs to become less concentrated and more dynamic. As our economy develops, we must ensure that financial decision-making is not concentrated in the hands of a few gatekeepers at banks and similar institutions. Richard C. Breeden, former chair of the Securities and Exchange Commission, has said:

> In countries where financial markets do not work as well as in the United States, investment decision-making is concentrated in the hands of just a

few dozen gatekeepers at banks and investment firms. The result is that financing tends to flow primarily to a cadre of established businesses with strong relationships to the old guard. By contrast, the United States has literally thousands of gatekeepers in our increasingly decentralized capital markets, many of them with a much higher appetite for risk ... It is not because our scientists are smarter than their scientists. It's because we're creating a system that provides capital more quickly to people willing to take big risks ... and our economy is reaping the rewards.[6]

We must ready ourselves to construct a financial system that enables us to compete in an increasingly integrated world market and helps to insulate us from financial contagion originating in other parts of the world.

Proper banking regulation is crucial to prevent or minimize the cost of banking sector failures, as banks dominate the financial sector. In recent years, some countries in our region have experienced banking system difficulties that have hampered growth and generated fiscal costs as high as 10 to 20 per cent of GDP, sometimes more. There is a threshold where, when these costs become high enough, the crisis inevitably enters the political arena. Evidence of this can be seen in Indonesia, where the fiscal cost of the Asian financial crisis was calculated to be nearer 80 per cent of GDP and the Suharto regime was toppled.

Many Caribbean states have therefore adopted reforms aimed not just at dealing with high-risk banks but also, more importantly, at strengthening banking supervision to reduce the likelihood of future crises. They have signed guidelines on financial prudence, established minimum capital requirements, adopted better systems to monitor asset quality, made provisions for bad loans, and imposed tighter limits on excessive concentration of risk, all factors in past banking crises.

Trinidad and Tobago must quicken the pace of structural finance sector reform, as it remains vulnerable to terms-of-trade and investor sentiment fluctuations, despite having taken the right measures to support financial sector stability. When oil and gas prices were high, Trinidad and Tobago felt it had the attractiveness and resources to become a financial centre in the region. Today, this idea no longer seems tenable. Indeed, with development of information and communications technologies, traders hardly need to use the traditional market. Computers are taking markets to traders, wherever they are.

The future may therefore hinge on maintaining the soundness and stability of our existing financial system through a proper regulatory framework along with continued deepening and widening of the financial system. This is why Trinidad and Tobago's firm policy at the

Central Bank is to comply with the Basel Committee's "Core Principles for Effective Banking Supervision."[7] In tandem with this, an integrated regulatory system that incorporates banking, insurance, and pension funds is now being designed for Trinidad and Tobago.

Monetary and Financial Policy

There are a number of issues concerning monetary and financial policy on the agenda for small states. Three issues are key to future policy planning. Competitive and open markets, the rule of law, fiscal discipline, and a culture of enterprise that is driven by innovation and productivity are all important factors in sustaining the growth process. Human expectations are always subject to bouts of euphoria and disillusionment, and our system must be strong enough to take such a diversion in stride. At one time, it was felt that stability would come from ensuring strong fundamentals. Today, that is simply not enough.

Is inflation targeting the way forward? Policymakers have traditionally used strategies such as controlling the growth of the money supply or pegging the exchange rate to a stable currency in pursuit of price stability. However, financial liberalization is leading to a breakdown of the traditional relationship between money and nominal income and may have reduced the ability of central banks to control inflation. With market pressures forcing some countries to abandon their exchange rate bands, monetary policy is losing its nominal price anchor, leading many central banks to search for an alternative framework that would engender stability and future growth.

In recent years we have seen a promising approach called "inflation targeting." The idea behind inflation targeting is to publicly announce and pursue specific target rates of inflation. Among other things, this approach calls for a central bank to be generally independent of politics, to have a mandate to pursue price stability, and preferably to have an explicit inflation target at which to aim. An excellent model comes from New Zealand, where the Reserve Bank has had full independence over the operation of monetary policy since 1990. The government set an inflation target of 0 to 3 per cent; any governor of the Reserve Bank whose performance to meet this target is deemed inadequate may be removed from office, and any change in this target must be debated and approved by Parliament.

Inflation targeting provides transparency and accountability. Its simplicity and openness also make it far easier for the public to understand the intent and effects of monetary policy, in addition to holding policymakers accountable for inflation performance. The announced target creates a penalty for failure and reduces the temptation for governments to spring inflationary surprises simply for short-term output boosts. With a credible target, the market is more able to predict how the central bank is likely to respond to internal and external imbalances.

Transparency of the monetary decision-making process is the key. Traditionally, central bankers have been secretive, but the new environment demands that we communicate more clearly with market participants if we wish to influence their behaviour and expectations. In Britain, minutes of the interest rate decisions taken at regular monthly meetings between the chancellor of the exchequer and the governor of the Bank of England are published swiftly. The Bank of England also produces an inflation report, which helps markets to understand the factors that guide the interest rate policy. In the United States, the Federal Reserve publishes the transcripts of its federal open market committee meetings. It also publicly announces all decisions to change the federal funds rate, rather than leaving it up to the market to work it out. There is credible evidence that inflation targeting has helped to boost monetary policy credibility in some countries. This could well be a suitable monetary framework for small states, which place a high value on a stable currency.

Ricardo Hausmann, former chief economist at the Inter-American Development Bank, puts the issue[8] of exchange rates this way. Every government faces a "trilemma": (1) if it wants a fixed exchange rate and free movement of capital, it should forget about managing interest rates; (2) if it wants to manage interest rates and keep the exchange rate fixed, it must control capital flows; and (3) if it wants to manage interest rates without affecting capital flows, it cannot have fixed exchange rate.

It is impossible to have all three things at the same time. One of the three has to be relinquished and the respective price must be paid. In a world of increasingly mobile capital, countries cannot fix their exchange rate and at the same time maintain an independent monetary policy. A choice must be made between the confidence and stability provided by a fixed exchange rate and the control over policy offered by a floating rate. In the Caribbean, our vulnerability to external shocks such as sudden shifts in commodity prices has been the deciding factor.

History is on the side of greater flexibility. Since the mid-1970s, the number of countries with flexible exchange rates has increased steadily. This suggests that global architects should be promoting and preparing for a world of floating currencies. Floating rates have affected countries with flexible rates, though the effect has been more severe for countries with fixed exchange rates. Confronted by sudden market panics, we have seen floating exchange rates overshoot guideposts and become highly unstable, especially if large amounts of capital flow in and out of a country. This instability carries real economic costs.

To get the best of both worlds, some countries have loosely tied their exchange rate to a single foreign currency, such as the US dollar, or to a basket of currencies. Others are tightly tied through a currency board or, even better, a currency union. Economists are deeply divided about what the optimal exchange rate regime is, but it seems that in the interest of stability, some form of linkage with more established currencies such as the US dollar is only prudent for developing countries in the position of those in the Caribbean.

It is clear that structural adjustment strategies have not met the expectations of rising living standards in an equitable manner when considering the quality of growth. The first generation of reforms adopted by Latin America and the Caribbean has largely failed to alleviate pressing issues of inequality and poverty. Based on a scenario of business as usual with continuing slow growth and recurring crises, the prospects for future reduction in the numbers of the poor do not look bright.

Poverty has always been a flashpoint issue, as we have seen through vigorous demonstrations in WTO ministerial meetings, at World Economic Forum meetings and, more recently, at IMF/World Bank meetings:

> The International Monetary Fund and the World Bank were set up together to help rebuild a post–World War Two economic system. Both came under fierce fire during the spring meetings of the two institutions when angry demonstrators said that the lenders were not doing enough for debt relief and that their policy prescriptions only deepened poverty in developing countries.[9]

The international financial system is under great scrutiny. The call for changes in its global agenda is becoming louder. This call, however, is not only for the system to deliver us from poverty, but also for changes in our analytical framework and our method of analysis. Some amongst us may argue that "quality of growth" objectives are utopian with no coherent, rational, or analytical grounding; but given the present economic, social, and political realities, small states may have little alternative but to face these new challenges.[10]

The Adaptive Response by Small States

Small states are experiencing a turbulent convergence of forces that are redefining their place in the global order. New economic borders are emerging, political options are widening, and new international regimes are redrawing the ties that bind them to the rest of the world. Yet small states still grapple with lingering problems: economic dualism, unemployment, low productivity, inequality, low saving and investment rates, and weak entrepreneurship.

We in small states sometimes believe that our size hinders development. In fact, size need not be an issue. There are many examples of small states that have grown rich and prosperous without significant natural resources or preferential trade accords. They did so by linking their economies with the world economy and by achieving external economies of scale rather than by relying on internal forces.

All nation states, particularly small states, may be called upon to cede some of their sovereignty in order to develop economically. The challenge is to do so without compromising the core principles of their sovereignty. Within this context, we will focus on some of the challenges facing small states in today's world. There are three broad areas of challenge: the first is to tackle volatility, vulnerability, and natural disasters; the second to transition to the changing global trade regime; and the third to strengthen capacities within small states.

How can small states take charge of this dialectic between nation state and markets? How can the state be transformed into an efficient developmental agent without forsaking its social and political responsibilities? A new worldwide system of economic relations is emerging, in which every nation state is being incorporated into the global economic system. Nation states must increasingly share their decision-making space with global corporate interest and civil society. For this reason, the state's role in development must be redefined, though not necessarily reduced. If the foundations of social life are not to be further eroded, this change in economic processes must be countered with "high-energy politics" involving intensified public participation and democracy.

Caribbean governments appear to be caught in a cross-current; stymied by introspection and indecision and unable to articulate viable economic strategies for lifting their countries to a higher-equilibrium economic level. Small states are indeed more vulnerable to external events, including natural disasters. Their greater trade openness, concentration of commodity exports, and dependence on net capital flows all serve to make them more vulnerable to external shocks. Income is equally vulnerable, and income streams can become very volatile. There is therefore a need to design a mechanism that would counter this whilst incorporating differing conditions in states, as both strong and weak states pose threats to global economic security. It is true that cross-border private capital flows have grown substantially in recent times. Small economies, however, are still viewed as riskier investments by private capital than larger developing economies, even if the former enact the right policies.

How can small states adapt to the changing international environment? International trading regimes are essentially devices of political economy: they are in place at least as much to protect nations from their own interest groups as they are to protect nations from each other. In this sense, the process of change and adaptation can be best analysed in a framework of political economy.

We must identify the winners and losers in this framework. Change is normally associated with altering the character of national expenditure to another set of expenditures that will usher in a new matrix of investment and consumption. But how can we do this? Losers are easily identified. They are the participants in the current economic structure and are normally adequately represented in the political system. They make appropriate noises and are satisfied by the status quo.

On the other hand, the winners belong to the next generation and are a product of as yet unrealized opportunities. They therefore cannot be easily identified or mobilized. Change is challenged by finding an appropriate incentive mechanism that would allow the losers to become winners. Caribbean societies can best adapt to their new trading environment if the framework for the political economy of change can be designed and an appropriate strategy developed.

At the international level, strategically targeted policies have been built into the trading framework, despite states' attempting to protect their allies and dependents from these trade barriers. These policies and other protectionist sanctions have been used by the United States, amongst others, and are clearly implied in "social clauses" on environmental and labour issues that have been seen by many to discriminate against exporters from developing countries.

Caribbean states' strategic approach must become more deliberate to adapt to the new trading environment. Such strategic policies will alter the pace, the time, and the scope envisaged in the change process. Another aspect of the political economy of change deals with the core-periphery dynamics of the new economic geography. Compact economic units no longer coincide with national boundaries. For example, it is argued that the triangular axis of New York, Washington, and Toronto represents one economic unit. So too does the block of California, Texas, and New Mexico. The boundaries of the Caribbean economy can no longer exclude Florida. Market forces must therefore work within this new economic-geographical arrangement.

There are two distinct and related processes that seem to be taking place: one is the relocation of industries and services in regions that are favoured with an attractive and richly endowed environment. The second is a specialization of economies that favours regions with established industries and attracts firms away from those with less developed initial conditions. New knowledge and insight into these aspects of the political economy of change – winners and losers, strategic policies, and economic geography dynamics – should form part of a scholarship agenda as Caribbean countries adapt to the new trading and financial environment.

CARICOM and Building Competitiveness

Building competitiveness is an exercise in political economy. We therefore raise two main issues. The first is reliance on the price factor – exchange rates, interest rates, commodity prices, and asset prices – in the typical adjustment strategy, as opposed to the non-price factor. It is true that the non-price factor is more of a medium-term goal towards building a competitive economy, but extreme reliance on the price factor can encourage Caribbean underdevelopment. This is so because markets are imperfect, and resource transfers emanating from changes in the price factor can have extremely negative effects. It has already been pointed out that the resource flows between multilateral institutions and Caribbean economies harm the region. The challenge of building a competitive economy cannot rely as heavily as in the past on price adjustments; rather, a better synergy between price and non-price factors must be worked into the adjustment matrix.

The second issue can best be described using a World Bank concept: "institutions matter." Many supporting institutions that develop competitiveness may need to be refocused towards understanding the strategy, public policy, or regulations. This remains an enormous link with the international economy, be it through economic intelligence, market strategy, public policy, or regulations, and an huge part of the change ahead. Our preparation to meet these challenges must come to grips with the argument that "institutions matter."

The limits of CARICOM must be considered. This is a matter of determining an optimal economic space, keeping in mind the theoretical underpinnings of the debates on regionalism, open regionalism, and multilateralism. Integration paradigms of the past are being challenged, as the pace of change of regional integration is outstripped by the rate of change of global integration.

The institutional structure of the integration process is less important than the economic structures that would grasp opportunities and withstand the risks of global integration. So far, much of the preparation in the integration agenda has been institutional, with concentration on WTO arrangements and the CARICOM Single Market and Economy (CSME).

These institutional frameworks are important, but CARICOM's potential is yet to be realized. The CSME is too much a minimalist position. Do we need a new platform on which to negotiate with other sub-regional groups and to expand trade, investment, and financial relations throughout the hemisphere?

William Demas, economic advisor to the prime minister of Trinidad and Tobago, has written extensively on the differences between development policies in small versus larger countries. While agreeing that the Caribbean region must be internationally competitive, he advised caution about the speed and extent of opening the Caribbean to the outside world. Scholars have referred to Demas's strong conviction that CARICOM must not be fragmented, and individual states must resist such trends in entering into economic cooperation agreements with third countries or groups of such countries.[11] At the same time, Demas urged the widening of integration with neighbouring countries in trade and collaboration in technology, education, and skills development. In a sense, William Demas, a key architect of Caribbean integration, foresaw the possibilities of a wider Caribbean convergence for its sustainability.

Caribbean researchers and scholars have promoted the establishment of more attractive business environments. They have written about export-led growth. They have warned about our local businesses being outcompeted. They have pushed the limits in searching for a theory of Caribbean development. The agenda for scholars must not reflect a state of under-development. Such a search – and the scholarship for it – must be rooted in history, philosophy, economic science, and politics, and may require a fresh synthesis in thinking.

In today's global economy, where new global imbalances are emerging, new frontier industrial policies are required. The global imbalances are reflected on three fronts: (1) in the simmering foreign exchange currency wars, apparent in the current "on and off" tension between the United States and China and the alignment of currencies in the world; (2) the emergence of a new food crisis resulting from the growing gap between supply and demand, which especially afflicts countries that are heavily dependent on the importation of food or the raw material needed for the production of such food; and (3) the continued ripples in oil and gas prices, as the politics of the world energy sector shifts to changes in technology.

These global imbalances are a reflection of the changing political order, and small countries like those in the Caribbean must be prepared to anticipate and, as far as possible, develop policy actions to protect our economies and the well-being of our people.

The challenge of change requires us to question the premises of past development strategies. A new view of development may emerge out of the following initiatives:

- We must re-invigorate seismic research to identify potential resources of hydrocarbons as we seek to expand private seismic data to an open data room and set the basis for renewed exploration in the hydro-carbon sector.
- We need to develop an aggressive program based on finance, technology, and management to make Trinidad and Tobago's economy more competitive. In this regard, the government has recently established the National Competitiveness Council along with the Economic Development Board to chart the new frontier ahead of us. Implicit here is the need to speed up our decision-making, and we are already engaged in a program to improve our ratings and the ease of doing business.
- Our international effort to promote new investment in on-shore and off-shore development must now expand our global reach to include Indian, Chinese, and Brazilian investment prospects. A new era of economic diplomacy will now inform our efforts to vigorously seek investments to support the new direction in our development strategy.
- No longer must we view the energy sector as a privileged enclave of a few; we must democratize this sector in search of opportunities to finance new economic space in our quest for inclusive development.

Finally, let us draw attention to key obstacles to change in the Caribbean by posing a penetrating question: What is holding back growth and development in the Caribbean? This is the question asked by Caribbean scholar Avinash Persaud, who argues that the anti-growth coalition, so deeply embedded in the socio-economic and political culture of the small states of the Caribbean, must be "broken" before any growth and development can take place.[12] The challenge, therefore, for policymakers, development strategists, practitioners, and those engaged in the field of economic change is how to break the anti-growth coalition.

10 The Quest for Equality and Sustainable Growth

PART A: BUILDING A KNOWLEDGE ECONOMY: ISSUES IN FINANCING HIGHER EDUCATION*

Knowledge is today a major driving force in development, fueled by changes in the globalized economy and the new information era. The building of a knowledge economy has become possible due to the creation of knowledge via research and advances in technology, investments in education, and a new openness to innovation. At the heart of this impetus is the search for competitiveness and sustainable development. Investment in knowledge infrastructure, including human capital, offers a new wave in economic restructuring, with "higher value-added products with closer customer linkages."[1] Finland was able to transform from a natural-base economy into a knowledge-based one in a short period, recently ranking as number one in the World Economic Forum's competitive index. The progress has been credited to investments in education and information systems.

Higher education is now at the centre of strategies for sustained growth and inclusive development. Coupled with a regime for innovation and information and communications technologies (ICT) infrastructure, investment in human capital has high "development dividends," as it prepares an economy to meet the challenges of competition in today's integrated global economy. In an aggregate sense, education influences the macroeconomy through its impact on productivity and technical change as it affects economic growth. Changes

---

* Part A of this chapter is based on Winston Dookeran, "Building a Knowledge Economy: Issues on Financing of Higher Education," chapter 9 of *Sharing Research Agendas on Knowledge Systems*, edited by Heather Eggins (occasional paper 16) (Paris: UNESCO, 2009).

in competitive structure increase the potential of development, while adaptation to an innovative system advances social cohesion and inclusiveness, and thus the well-being of society.

A recent World Bank publication argued that a country's competitive advantage in the global economy is linked to the converging impacts of globalization, knowledge as a main driver of growth, and the information revolution: "The proportion of goods in international trade with a medium-high or high level of technology content rose from 33 percent in 1976 to 54 percent in 1996."[2]

Opportunities are emerging from these challenges. Knowledge has become a primary factor of production. Building knowledge societies requires a sound incentive-based macroeconomic regime, a modern ICT infrastructure, a competitive innovation system, and high-quality human resources. The contribution of tertiary education is vital to the emergence of innovation systems and the development of human resources.

One of the main messages of the World Bank report is that "the state has a responsibility to put in place an enabling framework that encourages tertiary institutions to be more innovative and more responsive to the needs of a globally competitive knowledge economy and the changing labour market requirements for advanced human capital."[3] Three arguments that justify governmental support for funding universities are the existence of externalities from tertiary education, equity issues, and the connective role of tertiary education in the education system as a whole.

There is debate over whether education is a public or a quasi-public good. In the orthodox definition, education, while having the attributes of a public good, does not meet the test of Say's law – that demand creates its own supply – and it does confer private gains to individuals. But education is a significant generator of external benefits, and not all the rewards of education are captured by individuals. Indeed, there are significant externalities in the production of education, as the overall contribution of tertiary education to economic growth goes beyond the income and employment gains accruing to individuals. Externalities are crucial to knowledge-driven economic and social development, and permit workers to use new technology and boost productivity.

Apart from its contribution to economic growth, higher education has broad economic, fiscal, and labour market effects. There are linkages and spillover effects from the clustering of human capital alongside leading technology firms, as exemplified by technology-intensive groups in Silicon Valley in California, Bangalore in India, Shanghai in China, Campinas in São Paulo, Brazil, and similar groupings in East

Asia and Finland. Various studies have measured the positive correlation between increases in educational levels and consumption, tax base, and reduced dependence on medical and social welfare services. There are also non-economic externalities in the promotion of greater social cohesion and appreciation of diversity in societies. The World Bank UNESCO publication *Higher Education in Developing Countries: Peril and Promise* wrote that "they also attempted to widen access to higher education, and in some cases there was a belief that higher education could help make societies more democratic, while strengthening human rights."[4]

Joseph Stiglitz in his Nobel Prize lecture argued that each country must create a culture of knowledge in which government has a key role in encouraging creativity and scientific entrepreneurship. He has "highlighted the importance of market failure, macroeconomic stabilization, the important (but focused) role that governments must play in a predominantly market-based economy, the importance of promoting economic opportunities for the poor via strategies of equitable growth, and the key role of education and knowledge in advancing economic and social well-being."[5] When we consider the role of the state in education, a new challenge emerges, of offering financial incentives in higher education – and this goes hand in hand with the old challenges of promoting quality, efficiency, and equity. The rise of market forces and the recurring fiscal austerity facing governments have reduced the traditional state control model's ability to impose reform and have introduced a flexibility that relies on regulations and incentives.

Forces for Change in Higher Education

In the past, the dominant role of governments in the financing and provision of higher education was easily translated into a relationship characterized by a high degree of centralized control or by a great deal of institutional autonomy. Today there is a much more complex interplay of forces that rely on state regulations and financial incentives; participation and partnerships with industry, civil society, and professional associations; and competition between higher education providers (see Figure 10.1).

An initial step is to define a reform program within a coherent policy framework. Such a higher education development strategy should specify what type of system will contribute to growth in a knowledge-based economy, what the roles of the institutions within the higher education system are, and how the new technologies can be harnessed by individuals and enterprises. Several countries have attempted this

Figure 10.1. Interplay of forces for change in tertiary education

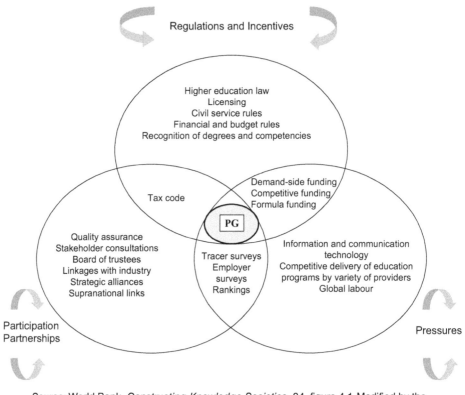

Source: World Bank, *Constructing Knowledge Societies*, 84, figure 4.1. Modified by the author to include vortex PG (political governance).

exercise, including New Zealand (*New Zealand's Tertiary Education Sector*, 1999); France (*U3M Plan for the Ile-de-France*, 2000); South Africa (*The Governance of Merger in South African Higher Education*, 2001), and India (*India as Knowledge Superpower*, 2001).[6]

Steps to design an enabling regulatory framework will require, in most cases, legislative measures, consensus-building mechanisms on cost sharing, quality assurance mechanisms, and financial rules and controls. In this context, government funding will remain the major source of financing for higher education in developing countries. "Negotiated" budgets based on historical trends may now be replaced with financial incentive formulae that steer higher education institutions towards compliance with quality, cutting-edge research, and efficiency and equity goals. Funding may be linked to performance, but it may also be linked to the mobilization of additional resources through increased cost sharing.

Some universities have established competitive funds to promote quality improvements. Under such systems, institutions may bid for extra-budgetary financial resources that are linked to proposals aimed at specific internal policy changes. Such policy changes may be within the faculties to help define their missions, market niches, development objectives, and action plans to achieve these objectives. The process must be transparent. Even in the academic world, successful organizations are those that challenge and re-invent themselves in the pursuit of more effective ways of responding to the needs of their clients and stakeholders. This view was articulated by Dr. David Kemp, Australian minister of education, who has written that "we need a framework that will encourage and support collaboration, accompanied by the exchange of technology and information, across the academic, industry and community sectors, between research institutions and users, research providers and business, across institutions and the nation and internationally."[7] Kemp has spoken of the uncertainty of the future and the need for flexibility of policy frameworks as they affect the funding of universities, and highlighted the importance of building institutions that are responsive to change.

There is growing recognition that the cost of higher education must be shared in a more equitable way among the various stakeholders. Higher education opportunities should be accessible to all qualified persons, and the state must play a crucial role in ensuring that no one is excluded by lack of financial resources. Any shifting of costs to students must therefore be accompanied by scholarship and loan programs that cover both direct and indirect costs (foregone earnings). This raises key issues of equity and management, as pointed out in the World Bank's international review of student loan programs, which highlighted serious shortcomings in the long-term viability of these programs. The report concluded that student loan schemes should meet the following conditions: (1) an appropriate marketing strategy; (2) transparent targeting to the most deserving students (academic and social criteria); (3) close supervision of academic performance of the student; (4) interest rate and subsidy rate to protect financial sustainability of the scheme; and (5) efficient management of the scheme.[8] Better results may be achieved when programs are financed and administered (with enforceable guidelines) by commercial banks. The challenges of "borderless" education across institutions and program types – life long and part time – requires a flexible management approach.

Financing Education: Some Findings

At the 2002 Salzburg Seminar Tony White said, of Ireland's phenomenal economic growth of 8 per cent between 1994 and 2001, that "there is no one factor responsible for this growth, but education policy … Education in Ireland has been viewed as an investment rather than as an economic drain. Over the years it has made a successful transition from elite to a mass education system; fully 50 percent of 18-to-24-year-olds attend university … Irish society believes in the value of education. Thus, higher education receives 81 percent of its funding from Government, 15 percent from fees."[9] This finding was elaborated on in chapter 6 of *Crisis and Promise* in relation to mechanisms for public financing of education in small countries: "Small states warrant different priorities. Partnerships with neighbouring small states have seen the establishment of a network university. Strategic choices to offerings are influenced by the countries' critical human skill requirements. Partnerships with external providers of tertiary education, including distance education, have been the traditional model. This approach is being overtaken by market developments, as cost incentives push foreign universities to locate special faculties in distant places that can be attractive to students and faculty. At the same time franchise partnerships are being developed between local private providers of university training and marketing arms of established institutions."[10] There are no empirically tested rules on the optimal ratio of expenditure on higher education in relation to GDP, but what is clear is that the development of human capital is highly connected to growth and quality of life.

The OECD/UNESCO 2002 report provides an analysis of the World Education Indicators (WEI) program launched by UNESCO, OECD, and the World Bank in 1997. The countries in the program were Argentina, Brazil, Chile, Egypt, India, Indonesia, Jamaica, Jordan, Malaysia, Paraguay, Peru, the Philippines, the Russian Federation, Tunisia, Thailand, Uruguay, and Zimbabwe. In its introduction, the report affirms that "education is an investment in the collective future of societies and nations, rather than simply the future success of individuals."[11] The report's comparison of the growth patterns of WEI and OECD countries supports the hypothesis that in the early stages of industrialization investment in capital is important, but as development deepens the role of human capital as a strong driver of economic growth takes over.

While investment in education promotes sustainable economic growth, it can also help equalize social disparities. One of the key findings of the OECD/UNESCO study is that "the goals of expanding education systems and maintaining [sustainable] equity are inextricably linked to questions of educational finance."[12] Demands on education

Table 10.1. Mechanisms for public financing of education in WEI countries

Mechanism	Goals	Constraints	Country
Direct public funding of private schools	Promote equity	Schools may increase fee or charge other fees	Argentina, Brazil, Chile, Paraguay, Philippines
Community grants/ community franchising	Promote equity; improve management capacity	Concerns about sustainability	Brazil, China, Zimbabwe
Grants/ scholarships	Promote equity	Targeting costs and difficulties; school may increase fee or charge other fees	Brazil, Chile, China, Jordan, Malaysia, Zimbabwe
Student loans	Promote equity and/ or cost recovery	Difficult to target; difficult to recover; often acts as subsidy	Brazil, Chile, Jamaica, Malaysia, Philippines, Thailand, Zimbabwe
Targeted bursaries/ school improvement funds	Promote access and equity; support local decision-making.	May not reach target population; social stratification; may be disincentive to schools	Chile, China, India, Paraguay
Vouchers	Promote choice, equity, and education quality	May results in selection practices; socially divisive.	Chile
Matching grants/social funds	Promote equity; improve management capacity	May have negative impact on poor students	Brazil, China, India, Philippines

Source: Adapted from UNESCO/OECD, *Financing Education*.

and demands for educational opportunities are growing in WEI countries. The resources required to meet these demands are highly dependent on macroeconomic stability. Apart from the issue of downturns, whether cyclical or contagious, the share of tax-based revenue as a percentage of GDP is also significant. In China this ratio is merely 6 per cent, while it is 40 per cent in the Netherlands. This restricts the public-sector capacity to fund education expenditure in many WEI countries. Combining public and private expenditure may help, but it might still be too little. In Indonesia this amounts to 1.8 per cent of GDP compared to 9.9 per cent of GDP in Jamaica. The World Bank estimates that an appropriate range of investment in education as a percentage of gross domestic product is between 4 and 6 per cent, of which higher education would generally be between 15 to 20 per cent. Table 10.1 outlines the wide array of mechanisms WEI countries use for financing education.

The issue of financing of higher education is linked to the issue of governance. State financial support for private education varies, ranging from 4 per cent in the United States to 12 per cent in France. Among WEI countries, governments in Chile and India are the biggest supporters of non-state education provision, although only about 10 per cent of that support goes to tertiary-level institutions. Since the cost of tertiary education can skyrocket, it has been argued that fees are justifiable for this level of education, but the level of private costs and the potential for excluding qualified students are important and sensitive policy concerns.

Perspectives in Higher Education

Bruce Johnstone discusses the finance and management agenda of tertiary education in the context of five themes: expansion and diversification of enrolments, participation rates, and number and types of institutions; fiscal pressure as reflected in overcrowding, poorly paid faculty, and major deficiencies in the university's hardware and software installations; the orientation towards the market in search of non-governmental revenues; the demand for greater accountability by all stakeholders; and the demand for greater quality and efficiency – "more rigour, more relevance, and more learning."[13] "Commoditization" refers to the conversion of education outputs into market products. It is argued that the production of high-quality learning materials at low unit costs will bring education to all: "In this way, teachers all over the world can be freed from the chore of reinventing the wheel. The Massachusetts Institute of Technology ... has shown the way by making its own web material available free. Let's hope this heralds a worldwide movement to commoditize education for the common well."[14] Another sign of the way things are going is that Apollo and Sylvan Learning, firms that sell higher education, are quoted on the US stock exchange. These agenda issues provide a framework that can be used to provide an empirical framework for educational planning.

In a keynote address at the 2002 Salzburg Seminar, Johnstone elaborated on certain trends in higher education worldwide: rising costs, institutional austerity, overcrowding, rising tuition fees, deterioration of quality, limitations on capacity and accessibility, deterioration of faculty morale and diminished public confidence in government.[15] The per student cost of higher education increases in response to high enrolment pressures, the move towards "massification," and the surge in faculty ambition. This means that there will be higher frontiers in the production possibility curve in education. Is there any innovation that will lower production costs in higher education? Information technology, yet to be fully explored, may have the potential. For now, higher education costs are to be met by revenue increases from taxpayers, parents, students, donors (philanthropists), clients, entrepreneurs, business, and consumers.

Technological change has posed a real danger of a growing digital gap among and between nations, clearly illustrated in the World Bank study: "Access to internet is essential for businesses, public institutions, and households to flourish in the modern economy. In the private and public sector, internet access can help spur productivity gains and deliver services more efficiently. For households, internet access can increase opportunities, build human capital, connect households to other parts of the country, and contribute to personal well-being. Yet Sub-Saharan Africa remains a long way from achieving universal internet access. According to the International Telecommunications Union (ITU), which tracks internet usage globally and across countries, only 1 in 5 in Sub-Saharan Africa used the internet in 2017. While internet access in Sub-Saharan Africa has grown rapidly in recent years, access rates remain well behind the rest of world."[16] Within countries, access to the Internet is heavily skewed in favour of high-income families, and there may even be a "digital gender gap." A well-functioning ICT system could reduce administrative and management costs, improve the quality of instruction and learning, and reap the economic gains to better access information cross-campus and across the globe. This is an opportunity for future funding by forging new university partnerships with business, manufacturing, and the extractive industries. Long-term finance instruments, either through the capital market or multilateral financial institutions, can be employed for capital funding. In that case, the state takes on the burden of such repayments and such finance programs are assessed from a national and regional perspective. In light of the state's finance limitations, multinational corporations with a stake and long-term interest in countries may be approached to be partners in the long-term financing of higher education. Since 1994, the General Agreement on Trade in Services (GATS) has included higher education on the list of services to be privatized.

In striving for financial viability, one requires policy strategies. For instance, one must work towards greater efficiency and/or supplement public revenue with non-governmental revenues. The introduction of revenue supplementation, also known as "cost sharing," can take a variety of forms, such as charging/raising tuition fees, increasing other fees, and freezing grants and other subsidies. Scotland has replaced tuition with loans to be repaid after graduation as a contribution to an endowment fund; Australia has adopted a higher education contribution scheme to be repaid after graduation (students may get a 25 per cent reduction if they pay upfront – which gives the appearance of a discount to those who can pay, or it may be seen as an incentive). Makarere University in Uganda has been heralded as witnessing a "quiet revolution" where student enrolment expanded, quality standards prevailed, and tuition fees have been systematically introduced.

Restructuring at Makarere had three central and interrelated elements: implementing alternative financing strategies, installing new management structures, and introducing demand-driven courses. The university encouraged privately sponsored students, commercializing of service units, and institutionalizing of consultancy arrangements. The results have been described as dramatic: in the space of five years, tuition fees were raised from zero per cent to 70 per cent. "Now over 30 per cent of revenue is internally generated. A relatively constant government subvention, combined with massive enrollment expansion, has brought a dramatic decline in the per capita cost to government."[17] Much of this achievement can be attributed to steady improvement in the country's macroeconomic performance and government's willingness to respect university autonomy. Within the institution, there was imaginative leadership that had "faith in the benefits of a market orientation and professional and participatory management, and their unambiguous sense of ownership of the reform process."[18]

The issue of tuition fees and cost sharing is not value free or politically neutral. Those promoting it claim equity or fairness (with parallel loans and grants), greater capacity and hence more equity, improved quality of teaching, and sustainability of finances. Finances will be volatile during public finance cycles. Those in opposition argue a loss of equality, the absence of a level playing field (some students have to earn incomes while studying), loss of public control, and a sub-ideal state. In order to be acceptable, tuition fees must supplement, not supplant, public revenue, or enrolments may not increase; and financial assistance programs must run in parallel. Also, increases in fees should be modest and regular. Some institutions have linked increases in fees to productivity expenditure, like better-equipped classrooms and laboratories, Internet access, new offerings, and savings.

Endowment and pension funds provide financial resources that need to be managed. Foundations and university endowments have traditionally been invested in government securities and equity holdings. In the United States, investment portfolios aim to "shoot for profits even in bad times" by investing in hedge funds. Universities appoint fund managers to implement a strategy for investment. Such managers determine the level of exposure and risk profile of the portfolio of investments. The returns to these investments represent an income stream, and the university must have the expertise to assess performance and advice on preferred investment strategy.

Most universities set themselves an entrepreneurial mandate. For instance, the University of the West Indies' report *Building an Entrepreneurial UWI* outlines the basic objectives of the exercise: "We are now pursuing a third major goal – Innovation and Entrepreneurship – as part of our overall developmental agenda. Innovation is a key driver of economic growth, and the University must perform a leadership role in promoting innovation and entrepreneurship across the region in order to realise this growth. Specifically, such activity is intended to

- produce a new class of university graduates with the skills and passion to start new businesses;
- initiate new revenue streams to the University by creating and commercialising intellectual property; and
- assist in realising infrastructural modernisation and regional transformation through the development of knowledge economies."[19]

Consulting firms often use university academics in their consulting engagements – this may apply more readily to programs with a high technical component, like engineering, science, economics, medicine, and management. The humanities do not easily offer themselves to market-based solutions in attracting new funding – sometimes with profit-sharing arrangements between faculty and university, other times on a purely private basis. In a period of rapid change, new training opportunities emerge as in the transition economies or the information industry. Decision-making at universities is not geared to respond in timely fashion to these rapid changes in the market; hence an entrepreneurial mandate emerges. In discharging this mandate, universities get opportunities to increase and diversify their sources of income, to explore new forms of thought and training, and to take on an entrepreneurial outlook. There is also a downside, as all departments may not have the same market power and there could be a diversion from the traditional canons of academic responsibility and integrity.

Philanthropy is big business in the United States, prompting higher education leaders to emulate the US experience, which provides another avenue to supplement public funds. Such contributions have thrived on favourable tax treatment, but the driving force is the existence of a culture of philanthropy. In many cases alumni associations provide the organizational platform for university fundraising activities. Such activities help in the expansion of capital programs, although there has been a recent trend to fund major areas of socially desirable research in fields like medicine, genetic engineering, and biotechnology.

In summary, the reform of higher education financing would include performance and incentive budgeting, expenditure reforms that include outsourcing of non-academic services, compensation reforms that include workforce planning systems, and devolution in spending authorities. Such reform may include radical restructuring of the system of higher education that may yield lay-offs, early retirements, and reassignment. Universities are known to resist change, and even more so radical change. Funding reform is an exercise in political economy, where the constituencies of "winners" in the change process must gain influence over the "losers." A major change agent in the university setting lies in the information revolution, as scholars have instant access to other scholars, thus simultaneously widening opportunities and competition.

Political Governance and the Marketplace

The issue of political governance of higher education was discussed by Teixeira et al. in the context of the challenges facing higher education systems and institutions and their struggle to deal with internal and external demands. In a later paper Amaral and Maglhães argued that "the government and higher education institutions are being challenged to widen access to higher education to improve the country's educational and economic performance, with the objective of attracting new publics and students from a broader range of social backgrounds."[20] These demands are reflected in changes in management and administrative structures for higher education. There also can be changes in performance that align education with national development, and in new models of public accountability resulting from rising demand for new and better education.

In addressing these issues – the distribution of power and the equilibrium between "winners and losers" among the stakeholders – matters of politics come to the fore. The forces for change in tertiary education, mentioned above, describe the links between regulations and incentives, participation and partnership and societal pressures. At the vortex is the issue of political governance as the core process that shapes the environment.

Economic growth and development are structurally linked to the knowledge economy, as merit-based, equitable, and efficient education is essential to economic transformation. Inevitably, decisions on these matters are made in a political process that has become more complex in today's world.[21]

Derek Bok, former president of Harvard University, has suggested that "universities show signs of excessive commercialism in every aspect of their work," but he is hopeful that the trend is not yet irreversible. He is probably right when he states, "In higher education, the cards are stacked against any institution that lacks an established reputation and a lot of money." Bok sees a major conflict between the commercialization of higher education and the need to protect the integrity of research and preserve educational values. Several scholars, he claims, have linked "the recent growth of money-making activity to a lack of purpose in the university." He does not agree; rather, he argues "that a university must have a clear sense of values needed to pursue its goals with a high degree of quality and integrity."[22]

The rise of market forces in higher education has opened the doors for additional cost-sharing avenues, but at a cost of turning universities into "knowledge factories." According to Stanley Aronowitz, "the learning enterprise has become subject to the growing power of administration, which more and more responds not to faculty and students, except at the margin, but to political and market forces that claim sovereignty over higher education."[23] The marketplace is now encroaching on the work of the universities, as it has done in hospitals, cultural institutions that have been thought to serve other values. These are bold assertions, and "a mute reminder that something of irreplaceable value may get lost in the relentless growth of commercialization."[24] Cheng has stated that the "foremost challenge is to manage commercialization to rise above short-term pressures and to take a more ethical stance towards education, a long-term strategic view."[25] Derek Bok argues that commercialization may undermine academic standards, by encouraging the appointment of professors who can bring corporate funding, or by restricting the full sharing of knowledge, reducing adherence to ethical behaviour, and introducing opportunities for private gain. In this environment, new challenges emerge for preserving educational and academic values, and new conflicts of interest will arise in protecting the integrity of research. The values of the university – promotion of social justice and equity, preservation and promotion of cultural values, generation of new knowledge – must not be sacrificed on the altar of commercialization.

Steps to Fast-Forward ICT[26]

Trinidad and Tobago's fast-forward agenda is all about transforming the country into a knowledge-based society. Government, working with the public and private sectors, has produced an exciting roadmap that charts a clear and determined course to an online society and a knowledge-based economy. Fast-forward provides far-reaching strategies for the development of a connected country that will adapt, flourish, and prosper in the new global information society.

NATIONAL ICT VISION
Trinidad and Tobago is in a prominent position in the global information society through real and lasting improvements in social, economic, and cultural development caused by deployment and usage of information and communication technology

NATIONAL OBJECTIVES
Our connectivity agenda will

- provide all citizens in our country with affordable Internet access;
- focus on the development of our children as well as enhancing the skills of adults to ensure a sustainable solution and a vibrant future;
- promote citizen trust, access, and interaction through good governance; and
- maximize the potential within all of our citizens, and accelerate innovation, to develop a knowledge-based society: Connected – Committed – Competitive – Creative – Caring – Community.

Towards developed nation status, our goals are

- sustaining strong economic growth;
- creating a competent, productive, and sophisticated workforce;
- improving efficiencies and service quality in public-sector agencies;
- improving education at all levels and increasing science and technology literacy through cutting-edge information and knowledge;
- improving social equity; and
- helping people become information sensitive.

PART B: THE DISTRIBUTION OF INCOME IN TRINIDAD AND TOBAGO, 1957–1976[†]

Income distribution is a vexing aspect of the economic condition and performance of developing countries. Reasonable growth rates in these countries over the last two decades have not been associated with a reduction in income inequality. Indeed, many Third World countries have

---

[†]   Part B of this chapter is based on Winston Dookeran, "The Distribution of Income in Trinidad and Tobago 1957–1976," *Review of Income and Wealth* 27, no. 2 (1981).

experienced a widening of income differentials within their borders, and in many instances there have been increasing levels of absolute poverty. A World Bank study summed up the situation as follows: "It is now clear that after a decade of rapid growth in underdeveloped countries, there has been little or no benefit to perhaps a third of their population."[27] Uneven income distribution patterns within developing countries are not unrelated to the world distribution of income, which is highly skewed. As well, estimates[28] indicate that the developing market economies of Africa, Asia, and South America, with 69.4 per cent of world population, account for 14.8 per cent of world GDP in nominal prices.

In response to these empirical realities, development economists and other social scientists are again focusing their attention on the mechanisms within differing economic systems that generate particular patterns of income distribution. The renewed interest in questions of distribution will hopefully offer new insights for economic theory, as theorists strive to integrate income distribution theories into the general methodology of economics. An important task for development theorists is to endogenize the distribution factor into the workings of the economic system and the economy and so provide a deeper understanding of distributional relations and their policy implications.

Trinidad and Tobago has shown relatively high growth in GDP over the last two decades, largely the result of events in the international economy. This small country with an open petroleum-based economy found its economic prospects and fortunes enhanced by the cumulative decisions of the Organization of Petroleum Exporting Countries.

In this chapter, I examine changes in national product and distribution of income in Trinidad and Tobago. To do so, I will estimate changes in GDP over the period 1957–76, and comparatively assess the behaviour of the size distribution of household incomes, listing some factors that may explain these changes in growth and distribution.

Growth Rate of the Gross Domestic Product

Over the period 1957–76, Trinidad and Tobago achieved an average annual growth rate of 13.3 per cent measured in current prices. Using the price index as a deflator, at constant 1970 prices the average annual growth rate for the period was 6.4 per cent. For the 1973–76 period, the annual growth rates were 33.4 per cent in current prices and 14.6 per cent in constant 1970 prices. These figures emphasize the impact that post-1973 petroleum prices had on the economy.

There has been some variance in the estimates given in different reports. Table 10.2 presents figures from the most recent reports, which

Table 10.2. Gross domestic product, 1957–76

	GDP (mTT$)				Rate of growth over previous year of GDP (%)			
	Current prices		Constant 1970 prices		Current prices		Constant 1970 prices	
Year	Value	Index	Value	Index	Annual average	3-year moving average	Annual average	3-year moving average
1957	654.7	40.3	968.5	59.7	–	–	–	–
1958	714.2	44.0	1,008.7	62.2	9.1	–	4.2	–
1959	793.1	48.9	1,074.6	66.2	11.0	–	6.5	–
1960	856.6	52.8	1,148.2	70.8	8.0	9.0	6.9	6.1
1961	946.3	58.3	1,255.0	77.3	10.5	9.8	9.3	7.7
1962	1,005.7	62.0	1,296.0	79.9	6.3	8.0	3.3	5.5
1963	1,094.2	67.4	1,357.6	83.7	8.8	8.4	4.8	5.2
1964	1,148.6	70.8	1,412.8	87.1	5.0	6.7	4.1	4.6
1965	1,188.0	73.2	1,448.8	89.2	3.4	5.1	2.6	3.6
1966	1,245.8	76.8	1,446.9	89.2	4.8	4.9	-0.1	1.9
1967	1,337.1	82.4	1,521.2	93.7	7.3	7.1	5.1	3.5
1968	1,521.5	93.8	1,598.2	98.4	13.8	10.5	5.1	4.3
1969	1,560.5	96.2	1,600.5	98.6	2.5	6.5	0.1	2.2
1970	1,622.8	100.0	1,622.8	100.0	3.9	5.2	1.4	1.8
1971	1,798.6	110.8	1,737.7	107.1	10.8	8.0	7.1	4.5
1972	2,034.4	125.4	1,798.7	110.8	13.1	10.5	3.5	4.0
1973	2,467.5	152.1	1,901.0	117.1	21.3	15.9	5.7	4.8
1974	4,003.0	246.1	2,524.5	155.6	62.2	39.1	32.9	18.9
1975	5,382.2	331.8	2,903.0	178.9	34.5	36.8	14.9	16.9
1976	6,220.8	383.3	3,040.5	187.4	15.6	26.2	4.7	10.8
Average 1957–76					13.3		6.4	
Average 1973–76					34.4		14.6	

Source: Dookeran, "Distribution of Income in Trinidad and Tobago."

were generally accepted as accurate. The table gives a detailed break-down of these growth rates. Over the period, GDP increased tenfold in current prices. In real terms GDP quadrupled between 1957 and 1976.

After a relative real increase in GDP in the fifties, the economy moved into a decline, setting in motion a secular trend from which there has been a minor and major respite. The minor respite took place around 1967–68 but was short lived, as the growth path moved back into the set pattern of the early sixties. The major respite occurred in 1973–74 and jolted the economy into a much higher level of economic activity.

Increased export earnings of the post-1973 period had the effect of reversing the balance-of-payments situation, multiplying government revenues and introducing an excess liquidity condition in the financial sector of the economy. Cumulatively, these changes resulted in a rapid increase in both the level and rate of growth of GDP. Although the level of the growth rate increased, the secular trend of a downward-sloping growth path remained unaltered. At least for the short run, it appears that the post-1973 boom has not affected the direction of the GDP growth path, which may be a reflection of the unchanging structure, and structural relations, in the economy.

The minor and major respites are both related to events in the international economy. High commodity prices and low inflation rates in the external markets partially explain the 1967–68 situation. Within the local economy, increased output in the petroleum and export commodity sectors complemented these external developments. As for the 1973–74 respite, the major contributory factors are the well-known changes in the world petroleum industry and petroleum prices. The possible advantage of high petroleum prices to an open petroleum-based economy was quickly reduced by a rising world inflation rate. Locally, the relative constancy of the population growth rate militated against a fall in real per capita GDP. During this period, net factor payments abroad were increasing at a faster rate than GDP.

Given the structural openness of the economy, the scope for excessive leakages from the system, and the overall dependence on the international economy, it is unlikely that market forces alone would generate responses that could push the economy towards structural changes. On the contrary, market forces may reinforce existing structural relations and hence sustain the net transfer of resources out of the local economy. Even within the domestic economy, resources are likely to accumulate at growth points. These processes may adversely influence the income distribution pattern, as there is no automatic mechanism to distribute increased value of output either on a spatial or target-group basis. The dependent market economy relies almost exclusively on deliberate public policy measures to achieve distributional objectives.

Economic strategy may deliberately seek to link the growth process with distribution targets. Otherwise, public policy may tend to strengthen the structural relations in the economy that create greater income inequality. For instance, the manner in which "excess" liquidity is injected into the system may distort price relations in the economy and create a boom in the speculator's market. Such a situation would influence the existing income distribution pattern, as speculation transfers wealth and has little impact on the net creation of wealth. Such a

Table 10.3. Movement of household incomes, 1957–76

	Average monthly household income at current prices		Price index	Average monthly household income at constant 1975–76 prices	
	Value (TT$)	% increase over previous period		Value (TT$)	% increase over previous period
1957–58	82	–	35	234	–
1971–72	220	268	55	400	170
1975–76	458	108	100	458	11.5

transfer process is more likely to increase the concentration of wealth. The condition is strengthened when the excess liquidity does little to increase the domestic productive capacity while at the same time it reinforces the foreign enclaved productive economy.

According to Table 10.3, average household income increased at an annual average of 27.9 per cent in current prices over the period 1957–76. At constant 1975–76 prices, the rate of increase was 9.8 per cent. The annual increase in GDP for the period was 6.4 per cent in real terms. These figures may imply that the share of income in total gross output was increasing over the period. Although income grew at a faster rate than output, it would be hazardous to infer that labour's share of total income increased over the period. Data on the disaggregation of income by factors is not accessible, and in this regard publication of national income statistics would be welcomed.

Movement of Incomes[29]

I note that although average income increased by 108 per cent between 1971–72 and 1975–76 in current prices, this amounted to only 11.5 per cent in real terms. This is due to the higher rates of inflation during this period, but could conceivably be the result of changes in the pattern of income distribution. For in comparing the average, we need not be comparing the same points in the distribution. Nonetheless, in the light of this small increase in real income, there is a need to explain the basis for increased spending in the economy since 1973.

Increases in income alone would not provide the full explanation. Average expenditure was 142.3 per cent of average income in 1975–76. It may be that rising monetary income and excess financial liquidity in the system together accounted for the increased spending in the economy.

Table 10.4. Income shares by deciles, % income shares

Decile of household	1957–58	Cumulative	1971–72	Cumulative	1975–76	Cumulative
1st–2nd	3.4	3.4	2.2	2.2	2.7	2.7
3rd	3.8	7.2	2.9	5.1	3.5	6.2
4th	5.3	12.5	4.5	9.6	5.4	11.6
5th	6.7	19.2	5.9	15.5	7.4	19.0
6th	7.9	27.1	7.4	22.9	8.4	27.4
7th	11.1	38.2	9.4	32.3	10.4	37.8
8th	13.2	51.4	12.5	44.8	12.8	50.6
9th	15.3	66.7	17.4	62.2	18.0	68.6
10th: first 5%	10.8	77.5	13.3	75.5	11.9	80.5
10th: second 5%	22.5	100.0	24.5	100.0	19.5	100.0

During the post-1973 period, expenditure increased at a faster rate than real income, which itself was increasing at a higher rate than gross output. The equilibrating factor must be intertemporal trade-offs among these variables. Current expenditure will have to be met by future income. It is not clear whether this expenditure is biased towards capital or consumption goods. A bias towards capital goods (provided they are productively "employed") will increase gross output and, *ceteris paribus*, real income in the future. Otherwise, there may be a widening difference among the values of these variables. As such, measures of income inequality may not be a faithful proxy for the level of economic well-being.

Patterns of Income Distribution

Table 10.4 compares the changes in income shares by deciles at three points over the period, in 1957–58, 1971–72, and 1975–76.

The calculations reveal that income inequality increased between 1957–58 and 1971–72. Between 1971–72 and 1975–76 there was a decrease in inequality. For instance, 40 per cent of households with the lowest income received 12.5 per cent of total income in 1957–58, which decreased to 9.6 per cent in 1971–72 and increased again to 11.6 per cent in 1975–76. At the other extreme, 10 per cent of households with the highest income received 33.3 per cent of all incomes in 1957–58, 37.8 per cent in 1971–72, and 31.4 per cent in 1975–76.[30]

Harewood calculated the Gini coefficients for the three distributions at different levels of aggregation and concluded that in Trinidad and

Tobago, "after increasing by about six percentage points between 1957–58 and 1971–72, by 1975–76 the ratios had returned to very nearly the same as in 1957–58."[31] Using the most disaggregated data, Harewood estimated the Gini concentration ratio to be 0.4313 in 1957–58, 0.5142 in 1971–72, and 0.4530 in 1975–76.

The Gini coefficient is a summary statistic and does not take into account the location of inequality in a distribution. Equal differences between two incomes (at any point in the distribution) affect the size of the Gini ratio in exactly the same way. It is conceivable, therefore, that those internal changes in the distribution pattern may not influence the size of this ratio.[32] The decile ratio test[33] may better detect the location of inequality in a particular distribution. Identifying the sixth decile as the median decile, I compared the ratios of each decile to the median decile. With respect to deciles below the median, lower numerical values indicate greater inequality. while for deciles above the median, higher numerical values indicate greater inequality. Table 10.5 gives these ratios.

From Table 10.5 we see that the 1971–72 distribution reveals more inequality than the 1957–58 distribution for all deciles except the seventh. The decile ratio test shows more inequality in 1971–72 than in 1975–76 for all deciles. The hypothesis that the distribution of income worsened and then improved over the period is corroborated by this analysis. The 1975–76 distribution, when compared to earlier work by Jack Harewood, appears to have remained roughly the same.[34]

Comparing 1975–76 to 1957–58, we see that for all deciles below the median except the fifth decile, the situation in 1975–76 depicts greater inequality than that existing in 1957–58. The difference in the fifth decile over the two time points is three percentage points. For deciles above the median, there was less inequality in 1975–76 than in 1957–58 except for the ninth decile. The change is most pronounced in the seventh decile, where the difference is in the vicinity of sixteen percentage points. The worsening of equality in the ninth decile for the 1975–76 distribution was also by sixteen percentage points.

These comparisons may be interpreted as follows:

1 Comparing the distribution of 1957–58 to that of 1971–72, the distribution of income worsened over the period for all income earners (i.e., inequality of income increased during the period).
2 Comparing the distribution of 1957–58 to that of 1975–76, the distribution of income worsened over the period for the 50 per cent of income earners below the median.
3 The distribution in the middle-income level broadened in 1975–76, suggesting an expansion of middle-income earners in absolute

Table 10.5. Decile ratios

Decile	1957–58	1971–72	1975–76
1st and 2nd / 6th	0.43 (3)	0.29 (1)	0.32 (2)
3rd / 6th	0.48 (3)	0.39 (1)	0.42 (2)
4th / 6th	0.67 (3)	0.61 (1)	0.64 (2)
5th / 6th	0.85 (2)	0.80 (1)	0.88 (3)
6th / 6th	1.00 –	1.00 –	1.00 –
7th / 6th	1.41 (1)	1.27 (2)	1.24 (3)
8th / 6th	1.67 (2)	1.70 (1)	1.52 (3)
9th / 6th	1.94 (3)	2.35 (1)	2.14 (2)
10th / 6th	4.22 (2)	5.11 (1)	3.74 (3)

terms. The disparity of income in the sixth, seventh, and eighth deciles was reduced.

4 The expansion of the middle-income grouping took place at the expense of both extremes. The incidence of cost in this change fell on the first, second, third, and the upper half of the tenth decile.

5 Overall, 1975–76 showed greater inequality than 1957–58. This point becomes clear only when the location of inequality is considered; otherwise the inference is hidden in the biases of statistical methods.

Real incomes of all households increased at an annual average of 7.4 per cent over the period 1957–58 to 1971–72. For the later period 1971–72 to 1975–76, the annual average increase was 4.5 per cent. The fact that the rate of increase for the lower-income deciles was below the overall average in the first period and above the overall average in the latter period corroborates the conclusion on income equality changes. However, the rising absolute increase for the lower-income group was not sufficient to overcome the degree of inequality that took place in the 1957–58 to 1971–72 period.

In absolute terms, 40 per cent of households in the lowest income group received a real income of 5 million dollars monthly in 1957–58. By 1971–72, this had increased in real terms to 8.1 million dollars. In 1975–76, this group received an absolute real income of 12 million dollars. In relative terms, these increases were lower than the overall average for all deciles. While real income for all deciles increased by an annual average of 7.9 per cent over the 1957–76 period, the increase for the 40 per cent of lowest-income households was 7.0 per cent. This situation was reversed in the 1971–72 to 1975–76 period, as the overall increase of 4.5 per cent was less than the increase in the 40 per cent lowest income group, which was 9.6 per cent.

Table 10.6. Total monthly real income for all households by deciles

Decile of household	1957–58 (TT$mn)	1971–72 (TT$mn)	Avg. annual % change, 1957–58 to 1971–72	1975–76 (TT$mn)	Avg. annual % change, 1971–72 to 1975–76
1st–2nd	1.4	1.9	2.4	2.8	9.4
3rd	1.5	2.4	4.0	3.6	10.0
4th	2.1	3.8	5.4	5.6	9.4
5th	2.7	5.0	5.7	7.6	10.4
6th	3.1	6.2	6.7	8.7	8.0
7th	4.4	7.9	5.3	10.7	7.1
8th	5.3	10.5	6.5	13.2	5.1
9th	6.1	14.6	9.3	18.6	5.5
10th–1st 5%	4.3	11.2	10.7	12.3	2.0
10th–2nd 5%	9.0	20.6	8.7	20.1	−0.5
Total	39.9	84.1	7.4	103.2	4.5

This information suggests that in the period of steady growth (1957–58 to 1971–72) the lower income groups benefited little in absolute terms and their relative position worsened. In the later period of rapid growth, the trickle-down effect did arrest the situation and generated a movement towards greater equality. It could be that the 1971–72 income distribution represented a chance variation from the "relative stability of income shares," a situation that was being restored by 1975–76. In that case the trickle-down effect would be a restoration process rather than a systematic improvement in the distribution pattern. The pattern of income distribution in the post-1976 period would provide insight into the sustaining nature of the trickle-down effect (see Table 10.6).

A Spatial Aspect of Income Inequality

From Table 10.7 we see that incomes in the rural area are lower than in the urban area. In addition, there is greater disparity of income in rural areas than in urban areas. Overall urban income is 1.24 times above median rural income, which was approximately $310 monthly in 1975–76. The urban/rural income ratio is lower in 1975–76 than in previous years. Ahiram[35] estimated an urban/rural ratio of 1.7 for Trinidad in 1957–58.[36] Notwithstanding the fact that Ahiram compared means rather than medians, the data may suggest that rural incomes are catching up with urban incomes.

This conclusion is inconsistent with findings regarding occupational groupings and place of residence. A close look reveals, however, that

Table 10.7. Percentage of households by income

Monthly household income	Urban	Rural	Trinidad and Tobago
Under $299	39.9	48.6	43.2
$300–$699	36.3	36.6	36.4
$700–$1,099	14.8	10.7	12.9
$1,100–$1,499	5.0	3.1	4.3
$1,500 or more	4.0	1.0	3.2

there has been a reclassification of areas in the data that may tend to lower the urban/rural income ratio: in the 1975–76 survey the urban area was expanded to include areas classified as rural in previous surveys.

There has been little statistical change in the spatial distribution of income over the years. This is probably to be expected in light of the reliance of economic growth strategy on "growth pole" accumulation and development. In general, the flow of resources continues to move from periphery to centre, reinforcing in the process the existing distribution of asset formation, capital levels, and income flows. The distributional component of the development strategy and policies does not have a clear spatial dimension, as balanced regional growth has had little recognition in public policy. In addition, the distribution factor is given low weight in project selection analysis. This is so for both private- and public-sector projects in Trinidad and Tobago

Tables 10.8 and 10.9 are self-explanatory and corroborate the general findings. From the point of view of income distribution, column 4 of Table 10.9 is of special interest. Because the "not classified" section amounts to 25 per cent of the sample, we must be cautious in drawing any firm conclusions from these data. Clearly, agricultural and production workers receive a share of the wage bill that is smaller than their respective share of the working population. It is of interest that income shares by occupational groupings may coincide with the sectoral contribution to GDP.

To the extent the above hypothesis is true (it is generally true for many developing countries), this may point to one of the major sources of large income disparity in Trinidad and Tobago. Structural dualism has been a feature of this economy, as very little attempt has been made, and less success has been achieved, in integrating the agricultural sector into the national economy. In addition, the informal sector remains a domestic enclave of the economy. One of the implications of this structural dualism is its impact on income distribution, where workers in peripheral

Table 10.8. Percentage distribution of occupational groupings by income, 1975–76

		Under $300	$300–699	$700–1,099	$1,100–1,499	$1,500 and over
Average monthly income		$142	$454	$858	$1,274	$2,017
Percentages						
All occupations	100	43.2	36.4	12.9	4.3	3.2
Professional	100	4.3	19.9	26.2	22.2	27.4
Manipulative	100	32.6	40.8	17.0	5.7	3.9
Agricultural	100	54.1	35.4	8.6	1.5	0.4
Production	100	32.5	49.8	13.8	2.9	1.0
Not classified	100	51.5	43.1	3.7	1.0	0.7

industries receive proportionately smaller shares of the national wage bill. This emphasizes the need for fundamental restructuring of the economic base as the surest path towards greater economic equality.

Expenditure-Income Pattern

According to the Household Budgetary Survey 1975–76, average expenditure per household exceeds average income for all income levels. Overall monthly expenditure was 1.42 times monthly income, while at the lower income levels the expenditure/income ratio exceeded 3.5. Regressing expenditure (E) against income (Y) and using cross-sectional area data, I found the least squares regression line to be the following:

$$E = 26 + 1.45Y \ (r2 = 0.72)$$

This is consistent with general economic hypotheses on this matter, for at zero incomes expenditure is positive. Also, the high expenditure/income ratio may be partly the result of increasing urbanization, as the propensity to consume is likely to be higher in the urban setting than the rural one. The "b" coefficient of 1.45 is statistically similar to the overall expenditure/income ratio of 1.42.

Table 10.10 reveals that the growth of commercial bank credit has been rapid, and this is particularly so during the 1974–76 period. Increases in bank credit were possible because of a substantial rise in bank liquidity in the post-1973 period. These data support the contention made above that credit availability may have influenced the increased spending in the economy to a large extent, as indeed did rising monetary income.

Table 10.9. Average income and income shares by occupational grouping, 1975–76

	Distribution (%)	Average monthly income ($)	Share wage bill (%)	Column 3/ column 1
Professional	8	1,157	20	2.50
Manipulative	22	529	25	1.14
Agricultural	11	339	8	0.72
Production	34	428	31	0.91
Not classified	25	328	16	0.64

Table 10.10. Index of commercial bank credit

	1968	1969	1970	1971	1972	1973	1974	1975	1976
Index	109.3	143.4	181.4	219.8	314.5	318.5	383.5	574.7	854.7

There may have been some degree of "money illusion" in the economy, a money illusion that may have been formed by the rapid rise in monetary income and the expectation of escalating inflation.

There is sufficient evidence to support the view that excess demand and spending in the local economy in 1975–76 was not based primarily on rising real incomes. What is not clear is whether the increased spending was investment for the future, was merely increasing economic well-being for the present, or was due to the need to maintain existing levels of living in an inflationary condition. Whatever the reason, the excess demand generated production bottlenecks, commodity shortages, and a rising import bill. These effects may unleash further inflationary pressure and consequently militate against an improving income equality pattern.

Income Distribution by Ethnic Groupings

This aspect has been documented in two articles,[37] and there is no evidence to suggest this situation has changed substantially over the last few years. Thus I will not deal with this aspect of the problem here; to do so would require more comprehensive data, especially since income data is no longer classified by ethnic groupings in Trinidad and Tobago. There is, however, an ethnic factor in the formation of distribution policy in Trinidad and Tobago. This is especially so with respect to government's social expenditure and public good entitlement. Scholars concerned about the development of an equal society may find research in this area of political economy rewarding.

11 Small-State Diplomacy and the Liberal Order[*]

The Liberal Order Is Rigged: Fix It Now or Watch It Wither is the title of Jeff Colgan and Robert Keohane's early analytical challenge to the Trump presidency. They argued that "the Brexit and Trump phenomena reflect a breakdown in the social contract at the core of liberal democracy" and attributed this to "populism defined by a faith in strong leaders and a dislike of limits of sovereignty and of powerful institutions"; they concluded that to "stave off complete defeat" political ideas must be rebranded and "substantive policies" must be developed "to make globalization serve the interests of middle- and working-class citizens" – or it will wither away.[1]

Amitav Acharya, in response to the "outpouring of anxiety over the future of the liberal order," quietly claimed that "Trump's ascent to power is a consequence – not a cause – of the decline of the liberal order" and that "the myths, limitations, and decline of this order have been anticipated and forewarned for some time." In any event, the liberal order, however defined, was "centered on the Atlantic littoral," and "the crisis of the liberal order has deeper roots, owing to long-term and structural changes in the global economy and politics"[2] – and, I may add, global power shifts.

Are We in a Post-Hegemonic Cycle in International Politics?

Maybe it was Acharya's insight that led Andy Knight to suggest that the "world seems to be crying out for an alternative ... which will depend on the convergence of interests and attitudes of the existing

---

[*] This chapter was adapted from the author's notes and on "Small States Diplomacy and the Liberal Order," paper presented to American University Annual Conference, Washington, DC, 2018.

preponderant powers and emerging powers, as well as on the willingness of the United States to accept a new role in a post-hegemonic world order."[3] Would the evolving world order focus on "ideas and ideology," and could that be decoupled from military, economic, and technological sources of power? This, in my view, is the dialectics necessary to sort out the contradictory processes working simultaneously in understanding the realpolitik in today's practice of statecraft and diplomacy.

The Dialectics of Realpolitik in Small-State Diplomacy

In the practice of diplomacy, there are three ideas I view as important: the advent of a multiplex world order, regionalism in the evolving world order, and the small states' rise to prominence in that order. In doing so, I am guided by John Bew's insight that "ideas were important in politics – increasingly so, in the democratic age – but their importance was to be judged by their political force rather than their purity or elegance."[4] In the conduct of international relations, we may be witnessing a reassertion of realpolitik, exercised in a world of extreme uncertainty or rapid transformation, and an attitude of "cynicism and cold calculation." Is this an ideological moment that "attempts to reconcile idealism with the pursuit of national interests"?[5]

In the search for a new vocabulary of international relations, Amitav Acharya urged scholars to remain "open to new concepts and theories … and new possibilities of a world order that have no precedents in history."[6] His journey into a "multiplex world order" is a lucid and logical response in a period of extreme uncertainty and points to a changing framework, but cannot claim to define a new order of things simply by "cross-cutting globalisms," as the new order will remain in flux in this "cycle of hegemonic decline." In transitions from one world order to the next, there is always a lag as certain resilient elements of the old order give way to the new. The transformation is never abrupt.

The dominance of the global economic and security order that has engaged world leadership in this era has overshadowed the key role of regionalism in the emerging world order. Focusing on regional public goods, global governance, and sustainable development, Estevadeordal and Goodman have shown how regional leadership – alliances and networks – fit together in the new frontiers of twenty-first-century cooperation.[7] Acharya, in a penetrating chapter in that publication, focuses on an alternative conceptualization of regionalism – hegemonic, integrationist, and multiplex – and concludes that "old regional mechanisms are evolving towards wider and more complex functions, and new mechanisms are emerging."[8] Regionalism will be confronted by new balance of power situations, and so will be forced to seek more leverage room for itself and for relations with non-regional actors.

Will this lead to less structured integration, and more "spontaneous" convergence among countries? If so, the study of convergence spaces may become more relevant than of integration models. Will the lines of distinction between private and public sectors become more blurred, where risk sharing takes a more critical place in the analytical calculus of development paradigms? These and other questions give credence to the insight that in regionalism, new mechanisms are emerging. One of the mechanisms that might be emerging is "subsidiarity," a social organization where political issues are dealt with for resolution at the most immediate level.

Increasingly, countries on the periphery have been searching for more "wiggle room" in the international order; as Robert Keohane observed several years ago, "one of the most striking features of contemporary international politics has been the conspicuousness of small states ... who through diplomatic innovation have risen to prominence, if not to power."[9] The underlying premise of this observation has been based on the pillars of the liberal order: free trade, multilateral diplomacy, the growth of democracies, and "values" in institutions of governance. The erosion of these pillars may pose a risk to the prominence of small states that have benefited from accepting policies rooted in the neo-liberal order. The vulnerabilities of small states extend beyond issues of geography, economics, and ecology, and now include policy shifts, resource flows, and the existential threats of natural disasters – as they affect the survival of these states. The world of small states, unique as it is in its problems and its solutions, will now search for more inviting alliances that could secure its sustainable development.

Cooper and Shaw argued that "small states continue to be disconnected from the most salient debates in international relations" and, using international relations theory, articulated the structural rigidities of vulnerabilities and resilience in the democracies of small states.[10] In a more recent publication, Baldacchino and Wivel examined the politics of small states across the globe today, admitting that "small states are more visible and prominent than at any other point in world history."[11] They argued that "globalization is a double-edged sword for small states – while allowing them to boost trade and avoid poverty but at the same time increasing vulnerabilities and dependency as a consequence of unconventional security risks stemming from mass migration terrorism, money laundering and environmental degradation."[12] Both sets of authors converge in their trajectories of the future challenges of diplomacy facing small nations like the Caribbean in the years ahead. From observing small states in Europe and learning from the experience of countries like Singapore and Qatar and island states of the Pacific and the Caribbean, I see emerging a synthesis of thought that could well lead to a general theory of small states, which is at the core of the thinking in this publication.

The Dawn of a New Discourse

At a recent CAF conference, Susana Malhotra urged new thinking on "a renaissance of the global system" as she addressed the new global dynamic in Latin America, noting that the unipolar order has been gradually eroded and the pressures "of modernity and globalization" are bringing business and political leadership together in almost every country of Latin America. This goes beyond the traditional private-public partnership, and focuses on the "catalytic" role of the state in forging new enterprises. A new dialogue on Latin America in world affairs has started, where lines of distinction between an Atlantic and Pacific Latin America are now blurred, and the international road map remains unclear.

At the first-ever UN Security Council meeting to invite small states, held under the presidency of New Zealand in 2015, the theme that global challenges demand collective responsibility was pervasive, no doubt predicated on the notion of multilateralism, a key pillar of liberal thought and the liberal order. Alicia Bárcena, executive secretary of ECLAC, called for "revitalizing multilateralism" to promote the 2030 agenda, and this is the cornerstone of small states' voice and influence in accepting collective responsibility for global challenges. In the circumstances, platforms for multilateral diplomacy for articulating small states' interests and their commitment for global responsibility will be redefined to reflect more willing advocates in the council of nations. This will be a tall challenge for small states in today's world of diplomacy.

At a recent high-level symposium in Argentina, Bárcena declared that "today more than ever, cooperation must be promoted and expanded on multilateral bases" – a theme she had raised earlier among leaders in Europe at the European Union–ECLAC Forum. At the symposium she described the current global context as "marked by the weakening of multilateralism and the return of protectionism" and called for more "dialogue space" in the "new context" for sustainable development, as outlined in the UN 2017 World Economic and Social Survey.[13]

Historically, Caribbean countries have been faithful to the prescriptions of the "Washington Consensus," as they agreed that the gains of globalization allow them a better insertion into the global economy. Rather than lament that the landscape of that order is now closing doors, a new diplomatic engagement to open doors will of necessity occur. This too signals the need for more inviting alliances, and poses a huge challenge to the conduct of international relations, at a time when global institutions are themselves engaged in responding to the realities of a flux in power relations.

I conclude with an observation: the challenge to the liberal order is not really a challenge to the values underpinning that order as much as it is a correction to the excesses of that order and the consequential shift in the structure of global power. Will this be a transient phenomenon, or will it have an ideological reach and so alter in a more far-reaching way the value premises of democratic societies, and add new momentum to a post-hegemonic cycle in world politics?

Small-States Diplomacy in Global Competitiveness[14]

There has been much doubt and anxiety as to the future of the liberal order in the geopolitics of today.[15] The spillover of this anxiety has opened a dialogue on the "new globalization" in a period of protectionism, weakening multilateralism, and a political assault on global competitiveness. Amitav Acharya, who was accorded the prestigious Distinguished Scholar Award in 2018 for his path-breaking scholarship in defining the political architecture of the emerging multiplex world order, cautioned international relations scholars not to be wedded to the conventional wisdom in the field and urged them to explore new ideas and possibilities of the world order that have no precedent in history.

This insight provides the setting for discovering new possibilities for small-states diplomacy in the upcoming period in economic advancement for small states in an uncertain economic order. The title of a keynote speech given by economist Enrico Spolaore, "Small States and the Future of Globalization," is of key relevance to the global challenges of our times.

The *Global Competitiveness Report 2017–18* states that "improving competitiveness ... requires the coordinated action of the state, the business community and civil society."[16] The report focuses on financial vulnerabilities as a threat to competitiveness, and on a nation's ability to finance innovation and technological adoption, spread the benefits of technological adoption, and provide worker protection in a flexible labour market.

Global economic institutions must now confront a new quest to design strategies and road maps for reform that will build on the achievements of the past, and cope with an increasingly new set of ripples that pose risks to the orthodox practice of development and ignite a search for a new kind of diplomacy. In this regard, small states have unique challenges, some of which were addressed by the World Bank in their 2017 publication *Small States: A Roadmap for World Bank Group Engagement*. With reference to small EU states, the road map identified financial deepening of the private sector – the cascade approach and blended finance approaches – as relevant to enhancing competitiveness strategies in small states in Europe. The mandate of its affiliate, the International Finance Corporation, is to enhance financial flows for small economies. Capital flow – its direction and sustainability – is key to building the resilience of the world's small economies. This task is anchored in economic analysis, but building a momentum to achieve results is essentially a diplomatic initiative.

The *Global Competitiveness Report* linked global convergence and competitiveness, as economies with higher convergence indices have witnessed greater competitiveness and have grown "significantly more strongly" than less competitive economies. The report identified "a comprehensive competitiveness agenda for reducing between-country inequality" as key to sustaining strong growth within and among clusters of countries.The identification of "emerging convergence spaces" has been on ECLAC's research agenda for Central American and Caribbean economies. The experience of the Pacific Alliance in pooling economic instruments in support of convergence has had promising results: the growth rate of those countries was more than double the regional average during the period 2014–16.

The World Bank road map for small states specifically linked financing to competitiveness by carefully identifying several priority areas in which there is need to develop a global practice. This practice "include[s] multiple efforts to mobilize concessional and private resources to serve small states clients[']" development finance needs, particularly addressing financial vulnerabilities. Some of these needs as they apply to small EU states are predictability of affordable financing, debt sustainability, access to financial markets, and diversification of small economies. With respect to deepening private-sector involvement, the "IFC is committed to helping expand the limited set of economic opportunities leveraging the full weight of resources of the world bank group, ensuring obstacles for the poor and the bottom 40 percent of the population to access these economic opportunities are reduced."[17]

One of the flagship economic reports that measures business competitiveness rankings is the World Bank "Doing Business" index. These indicators carry considerable weight in investment attractiveness, and include regulatory hurdles, tax and exchange rate issues, and other measures that make a "better" business environment. The methodology applied in constructing this index and the integrity of its findings have been questioned;[18] there have been calls to ditch the "doing business" rankings, in light of a diplomatic war between Chile and the editors concerning the political bias of the findings. Nonetheless, this index attracts extensive international media coverage and its findings are used by countries against each other to improve their standing.

The *Global Competitiveness Report* recently developed a proposal on "the future of competitiveness benchmarking" that offers an opening for technical negotiations and conceptual innovations in the design challenges. This index is a valuable measure of a country's progress in building structures and processes to support policy initiatives on a global competitiveness framework. As well, my colleagues and I, drawing on the pioneering work of Lino Bruguglio on resilience, constructed a methodology to measure Caribbean external vulnerability and then argued that trends in financial flows are key to building economic resilience – by examining the "structural variable" of vulnerability, the "process variable" of fragility, and the "challenging policy variable" of resilience – to generate inflow of funds, sustain competitiveness, and increase the well-being of citizens. While the methodology is applied to data from Caribbean countries, its logic and methods can be applied with equal rigour to small economies in general.[19]

To make progress, technical analysis will need to build a momentum for effective results. As such, the search for diplomatic interventions becomes necessary, within global institutions and in the global policy frameworks that are being framed. A global dialogue is in the making, and small economies have a vested interest in being part of that dialogue, which is not only technical but also a matter of diplomacy. Tom Long has argued that "small states can influence institutional rules and procedure … just as for rules shaped by greater powers,"[20] and many scholars suggest that "small states can ⬚punch above their weight.'"[21] According to Long, "Luxembourg has been a founding model member of European institutions, and it has used this to pressure for favorable EU policies, while seeking to strengthen institutions as a bulwark against historic German French rivalry."[22] Serge Allegrezza discussed this in a seminal article,[23] and drew attention to a "competitiveness observatory" set up by the social partners in Luxembourg and the measurement of the competitiveness scoreboard that was discussed in "a special parliamentary session" on competitiveness and growth.

Long's suggests that "small states have a greater capacity to influence the agenda in world politics and play a critical role in the evolution of

European integration than is commonly understood ... inside European institutions, small states can construct a 'a position of authority' through diplomacy – by influencing rules and voting procedure."[24] In this sense, small-states diplomacy is an essential component of those states' advancing their interests in global competitiveness.

In search of twenty-first-century cooperation, Estevadeordal and Goodman show how regional leadership – alliances and networks – fit together to link public goods with sustainability, and Acharya called for a new conceptualization of regionalism that will embrace more complex situations in a changing "balance of power."[25] Could small states shift global economic structures to favour their interests? Would small states benefit from open trade systems? How could small states overcome their "smallness" and develop diplomatic leverage? These and other questions were addressed by Henrikson, and Alesina Alberto and Spolaore provide a critical body of thought that informs the agenda of small-states diplomacy in today's world.[26]

Regional public goods have once again been cited as important in the context of twenty-first-century international relations. Michelle Egan traced the pivotal role of European public goods in the foundations of European integration. These public goods include competition policy and market access, common external tariff and trade matters, transportation and cross-border services, environment and negative externalities, economic convergence and income and wealth disparities, macro-economic stabilization and the euro, and internal security and border control. Egan concluded that "despite the growing chorus if disenchantment in Europe – with the concerns for inequality, productivity and migration – there remains a role for regional organizations to act as catalysts for collective action by providing regional public goods." But he hastened to add that public goods "can also weaken democratic institutions and can collapse trust in European institutions."[27]

Small states in Europe are strategically placed to recalibrate its approach to regional diplomacy – in its quest to promote and sustain growth and equity in its development goals. As such, those states can bring important lessons to the attention of other small states in the world and add considerably to the expectations of this exercise in global analytical leadership.

12 Getting Governance and Development Right[*]

The Challenge for Small States

Principled leadership must rest on consensus-building structures. Democracy is the vehicle, but the Western liberal model often ignores the roles of inequality, liberty, human and property rights, and capabilities in the developing world. Dr. Ricardo Hausmann has suggested a new definition of development that centres on diversity of products and competitiveness based on capabilities.[1] Small states have the potential to play a critical role in shaping governance in the democratic order of our times. From a global perspective, there are approximately 200 nation states: 134 classified as small developing states, 105 with less than 5 million people, 45 with less than 1.5 million people, and 34 island states, including those in the Caribbean and the Pacific. It was always questioned whether small states would survive. As small states passed that hurdle, the issue then became whether they could build the resilience to cope with internal and external risks. This continues to remain a key challenge. The question now is whether small states can be sustainable with the new shifts in global politics and economics.

Societies in small states are caught in a profound wave of change as they respond to a different globalized order. The political and economic paradigms of yesterday have lost their legitimacy to promote workable solutions for an impatient generation with higher expectations. It could be argued that the realignment of the political culture towards citizens' interests and rights or entitlements to higher standards of living should

---

[*] This chapter was adapted from Winston Dookeran, "Getting Development Right: Leadership and Governance in Small States," in *Power, Politics and Performance*, 28–58 (Kingston: Ian Randle, 2012).

have been achieved with independence. However, two generations have failed in this task. The stage is therefore set for exploring new approaches.

Politics has emerged as a formidable obstacle to the process of economic change in almost all Caribbean societies. The premise of the old Caribbean politics as the sustaining culture supporting integrity, equity, and political rights in the workings of the political process is constantly under scrutiny, and undermined by a new oligarchy of corruption that dominates the present power structure. Societies rooted in pluralistic divisions retreat, rather than advance, when confronted with the challenge of embracing a new political and social belief system.

Economic growth is the engine of development, but development is about people, about expanding their possibilities, improving their quality of life, and enhancing their capabilities. Nation states are in a constant search for justice and for identity in striving for character and a purpose to economic and social advancement. For almost half a century, scholars sought to respond to the desire of independent people to live their lives, to give expression to independent thought, and to advance the cause of a critical tradition.

In the immediate postcolonial period, the focus was on development of the political economy. Today, after several decades, the focus is on the political economy of development. What is the difference? Put briefly, development of the political economy relates to the tasks of state and nation building. It is about designing and devising political and economic systems compatible with national realities and aspirations. In contrast, the political economy of development relates to changes in the balance between winners and losers in the process of advancement, defined to include sustained growth and inclusiveness. The political economy of development must not only be sensitive and responsive to vital national and regional interests, but also take cognizance of shifts in a changing world order.

The first reform wave was about "getting the macroeconomics right." The second wave was "getting the institutions right." If development is the goal, "getting the governance right" is the current wave, which acquires a special meaning, as it can influence sustained growth and inclusive development. Politics and economics must be treated as inseparable in the analysis of development. In the final analysis, right policies will yield right outcomes.

The Issue of the "Crisis Economy"

While this analysis is rooted in the experience of Trinidad and Tobago, the economy with the largest GDP in the Caribbean community, it is relevant to a wider regional economy. Tracing the context of the economic debate from the first wave of macroeconomic stability – the Washington Consensus – to the second wave – Institutions Matter – we might now ask: what next? The answer to that question lies in the risks faced by Caribbean economies due to current global economic imbalances and the political dynamics of resource-rich countries falling into a downward spiral. It is apparent that once this downward spiral begins, it is hard to stop. The local risk factors of emerging fiscal deficits, falling competitive advantage, and secular decline in productivity in the Caribbean economy cannot be mitigated through short-time cyclical capital inflows.

What is required is radical reform of a development strategy to construct a knowledge-based economy, which challenges leadership to a better macroeconomic management approach. It has been argued that development today is elusive, as economic linkages are missing and growth is limited by cycles in world prices.

The structural issues of inequality and poverty will not be solved easily in the context of a political economy where those controlling natural resource wealth use that wealth to maintain their economic and political power, or in a currency reserve system where international dollar reserves are equivalent to the United States borrowing from the rest of the world.

Politics and Development

Development is about closing the gaps in social equity and the growth potential of the society. How to acquire and consolidate power depends on the nature and outcome of the mechanisms of the political system. How to compensate the losers is part of the process of reshaping the society's social welfare. The politics of development is often viewed in narrow terms of the distribution of income and opportunities, but greater weight should be assigned to the goal of reducing inequality and injustice in our global economy. The market works by rewarding countries and individuals with the most productive assets; it fails by generating negative externalities for the vulnerable and by increasing the risks faced by the weak.

Is there a great transformation in developmental economics ahead of us?

The art of good governance is critical to reconciling the conflicts between economics and politics in development. A greater demand for good governance needs to be created. Unless this demand exists, there is less possibility for the emergence of a supply of good governance.

Here, the interaction between policy, institutions, and the market becomes a critical ingredient in the growth strategy, a lesson learned from the experience of the reform process. The first wave of reform policies concentrated on issues of macroeconomic stability: putting the house in order. The main measures of macroeconomic stability were: opening up the economy to become competitive, removal of persistent budget and non-budget deficits, control over liquidity and inflationary excesses, and altering the supply structure of private and public goods.

Political Economy of Development

Waves in New Thinking

The 2008 inauguration of the Foundation for Politics and Leadership raises fresh hopes for a new direction for politics and leadership in the Caribbean. Several commentators have suggested there is an emerging consensus that it is time for a new point of departure in Caribbean development. David Jessop[2] calls for Caribbean think tanks, study groups, and corporate retreats to look over the horizon and react to the new trends and developments that will shape the future.

There is no single or simple answer, but there is an answer, and the search for real solutions must inform the creation of that future. The hope is that the Foundation for Politics and Leadership will advance Caribbean thinking well beyond what was carefully documented in the 1990s West Indian Commission's report *Time for Action* (1992). The report was a static expression of unfulfilled Caribbean dreams. What we need now is a road map for creating new energies in Caribbean development – a new departure point.

The Context of the Economic Debate

The history of political economy has always had departure points and shifts in the prevailing economic paradigm, putting the economy on a different path. One such departure point in the hemisphere and the Caribbean region was in the 1980s. In Trinidad and Tobago there was a shift from a commanding-heights economy to a market-driven economic process. The economic strategy of the Washington Consensus was embraced and the answers to the following questions sought: What macroeconomic measures are required to stabilize the economy? How do we liberalize our markets to exploit opportunities abroad? Why do we need a better relationship between the private and public sectors?

The answers to these questions are the first-generation reforms, a challenge of structural adjustment. The political process was emphasized, culminating in a failed coup attempt in 1990 that threatened the new direction. The first-generation reforms were soon seen to be insufficient, giving basis to a second generation of reforms focusing on building institutions.

These institutional reforms required a change in the exchange rate regime, a new regulatory model in telecommunication and technology, meeting of international banking standards, and creation of new delivery systems for public goods like water, electricity, postal services, roads, bridges, education, and health. Institutions do matter, and major policy changes do require alterations, rousing populist discontent and resistance from vested interests and threatening a rollback of the policy choices adopted, even when decisions are taken at the highest political forum.

The Expression of the Crisis

Protest politics emerged in the first decade of the twenty-first century, leading to the election of leftist governments in Bolivia, Brazil, and Venezuela. In the Caribbean, "change" governments came into office in Barbados, Jamaica, St. Lucia, Belize and, recently, Grenada. Globally, there was a fervent passion for political change as expressed in Australia, Kenya, Zimbabwe, France, and the United States. These political changes were taking place in the midst of an evolving global and national crisis.

In the April 2008 issue of *The Economist*, the cover page headline read "Fixing Finance … and the Risks of Getting It Wrong." The "home rage" in America's mortgage market raised issues of confidence and faith in open financial markets. First, there was disbelief and denial, then fear, and then came anger because three decades of public policy were dominated by the power of the markets. Finance stumbled with sub-prime lending, the credit crunch, and weak business and consumer confidence, laying the conditions for the onset of a recession in the United States. Other countries like Canada, Mexico, the United Kingdom, and Japan were at risk of contagion effects.

Some major countries took action to neutralize market fears by bringing real interest rates to near zero. Trade deficits rose, which led to a weakening of the US dollar. In Trinidad and Tobago's economy, between 2002 and 2007 the energy sector's contribution to GDP rose from 26.2 to 43 per cent, total revenue from 29.9 to 56.0 per cent, and exports from 73.3 to 89.4 per cent. This increased exposure to adverse financial shocks and emphasized the "natural resource curse" and vulnerability of this energy-based economy.

Particularly worrisome was the growth of the non-energy deficit, or the level of net domestic fiscal injection from 7.6 per cent in 2003 to 15.4 per cent of GDP in 2007, which increased further in 2008. This was a key source of domestic inflationary pressures. These statistics confirmed that the US economy was facing structural imbalances that reflected a sustained inflation surge and the creeping up of fiscal pressures that would soon create a chronic deficit in public finance.

Confidence and Risks in the Global Economy

Underlying this development was the huge risk of the global economic imbalances – few rich countries were receiving large current account deficits. The United States deficit was about three and a half times larger than the deficits of all other countries of the OECD combined. It is estimated that the average growth rate of energy during the next years will be about 5.5 per cent, and given the supply constraints, this will lead to dramatic price escalation. Global growth will be negatively affected. There will, however, be more resilience in the major markets of the developing world.

Historically, once resource-rich countries begin to fall into a downward spiral cycle is hard to stop. Economist Joseph Stiglitz argues: "the political dynamics of resource rich countries often lead to high levels of inequality; in both developed and less developed countries, those controlling the natural resource wealth use that wealth to maintain their economic and political power – which includes appropriating for themselves a large fraction of the country's resource endowment."[3]

Can you imagine Trinidad and Tobago without an energy sector? We are sitting on the cliff of a crisis economy in a global economy that is on the verge of major macroeconomic adjustment. A key element of this adjustment will come in reforming the global reserve system and in the expected global crisis in food and water.

The global reserve system is at the heart of the weakness of the global financial system. In the dollar-denominated reserve system, the reserves are tantamount to borrowings of the United States, but the return on these lendings is much less than if it had been invested in other commercial projects. Stiglitz estimated that the cost of holding reserves is in excess of US$300 billion per year[4] – which is four times the level of foreign assistance from the whole world.

The key risk issues ahead are a global recession, adjustment in macroeconomic imbalances, global reserve reform, and erosion of competitiveness. These risk factors pose challenges to the resilience of Caribbean economies, already vulnerable to external shocks. On the local radar screen, new expressions of internal balance will surface because of the coming trends in economic behaviour. The twin deficits in the fiscal and current account may once more recur as a key policy concern. The reasons why this may now emerge as a risk are: the emergence of a growing non-energy fiscal deficit notwithstanding the persistence of buoyant revenues, the continuous fall in competitive advantage on an economy-wide basis, and a secular decline in productivity in the Caribbean economy over the last twenty-five years. These risk factors may be mitigated in the short term by energy financial inflows. However, recent developments in the behaviour of energy companies operating in Trinidad and Tobago – cutting expenditures and seeking more tax breaks – suggest an end of sustained growth in this sector. This is further reinforced by revelations of limitation on gas supplies in wells and high depletion rates in the industry.

Crossroads and Changing Directions

The economy is now at another crossroad; we stand at yet another point of departure. The gains made during the first and second generations may have reached their end. CARICOM has long since reached its limits. In spite of the recent breakdown of the Doha Development Rounds of trade negotiations, the Caribbean countries remain defensive in their trade negotiations. In short, the economic space in which the region operates is perhaps receding. New thinking in the political economy is now a necessity. What are the new pillars for building another generation of economic leadership? In the immediate future, preparing for the adverse risks ahead is the key challenge. There are positive risks that we must address upfront. How do we go about that task?

Energy flows converted into public investment are limited in returns because such public investment, rather than generating income and output in the national economy, makes more demands on further recurrent expenditure. Infrastructure development for building productive capacity in a competitive economy is the direction in which we should be heading. This calls for a radical altering of development strategy to deal with structural inflation; that spells serious economic instability. Such instability may lead to social pressures that cannot be contained by the political process. Economic leadership must shift from targeting a dateline for development to managing risks on a current basis – risks associated with the falling dollar. And the expected fortunes of the energy sector must be carefully simulated in a model with foresight. In this forecast the following risks must be factored: the exchange rate and interest rate volatility, shortages and rising prices in an overheated economy, and a fall in the real value of the local currency.

New directions in building institutional capacity for delivering public goods must be top of the economic leadership agenda. The old institutions may have lost their relevance, calling for new models for cooperation among private, public, and civil society. The role of the state must respond to the delivery and equity issues confronting the society. The bureaucracy and the judiciary are essential institutions that must be included in the matrix of governance fundamentals.

New directions are required in the models of political leadership. Kelvin Dalrymple, former chief research economist of the Caribbean Development Bank, in discussing the role of leadership in economic development, characterized the models of Caribbean leadership as "personality," "autocratic," "dynastic," "crisis," and "situational."[5] The political structures that support these styles of leadership must be assessed in the context of development and good politics. The economy is on the edge on a cliff, with the expectation that the bubble will grow in response to a global rise in prices and non-performing energy output in the local economy. A fall is inevitable, at which time the stabilization fund (still underfunded) may have to be accessed and the national debt increased. Where do we go from here?

Choices for the Future

The Foundation for Politics and Leadership provides a forum to critically define these issues and construct solutions. The following questions provide a framework for an action agenda:

- How do small nations sustain development in a constantly changing global information and competitive market environment?
- What is the relationship between a state-centred economy, use of state funds, natural resources, and sustainable development?
- What is the relationship between the state and the development of a market economy and healthy private sector? How can the new network power – social networks and connectivity – be used as a catalyst for creating new leadership in development?

The time has come to introduce a paradigm shift in economic leadership. Trinidad and Tobago is a classic resource-based economy. In such economies development is elusive, as economic linkages are missing and growth is limited by the cycles in world prices. The imperative is now to search for new choices for the future. Resource- and investment-driven industrialization strategies cannot deliver sustained development.

Structural transformation to a knowledge-driven economy may better prepare us for a secure future. Small economies can build a competitive edge by focusing on infrastructure that enhances productivity, incentives that facilitate technological leapfrogging, and investments that quickly penetrate the global market. Once these goals are set, a program must be implemented to direct private and public national expenditure towards these choices. This will demand a deep understanding of the political economy of change, including the challenges of building capacity in the education, information, telecommunication, and innovative sectors.

A risk-management approach to macroeconomic management should be adopted. The basic elements of the first- and second-generation reforms must be kept, but a third point of departure is now mandatory. The world economy is not standing still, and global markets are more integrated. This raises adverse risks and positive opportunities in economic management. Visioning and consensus-making mechanisms must be seen as part of a continuous process in framing strategies and executing plans.

The first question is whether small states will be able to survive. Given that they are limited by geographical space and capacity, this seems an impossible objective, especially in a world based on reciprocity and competitiveness. Yet Lino Briguglio and colleagues make a strong argument that small states have been surprisingly resilient in responding to their vulnerability to external shocks, their inherently narrow range of exports, and their structural openness. This resilience, they claim, is based on policy interventions in four principal areas: macroeconomic stability, microeconomic efficiency, good governance, and social development.[6] This provides a framework upon which a risk management matrix could be designed for decision-making in the present. The question for small states now is: is resilience a necessary condition for sustainability?

Political Economy of Small States

The political economy perspective sets the backdrop for the future agenda. The new feature to this perspective is a regional approach to small-state economic resilience. Small European states share the characteristic of having achieved a high degree of economic and political success. In addition, like all other small states, they have to continuously adapt to the changing world economy. How have they succeeded in their development?

Peter Katzenstein provides an analysis of the industrial adjustment strategy of the small European states of Sweden, Norway, Denmark, Netherlands, Belgium, Austria, and Switzerland, describing how these states have coped with changes in the international economy.[7] The social agenda asks to build social cohesion and to promote basic needs and capabilities; it asks for the delivery of basic social services to consider regional social impact. The political agenda wants reform of systems and governmental institutions, electoral reforms, a demand for greater accountability, and the effectiveness of public policy.

The private-sector agenda should include private-sector leadership and involvement, encourage investments and entrepreneurship, provide incentives for small and medium enterprises development, and institute governance of the private sector and microfinance. The scholarship agenda is about linking political and economic logic, about more process analysis, about directions for capacity building and good governance. It deals with charting demands for good governance and generating new ideas to cope with global changes.

Due to their small size, these European states are dependent on the international markets. They have pursued a policy of adjustment with economic change through a variety of economic and social policies that prevent the costs of change causing political crises. They have cultivated a strategy that responds to, and reinforces, domestic goals that mitigate the political impact of economic changes. The leadership in these states has maintained the legitimacy of the political arrangements through good governance policies.

As Katzenstein notes, the yardstick for measuring their success is the extent to which social coalitions, political institutions, and public policies facilitate shifts in factors of production that increase the economic efficiency with due regard to the requirements of political legitimacy. This model of "democratic corporatism," or social partnership, covers all areas of economic and social policy that are able to diffuse conflicts and accommodate the different interests of the stakeholders. It demonstrates a culture of compromise reflected through political arrangements, reinforcing shared interpretations of the collective good.

Their social partnership provides these European states with the space to respond to changes in the international economy. In their effort to cope with constant change, they pursue a combined strategy of liberalization, domestic compensation (or distribution), and flexible industrial adjustments. Hence, their strategy is flexible, reactive, incremental, and constantly improvising to cope with change. Their policies are aimed at identifying and anticipating changes in the international economy and helping the social partners (private sector, trade unions, and government) to adjust to the changes without causing political instability.

In another comparative historical study of the development of European states, Dieter Senghaas traces the development paths these countries have followed, and asks why some parts of Europe developed while others did not.[8] This Eurocentric analysis draws lessons from the varied recent history of European development. Senghaas's discussion focuses on Friedrich List's theory of how delayed development is possible in a world economy characterized by growing development differentials. He examines the relationship between three types of development paths: "associative" (export-led), "dissociative" (opening up of domestic potential), and "autocentric" development or "peripheralization."

Among the smaller states of Europe, Belgium, Austria, and Hungary pursued a dissociative strategy. Switzerland and the Netherlands adopted an associative development path. A third set of small states – Denmark, Sweden, Norway, and Finland – pursued an associative-dissociative development history. These states illustrate how a redistribution process preceded industrial growth in successful delayed development. This "distribution-before-growth path" in Europe contradicts conventional development theory that puts growth first and redistribution later.

Briguglio et al. in *Small States and the Pillars of Economic Resilience* defines the economic resilience of small states as the ability to generate and manage a relatively high GDP per capita in comparison to other developing countries. This ability, given the small states' vulnerability, is associated with policy-induced measures to adjust to external shocks. These policy measures – macroeconomic stability, microeconomic market efficiency, good governance, and social development – called "pillars of resilience," and deficiencies in any one of them are likely to compromise a country's ability to withstand exogenous shocks.

The macroeconomic aspects of resilience building are stability, stewardship, and competitiveness. The regulatory framework needs to promote competitiveness, stability, and predictability. Since small states have limited scope in setting discretionary fiscal and monetary policies, they need to concentrate on factor and market flexibility. Policies to promote microeconomic efficiency have to focus on market efficiency and right resource allocation. There is a greater role for the private sector in developing small-state resilience. It is crucial to create a favourable environment for the growth of a healthy private sector and entrepreneurship. Policies have to promote competition in domestic, regional, and global markets.

Claudius Preville has noted that development has a wider connotation than economic resilience.[9] He associates resilience-building with social and environmental concerns that cannot be considered in isolation from economic realities. Furthermore, social cohesion negatively affects small states experiencing political and/or ethnic conflicts. Policies need to take into account the wide divergences in income among different groups.

A social policy that promotes social cohesion enhances the chances of economic success. In another study, Sudha Venu Menon shows how the multicultural small state of Singapore is a classic example of good leadership and public management in realizing the country's development goals.[10] Governance and leadership are put forward as central forces in fostering economic growth in that country.

Looking Ahead

Leadership and governance have been important to the development of appropriate institutional frameworks for sustained dynamic development and constant innovation to adapt to changing external realities. The social partnership policies of certain small states have provided the basis for economic resilience. From Briguglio et al. we can infer that in the area of good governance, small states need measures that are more specific to their respective contexts. The important elements of governance are openness, transparency, government accountability, administrative efficiency, respect for human rights, and the rule of law. Venu Menon also notes the importance of leadership and governance in the development of small states. A *Sunday Times* column states that history provides us with a plethora of evidence that a country's development is dependent on its leadership, irrespective of whether that history is of Western advanced countries or the post–Second World War emergence of nations.[11] Leadership is vital in meeting the goals of development. So is good governance.

The "Caribbean States in 2020: Sinking, Surviving or Prospering?" report on the Wilton Park Conference observes that the era of preference is now effectively over and globalization poses the major challenge to the Caribbean region.[12] The region must therefore develop strategies and policies to enhance resilience. The report raises the following urgent needs of the region: to develop modern skills like information technology, to enhance entrepreneurship skills and education, to promote small and medium enterprises, to address food and energy security, and to make the region more attractive to investors. The report notes that the promotion of good governance is an important issue. The region has also seen recent changes of governments, with a new generation of leaders and the expectation of fresh thinking. What should that fresh thinking involve for leadership and development of small states?

The reform of the state is a perennial issue in the Caribbean. In spite of several attempts to tackle this issue, it remains largely unresolved after more than a half-century of independence. Several scholars, such as Merilee Grindle and Vaughan Lewis, have identified the governance model and the politics of reform as key obstacles to success.[13] Others, like former prime ministers Owen Arthur of Barbados, P.J. Patterson of Jamaica, and James Mitchell of Saint Vincent, have spoken eloquently on the subject. Apart from some cosmetic changes, like moving from a monarchy to republican status, the essence of the state structure remains the same. Some see this as a sign of stability, other as a sign of intransigence.

The elitist power structure in Caribbean societies has, from time to time, inhibited such reform, and the distribution of power in these societies reinforces the status quo. The population, often in silent protest that occasionally erupts, has viewed the structure as oppressive, undemocratic, and not aligned with the changing political sociology and demographics of the people. In modern times, there have been some major eruptions – in Guyana in 1964, Grenada in 1983, and Trinidad in 1990 – as well as many expressions of protest in Jamaica and Haiti. But protests have not been the only means for expressions of discontent, as the tone of politics has also been influenced by silent urgings for reform of the state.

Constitutional and electoral reform have had attractive and populist appeal, but even those who advocate them for electoral gains refuse to act when the electorate awards them the reins of power. The court system is often used as an arbiter and a substitute for the expression of will of the people. Nonetheless, the structure of the state and the system of governance remain solidly intact. It is no wonder good-governance mantras have replaced state reform in these tiny Caribbean democracies. The question is: will the fate of those in the Caribbean who advocate good governance be any different from those who advocate reform of the state?

The key factors in the new political economy of development are leadership and good governance. Political leadership today must face up to the new notions of formal and functional sovereignty and the exercise of pooled sovereignty in relations between nation states. Development involves some of the hardest choices between the development path and distribution of public resources. In the current context, governance is about the way in which trade-offs are made between keeping pace with global developments and being sensitive to local and regional aspirations. Global economic trends are bound to affect domestic and regional politics. Future problems will be in the area of human security, and will need to be addressed by a combination of innovative domestic policies and international cooperation via various dialogues and formal institutional agreements.

The task of leadership is to find a synergy between economics and politics in the development of small states. Managing natural resources in a sustainable manner is another major agenda for those states. The economic growth prospects of small island states will depend on management to mitigate the future impacts of climate change.

Forging Social Cohesion

Good governance or quality governance involves leadership that can forge social cohesion in a plural society. The future agenda of leadership has to promote the basic capabilities that cannot be left solely to market forces. Social objectives can, however, contribute to economic growth and human capital. This implies improving government resources and the capacity to implement social policies and deliver basic services. And this in turn calls for a fresh look at appropriate governance structures and delivery mechanisms.

Choices about future governance and development should involve a "regional social compact," that is, it is necessary to demonstrate renewed commitment to building a regional institution that will foster economic growth and development, namely the Caribbean Court of Justice. This institution will ensure the legal commitment and obligation to implement decisions taken at the regional level after substantial consultation and negotiation among relevant parties. The future of the Caribbean will be brighter once we find the confidence to make something as vital as a regional court function as intended, rather than remain in its present imbroglio.

The Challenge of Political Reform

Many small states are today facing the challenge of political reform of the system and institutions of government. During the past fifty years since the Caribbean states attained independence, the Westminster system of governance has been subject to intense scrutiny and a call for fundamental political reform has emerged. This is currently a serious issue in popular, political, and academic circles. The issue of electoral reform in Caribbean countries continues to surface in the context of the Westminister system of government to which most of the

English-speaking countries of the Caribbean are wedded. This issue raises wider concerns about constitutional reform and the separation of powers and independence of institutions for governance. Recent developments of an electoral nature have also raised the issue of the plurality of the electorates in Caribbean countries and the capacity of the political system to accommodate them in a democratic framework. These concerns have become key matters for sustaining democracy in these small states.

At the beginning of the twenty-first century, the intersection between politics and technology is part of the new political scenario in connecting minds and shaping political behaviour. Electronic voting is already being promoted as a viable system in this global community. So too are changes in the new media that will enhance information flow in the quest for good governance. Electoral reform is a major requirement for small states attempting to bring people closer to government and so strengthen the pillars of democracy.

The process of constitution-making has come to the fore as nation states strive to alter their worn-out constitutions, embrace new approaches to stop the abuse of power, demand greater accountability of the executive power, and enhance the effectiveness of public policy implementation. In addition, plural societies face special challenges in reforming constitutional structures that promote social cohesiveness, national character, and justice.

The Single-Market Economy

The Caribbean Single Market Economy (CSME) is a key institution in the integration process. Whether it will drive Caribbean development remains an open question. Of course, the CSME has operational capacity to protect trade within the region, but more than this is required to encourage development. This raises the question of the viability of CARICOM itself. While CARICOM may be necessary for the region, is its design suited to Caribbean development? I have argued that the integration process in the region must adjust to a convergence model for more economic space, thus giving it more political legitimacy.

Against the backdrop of the CSME, individual state governance as well as regional governance needs to be addressed. Given the deepening of interdependence, the regional institutional capacity for good governance and management has to be improved. The fresh thinking should, then, be in terms of consolidating regional governance. While it is important for the region to reorder its relations with the rest of the world, leadership and governance will have to position the development goals of the region as the guiding principle of the relationship. A new CSME cannot be achieved and made to work relying on the existing regional organs, such as the Council for Finance and Planning (CO-FAP) and the Council for Trade and Economic Development (COTED). Establishing a regional development fund would go a long way towards fostering new institutional capacity.

Expanding the Private Sector

A Caribbean business council should be created, since a new CSME will also be driven to a large extent by: the private sector. This council will facilitate greater private-sector leadership and involvement in all aspects of the creation and management of the CSME. Given the need to expand the private sector and to create jobs in small states, the new agenda is to provide incentives to encourage investment and entrepreneurship. New and innovative approaches are needed to ensure that there is a continuous process of building local capacity in the region.

In an environment offering limited alternative employment opportunities, self-employment and small and medium enterprises (SMEs) will continue to grow in the region and improve in competitiveness. Addressing their credit needs is crucial to fostering their development and promoting entrepreneurship. Microfinance is critical to broadening the small-scale entrepreneurial class and vitalizing the informal sector. Apart from providing access to credit, microfinance institutions act as catalysts for training, provide access to markets, and provide quality assurances in the market place. They are a vital bridge to empowerment of and social benefits for less endowed but creative clients.

The current regulatory environment in the region does not favour the microfinance sector, as there is no policy or regulatory framework specifically addressing the unique and specific needs of microfinance. The CSME will also affect the SME sector and the microfinance industry, which will become central to the region's future development policy.

Governments and financial institutions at the national and regional levels have to take a fresh regional look at financial regulation to place microfinance and SME policies within the Caribbean region's development goals. The way forward is to create an enabling policy environment to support an integrated approach to SMEs. This implies improving the institutional governance for the private sector and microfinance.

Keeping Ahead of the Curve

Global trends are constantly changing. In order to be resilient, small states will need to keep pace by generating new ideas to cope with the changes. This calls for a regional scholarship agenda that raises the following fundamental issues for the future of leadership and development of small states: How do we reconcile economic/development outcomes with political democracy? What are the new challenges to development and what should be the appropriate responses?

Answers to these questions will require an analytical framework to link political and economic logic; a shift in emphasis from policy to process analysis; and a methodology to identify the synergy between political capacity and good governance.

Epilogue

A book rarely stands on its own – it comes from somewhere and sometimes travels unknown paths.

The Caribbean on the Edge is an anthology of ideas and writings that shaped my thinking over decades of work on development and on the Caribbean. Throughout my academic and political life, I strove constantly for a way forward in the interests of Caribbean progress and development – which often led me to challenge the lazy orthodoxies of our times. I believe that status quo solutions will not solve the complex political, social, and cultural challenges we face, and more so beyond the times of the pandemic.

I have learnt that the synergy of the logic between our economic aspirations and our political actions is the crucial factor in designing a pathway for sustainable development. Such designs require both data analysis and vision. Leadership, too, ignites action, and our institutions are in need of continuous renewal. Our political system must be strong enough to weather the storms. And the society must navigate its place in the global order of things.

This journey has many starts and no end, and this epilogue is a message to future students of economics, politics, and diplomacy. The analytics of the past are constantly in search of new thinking, different approaches, and effective outcomes. The discovery process never ends, but delivery to society must always happen for the flow of progress.

Today, as we navigate a global pandemic, small nations must confront the new order of things – leading to a rethink in economics, a continuous review of power relations, a reordering of the priorities of society and strategies for advancement. In other words, a new analytics is needed, as survival is a higher order of urgency than sustainability. Yet it is sustainable policies that will buffer and insulate our population over time and lead to a better world. Now, policy analysis must be anchored with a philosophical tone.

Minouche Shafik in her 2021 book *What We Owe Each Other* asks two questions: "What does society owe each of us?" and "What do we owe in return?" Her book "shows us the way to a new social contract, one that fits the twenty-first century … a new paradigm is needed if we are to adapt to the world we face and rebuild the mutual trust and support on which citizenship and society is based."[1] She invokes W.B. Yeats's poem "The Second Coming" – "things fall apart; the centre cannot hold … Surely some revelation is at hand" – and writes that the poem "captures a sense of foreboding, when change seems inevitable."[2]

At a recent conference[3] I spoke on the theme "The Pandemic as Global Political Stress Test." In the coming year, America will undoubtedly be expected to return to its seat at the head table of global affairs. However, it will be confronted with a new seating arrangement, one in which its sphere of influence cannot be taken for granted. I am referring, of course, to this "age of contagion" to which the jarring pandemic of today testifies. And with it come shifting alignments of political forces.

Some postulate that these unprecedented times threaten the "breakdown of global order" – and whether or not you are in agreement, it is undeniable that the world will face a global political stress test in the years ahead.

Attempts to recover from the devastation of the pandemic have already seen changes in the logic of economic management, as the alarm once felt over deficit financing has given way to the need for it. As the *Economist* puts it, "the old paradigm looks tired."[4] Health security is on the daily radar screen, the risks are widening and increasing, and new risks are surfacing. The dynamics of world politics are shifting in many directions.

The actions of leadership – emerging from the pandemic and the global recovery efforts – will pose some immediate questions:

- Will the orthodoxy of "recovery economics" work today?
- Will the G7 and G20 summits rise to the full challenges facing all of humankind?
- Will vaccine diplomacy leave poor countries and people exposed to the peril of all?

In global politics:

- Will the multilateral frame for global politics be fair to all countries?

- Will there be more diplomatic leverage for the continent of Africa?
- Will Latin America be left out as the world "connects the dots" in a new era?
- Will Europe's strategic autonomy allow for a more resilient politics?
- Will big power rivalries wreck the resetting of a different economic order?
- Will small countries survive or sustain in a fragile period?

Small nations must address key agenda issues on health security and governance. Health security issues include

- the effectiveness of regional pandemic surveillance and coordination of health security measures;
- the adoption of sustainable self-financing instruments to provide universal health coverage for society, including the poor; and
- democratization of access to global research and products in medical science – like the COVID-19 Vaccines Global Access Facility – which will require a revitalization of the World Health Organization.

Governance issues include

- resetting of the platform of financial flows in the reworking of international financial institutions and the global marketplace;
- a diplomatic initiative to establish channels of communications with the centres of global power; and
- a focus on the technical issues as "universal vulnerabilities index" and the subject of "ocean governance and security" for Small Island Developing States.

The pandemic has been a global political stress test – capable states with good leadership who embrace reforms become stronger and more resilient, while those with weak state capacity – political and economic – will be in trouble and set for stagnation.

The COVID-19 pandemic is forcing a rethink in economics and generating geostrategic shifts in the world of diplomacy. Small states face complex challenges in the formulation of growth strategies in the loop-type shock cycles as the old paradigms "are looking tired." At the same time, the liberal order upon which global institutions were premised is in flux and the changing geopolitics is opening up strategic shifts in areas of diplomacy, particularly for small states.

Below are some of the theme issues that will have an impact on the Caribbean.

The Great Reset and Realignment of Global Cooperation

According to the Great Reset theme of the World Economic Forum,[5] COVID-19 may reverse global human development in living standards, and Small Island Developing States will be particularly challenged to sustain the vaccination effort and ignite an economic recovery.

There is a temptation, beyond COVID, to view the shake-up in public policy as being temporary, after which "normalcy" will soon return. There are several areas in which this "normalcy" will be structurally changed – global digitalization, finance, and health care. In each of these areas, small countries will face negative global externalities. This calls for a fundamental re-engineering of the system and protocols for global cooperation that includes small nations.

The Next Chapter in Globalization

The next chapter of globalization will be "digitalization" – a huge revolution is in process, and the relevant infrastructure in small nations will be tested, as well as the economics that underline this transformation. The World Economic Forum, in its urgency to define the Great Reset and its desire for inclusivity, could find a ready platform to engage small countries in its efforts. Otherwise, its words will be mere platitudes and its credibility will be shaken. Associated with this is the trend to regionalism as opposed to globalism, putting more focus on resiliency than efficiency, and the rising incidence of inequality. The pathway for small states in the post-COVID world will, in itself, spell a different dimension to the global paradigm of development.

Small States' Response to Global Financing

Financing in the pandemic period, particularly in the G7 and G20 countries, has radically altered the way deficit financing is viewed – once seen as an alarm, now seen as a need. Even small countries have followed that pathway, notwithstanding their own limitations. Development financing will become more complex. We live now in "an age of contagion," and the impact of this will be clearly seen in the new world of finance, both of a Bretton Woods vintage and in the wider private-sector global flow of funds. Small countries will not have an automatic place – no hegemons, no multipolar or even multiplex world – and with challenges of cyber and information technologies, will resort to hedging and floating coalitions to leverage their financial space. The

G7-G20 proposals for financing in the post-COVID world may merely add new inequities to the world economy.

Small States' Agenda in Global Health Diplomacy

The global health care industry will undergo a major technological and behavioural transformation. Democratizing access to global research and products in medical science, through such as the COVID-19 Vaccines Global Access Facility, will rise in significance, if only due to humanitarian causes. Already vaccine diplomacy and the reform of the World Health Organization are on the global agenda. In addition, there is an urgent requirement to design sustainable financing instruments for full health coverage for all of societies, including the poor. In this regard, the global adoption of a universal vulnerabilities index will be of paramount importance to small island developing countries. Small countries will be called upon to play a greater role in global health diplomacy.

I hope that the chapters in this book will provoke insights that encourage future studies. This epilogue of *The Caribbean on the Edge* provides but a brief glimpse of the year ahead. As I write these final words, I am mindful of Yeats's poem with its sense of foreboding, and urge the scholars of tomorrow to build new structures for a hopeful framework in Caribbean scholarship. Such structures include not just Shaik's new social contract, but also a shift in thinking regarding the diplomacy of small states.

Yee-Kuang Heng, in exploring the power capabilities of small states, asserted that "small states behavior can in fact reveal deep-seated structural changes in the international system and provide significant insights into the management of power asymmetries."[6] Shifting away from the traditional assumptions of weakness and vulnerabilities of small states that permeated earlier studies, Heng reviewed small states' foreign policy initiatives in world diplomacy, citing several instances where these initiatives have shaped discussions on the global stage. For example, he referred to the instigation of a group of four – Brunei, Singapore, Chile, and New Zealand – who initiated discussion on the Comprehensive and Progressive Agreement for Trans-Pacific Partnership. He cited the Nordic states' adoption of a niche strategy to have co-decision power through a regional coalition of small states, and mentioned Trinidad and Tobago, along with Singapore and Djibouti, for using "adroit diplomatic strategies with their geostrategic locations" in their diplomatic thrust.[7]

Citing visionary leadership from small countries such as New Zealand in the wake of the horrific Christchurch mosque shootings in 2019 to coordinate counterterrorism efforts, drawing on smaller nation's particular strengths in conflict mediation, and dealing with extremist groups, Cohen and Fontaine made a compelling case for microlateralism, asking how small states can lead global efforts and arguing that "leadership by small states can make multilateral efforts more palatable to rival powers."[8]

While the world still needs the United Nations and its advocacy of multilateralism, that framework lacks flexible approaches that are genuinely inclusive and embracing of the special talents of small states. Microlateralism offers new space for small countries to play a strategic role in shaping solutions on issues of global politics and diplomacy. Small states are not necessarily hapless, and their capabilities in managing their relationships with the big powers are fertile ground for strategic studies on small states diplomacy.

Notes

Preface

1 Opening remarks to the IMF-World Bank spring meetings and Forum for the Future of the Caribbean. Washington DC, 16–22 April 2018.
2 Dookeran, *Power, Politics and Performance*, xi.
3 Dookeran, *Crisis and Promise*, x.
4 Dookeran and Elias, *Shifting the Frontiers*.
5 Piketty, *Capital in the Twenty-First Century*.
6 Dookeran and Izarali, *Frontiers, Flows and Frameworks*.

The Evolution of ECLAC's School of Thought and Its Influence on the Caribbean

1 Prebisch, *Problemas practicos y teoricos*; Prebisch, *El desarrollo económico de América Latina*; Prebisch, *Problemas teóricos y prácticos*; translation mine.
2 See Smith, *Wealth of Nations*.
3 Prebisch, *El desarollo económico de América Latina: Problemas, teóricos y práticos*.

1. Caribbean Development: Setting the Framework

1 West Indian Commission, *Time for Action*, 449.
2 Stiglitz, "The State," 7.
3 World Bank, *Annual World Bank Conference on Development Economics*, 34.
4 Stiglitz, *An Agenda for Development*, 34.
5 Alesina, *Political Economy*.
6 For an analysis of the two-level games of international relations and political policies, see Putnam, "Diplomacy and Domestic Politics."
7 Bhagwati, *Regionalism and Multilateralism*.

8 Bhagwati, *Regionalism and Multilateralism.*
9 On this and related issues, see Galbraith, "The New Dialectic."
10 Examples of the confusion surrounding these issues are readily apparent: the Mercosur trade bloc (Argentina, Brazil, Paraguay, and Uruguay), for instance, which formed the world's second customs union in January 1995, will not establish a supranational court to settle trade disputes, as some members felt that it would reduce their sovereignty. Many in the US Congress – even those considered free-traders – were reluctant to pass the Uruguay round legislation in late November–December 1994; they feared that the WTO, by eliminating the one-country veto and establishing tribunals to rule on trade disputes, would dilute US sovereignty and force changes in a wide range of US environmental and labour laws. In a nationwide referendum, Norway voted not to join the EU, feeling at least in part that its resource base was strong enough to keep foreign bureaurocrats from interfering in its internal affairs. And the Caribbean Community Common Market heads of state were determined to keep its expansion under the ambit of elected governments, in part because they feared development of their sovereignty. In each case there were serious debates as to what constituted national interests and how integration would affect national sovereignty.
11 See Wolf, "Myth of Empty Sovereignty."
12 Ohmae, *End of the Nation State*, 2.
13 *End of the Nation State*, 4.
14 *End of the Nation State*, 5
15 Ito, *What Can Developing Countries Learn*, 2.
16 Pantin, *Industrial Policy.*
17 Birdsall, "Adjustment, Reform and Growth."
18 ECLAC, *Summary.*
19 Dookeran, *Policy Reform in the Caribbean.*
20 Dookeran, "Preferential Trade Arrangements."
21 For a discussion of this topic, see Ostry, *Post–Cold War Trading System*, chap. 7.
22 Payne, "Westminster Adapted."
23 Lijphart, "Political Consequences," 481.
24 Smith, *Plural Society*, xi.
25 Lijphart, 1990, 36.
26 This section draws upon Griffith, "Caribbean Security," and Dominguez, "Caribbean in a New International Context."
27 Dominguez, "Caribbean in a New International Context."
28 Bernal, "Paths," 3.
29 This section is based on Huggins, *Green Paper*, and ECDPM, "Synthesis."
30 Huggins, *Green Paper.*

31 See https://ecdpm.org/wp-content/uploads/PMR21-Future-ACP-EU
    -Relations-PEA-January-2016.pdf.
32 See https://library.fes.de/fulltext/iez/01115001.htm.
33 Gonzales, "Europe and the Caribbean."

2. Caribbean Policy Analysis: Shaping the Issues

1 This scenario is of particular concern, for "despite the rhetoric of the new
   age of global economy, there are plenty of signs today that we are repeat-
   ing the dangerous gamble of competitive devaluation of the interwar
   period: the worldwide currency chaos in mid-September 1992 and the U.S.
   effort to undercut the competitive advantage of foreign producers through
   exchange rate manipulation … are just two recent startling examples of
   this sort. Furthermore, many developing countries are too small to be optimal currency areas, as the costs of floating their exchange rate exceeds the
   benefits" (Cui, "International Chapter 11 and SDR," 4).
2 See Bernal, "CARICOM."
3 For a more comprehensive view of these issues, see Dookeran, "Preferential Trade Arrangements."
4 Knight and Persaud. "Subsidiarity," 43.
5 Lewis, *Caribbean Sovereignty*.
6 Galbraith, "The New Dialectic."
7 The Free Trade Area of the Americas (FTAA), formed in December 1994,
   seeks hemisphere-wide free trade by 2005. The EU is currently expanding
   its borders into Eastern Europe and the southern Mediterranean; and the
   eighteen members of APEC (Asia Pacific Economic Cooperation forum)
   have just signed an agreement to establish a free-trade zone among developed nations by 2010, while developing nations in the region will meet
   these requirements by 2020.
8 Distinct from human capital and social expenditures, social capital, as
   defined by Putnam, "refers to features of social organization, such as
   networks, norms and trust, that facilitate coordination and cooperation
   for mutual benefit. Social capital enhances the benefits of investment in
   physical and human capital … and seems to be a precondition for economic development, as well as for effective government. Development
   economists take note: Civics matters" (Putnam, "The Prosperous Community," 35–7; see also Putnam, *Making Democracy Work*, chap. 6). While
   social capital is specifically concerned with the grounds for public policy
   and institution-building, on another level it is reflected internationally in
   the emerging norms for cooperation, multilateralism, and shared concerns
   and responsibilities, as opposed to traditional opportunistic, unilateral
   models of international relations.

9 Keohane, "Sovereignty, Interdependence."
10 Etienne, "The Limits of Integration?," 3.
11 Keohane, "Sovereignty, Interdependence," 91.
12 Prime Minister A.N.R. Robinson of Trinidad and Tobago took the initiative in establishing the West Indian Commission in the late 1980s, in order to examine the issues facing the future of the Caribbean. Its six-hundred-page report, *Time for Action*, contained more than two hundred specific recommendations.
13 Twenty-four states signed the convention establishing the ACS on 24 July 1994 in Cartagena, Colombia. Those who became full members are: Antigua and Barbuda, the Bahamas, Barbados, Belize, Colombia, Costa Rica, Cuba, Dominica, the Dominican Republic, El Salvador, Grenada, Guatemala, Guyana, Haiti, Honduras, Jamaica, Mexico, Nicaragua, Panama, St. Kitts and Nevis, St. Vincent and the Grenadines, Suriname, Trinidad and Tobago, and Venezuela. The non-independent territories and countries eligible for associate membership are: Anguilla, Bermuda, the British Virgin Islands, Cayman Islands, Montserrat, Puerto Rico, Turks and Caicos Islands, the US Virgin Islands, France (for Guadeloupe, Guyana, and Martinique), and the Netherlands (on behalf of the Netherlands Antilles and Aruba).
14 For a discussion on how Caribbean open regionalism might be built, see Dookeran, "Caribbean Integration." For a comprehensive treatment of this subject, see ECLAC, "Open Regionalism."
15 Twenty-four states signed the convention establishing the ACS on 24 July 1994 in Cartagena, Colombia. Those who became full members are: Antigua and Barbuda, the Bahamas, Barbados, Belize, Colombia, Costa Rica, Cuba, Dominica, the Dominican Republic, El Salvador, Grenada, Guatemala, Guyana, Haiti, Honduras, Jamaica, Mexico, Nicaragua, Panama, St. Kitts and Nevis, St. Vincent and the Grenadines, Suriname, Trinidad and Tobago, and Venezuela. The non-independent territories and countries eligible for associate membership are: Anguilla, Bermuda, the British Virgin Islands, Cayman Islands, Montserrat, Puerto Rico, Turks and Caicos Islands, the US Virgin Islands, France (for Guadeloupe, Guyana, and Martinique), and the Netherlands (on behalf of the Netherlands Antilles and Aruba).
16 See https://www.norden.org/en/news/new-presidency-focuses-vision-2030.
17 The basic strategies of structural adjustment programs include reduction of domestic demand, resource reallocation, increased foreign and domestic savings, and increased economic efficiency in the use of resources. Thus, the emphasis is now on the quality and efficiency of government spending, which can be improved by concentrating on pro-poor growth and pro-poor budgets, flexible fiscal targets, strengthened public expenditure management systems, citizen accountability, and a gender-equitable focus in public expenditure management and budget process (see Norton

and Elson, 2002).See Norton, "Agricultural Issues"; for specific economic measures, see IMF, *Fund-Supported Programs*.

18 Unger and Cui, "China in the Russian Mirror," 85.
19 Callaghy, "Toward State Capability," 33.
20 Sir W. Arthur Lewis, a leading West Indian economist, won a Nobel Prize for economics in 1979.
21 Piketty, *Capital in the Twenty-First Century*.
22 Osmani, "The Sen System of Social Evaluation," 22.
23 Sen, "Identity and Justice," 103.
24 Cappelletti, "Repudiating Montesquieu?"

3. Caribbean Catalogue: Recasting the Strategies

 1 Here, I count the Caribbean countries as Bahamas, Belize, Cuba, Dominican Republic, Guyana, Haiti, Jamaica, Suriname, and Trinidad and Tobago and member countries of the Organization of Eastern Caribbean States (OECS), which include Antigua and Barbuda, Dominica, Grenada, and St. Kitts and Nevis, St. Lucia, St. Vincent and the Grenadines.
 2 World Bank Joint Task Force, *Small States*, ii.

4. Policy Response to the Pandemic

 1 "WHO Director General's Opening Remarks at the Media Briefing on COVID-19, 11 March 2020," https://www.who.int/director-general /speeches/detail/who-director-general-s-opening-remarks-at-the-media -briefing-on-covid-19---11-march-2020.
 2 Dookeran, "Reflections."
 3 Allen et al., *Roadmap to Pandemic Resilience*.
 4 Cliffe, "Pandenomics."
 5 Wolf, "The World Economy Is Now Collapsing."
 6 Dookeran, "Reflections."
 7 Sabia, "Governments Will Face Three Tests."
 8 Shankarjha, "Modi's 'Stimulus Package.'"
 9 Young Professionals, "Resetting T&T's."
10 See Floyd, "Foreword: Whole of Government Approaches."
11 OECD, "Evaluating."
12 OECD, "Evaluating."
13 See Al Omian, "Are We Witnessing?" Also see Bárcena, "Measuring the Impact of COVID-19."
14 Mohamed El-Erian. "The World after COVID19 – The Future of the Global Economy." Munk Debates, 23 April 2020 (podcast). https://munkdebates .com/podcast/mohamed-el-erian.

15 Ndii, "Memo to #UpperDeckPeopleKE."
16 Drezner, Krebs, and Schweller. "The End of Grand Strategy."
17 Drezner, Krebs, and Schweller, "The End of Grand Strategy."
18 On complexity, see Arjoon, "What Drives Economic Complexity?"
19 Turner, "*Monetary Finance Is Here.*"
20 Al Omain, "Are We Witnessing?"
21 This section draws from a speech given by Gertjan Vliege, external member of the Monetary Policy Committee, Bank of England, titled "Monetary Policy and the Bank of England's Balance Sheet," April 2020.
22 This refers to large-scale asset purchase (quantitative easing, or QE) where the central bank purchase of government bonds or long-term securities restores confidence and adds liquidity back into the market. The US Federal Reserve Bank announced a new round of QE in March 2020.
23 The Bank of England's response includes, for instance, a facility for corporate financing and another for repo market stability.
24 Wenner, "Caribbean Diaspora."
25 See Alleyne and Karagiannis, *A New Economic Strategy for Jamaica.*
26 OECD, *OECD Guidelines.*
27 Berkowitz, Ma, and Nishioka, "Can State Owned Enterprises Restructure?"
28 Musacchio and Pineda Ayerbe, *Fixing State-Owned Enterprises.*
29 Berkowitz, Ma, and Nishioka, "Recasting the Iron Rice Bowl."
30 See https://www.imf.org/en/About/Factsheets/Sheets/2016/08/02/19/55/Rapid-Financing-Instrument.
31 See Bárcena, "A Development Allocation of SDRs."
32 Dookeran and Campanella, "The COVID-19 Symmetric Shock."
33 "UN Secretary-General Antonio Guterres Appointed to Second Term," Anadolu Agency, 18 June 2021, https://www.aa.com.tr/en/health/un-secretary-general-antonio-guterres-appointed-to-second-term/2278556.
34 See Morris and Shin, "Catalytic Finance."
35 Saunders, "Tied to No One's Apron Strings."
36 See Acharya, *Constructing Global Order.*
37 The CARICOM Commission on the Economy was re-established in July 2019 by the heads of governments under the chairship of Professor Avinash Persaud.
38 For a full explanation of the region's policy impact to COVID-19, see IDB, "The Fragile Path to Recovery."

5. The Politics of Development

 1 World Bank, *The Growth Report.*
 2 UNU-WIDER Conference on Country Role Models for Development Success, Helsinki, 13–14 June 2008.

3 Birdsall, *The World Is Not Flat*. Birdsall argues that global markets alone will not increase wealth and welfare in the global economy, and there is a need to address the fragile global polity.

4 Stewart, "Do We Need a New 'Great Transformation'?" Polyani in 1944 wrote his path-breaking book *The Great Transformation: The Political and Economic Origins of Our Times*, in which he traced the pre-market, pre-industrial system to the market-dominated industrialization of the nineteenth century and the "succession of changes that were provoked by the predominance of the market model" (Stewart, 614–40).

5 Dookeran and Jantzen, "Prospectus," 7. The Foundation for Politics and Leadership, a think-and-action initiative, was launched in Port of Spain, Trinidad, on 4 June 2008.

6 Weder and Weder, "Switzerland's Rise." They write: "the Swiss political system with its direct democratic elements and the implemented principle of subsidiarity created political contestability that maintained government efficiency and led to political stability throughout history" (1).

7 Csaba, "Country Study, Hungary."

8 Fosu, "Anti-growth Syndrome in Africa."

9 See IMF Staff, "Globalization," quoting Stiglitz's *Globalization and Its Discontents*, 4.

10 Mavrotas and Shorrocks, *Advancing Development*.

11 Emmerij, "Turning Points."

12 Sen, *Development as Freedom*. See also Nafxiger, "From Seers to Sen."

13 Mannermaa, *Democracy*.

14 Scalapino, *Politics of Development*.

15 Yao, "The Disinterested Government."

6. Political Economy and Strategy

1 This section also draws on Dookeran, address to the Conference on Global Governance and Reform.

2 See Kumar and Messner, *Power Shifts and Global Governance*; Moon, "Power in Global Governance"; Stephen, "Emerging Powers and Emerging Trends."

3 https://www.un.org/en/ga/69/meetings/gadebate/26sep/trinidad .shtml.

4 See ECLAC, *Education, Structural Change and Inclusive Growth*, 5; Buvinić, Mazza, and Deutsch, *Social Inclusion and Economic Development*; World Bank, *World Development Report 2006*, 4.

5 World Bank, *Caribbean Economic Review*, 7–8.

6 Acemoglu and Robinson, *Why Nations Fail*.

7 Gates, "Good Ideas, but Missing Analysis," review of *Why Nations Fail: The Origins of Power, Prosperity, and Poverty*, Gates Notes (blog), 26 February 2013, https://www.gatesnotes.com/books/why-nations-fail.
8 Berg and Ostry, "Inequality and Unsustainable Growth."
9 This view was also expressed by the author in an address he gave at the Regional Forum on Cluster Development, "Inequality Restricts the Space for Economic Growth: Notes for Phase One, New Growth Development," 9 November 2011.

7. Political Logic and Economic Logic

1 Ramsaran, "Aspects of Growth and Adjustment"; National Planning Commission, *Medium Term Macro Planning Framework*.
2 Ramsaran, "Aspects of Growth and Adjustment."
3 Dookeran, "Facing the Issues," 6.
4 Berg and Ostry, "Equality and Efficiency"; Ostry, Berg, and Tsangarides, *Redistribution, Inequality, and Growth*; Ostry, Berg, and Loungani, *Confronting Inequality*.

8. The Imperative of Caribbean Convergence

1 Dookeran, "Forum Looks to Set New Strategy."
2 Karim, "Good Leadership."
3 The CARICOM region celebrated the fortieth anniversary of the signing of the Treaty of Chaguaramas on 4 July 2013.
4 For more on emerging markets and global political economy, see World Bank, "The Role of Emerging Market Economy Demand"; World Bank, *Multipolarity*; Hanson, "The Rise of Middle Kingdoms"; Fornes, "Emerging Markets"; Aizenrnan, "Large Hoarding of International Reserves"; Zoellick, "After the Crisis."
5 See Griffith-Jones, "Perspectives."
6 For more on BRICS see the Goldman Sachs report "Dreaming with BRICs," and Lawson, "Dreaming with BRICs." Sujay Mehdudia, "The Way Forward," speaks clearly to the need for action by moving from "policy discussions to delivering tangible benefits."
7 Sachs, *Common Wealth*.
8 McCloskey, *Bourgeois Dignity*, 122.
9 Dookeran, *Crisis and Promise in the Caribbean*, chap. 14.
10 ECLAC, *Opportunities for Convergence*.
11 Dookeran. "Una nueva frontera para la convergencia del Caribe: La intergración sin fronteras" (speech). April 2014, Santiago, CEPAL.
12 Malaki, "A Partnership Approach," 86.

13 Ramphal, "Vision and Leadership."

14 Dookeran, "Caribbean Convergence."

15 P.J. Patterson, keynote speech at book launch of Sir Sridath Ramphal's *Caribbean Challenges*, Jamaica, 18 June 2012.

16 Dookeran, plenary speech at the Caribbean Growth Forum Launch Event, 18–19 June 2012, Kingston, Jamaica.

17 ECLAC, *Opportunities for Convergence*; ECLAC, "The Politics of Global Financial Regulation Rulemaking."

18 ECLAC, *The Caribbean Forum*; Adam and Niels, *Practice Makes Perfect?*

19 Andonova, "Globalization, Agency and Institutional Innovation."

20 ECLAC, "The Politics of Global Financial Regulation Rulemaking."

21 Bissessar, UN General Assembly Thematic Debate.

22 Keijzer et al., "ACP-EU Relations."

23 ACS, Fifth Summit, "Draft Plan of Action."

24 ACS, "Draft Declaration of Haiti," Preparatory meeting for the 6th extraordinary meeting of the ACS ministerial council, Peton Ville, Haiti, 23–24 April 2013.

25 ECLAC, *Opportunities for Convergence and Regional Cooperation*.

26 Gonzales, "Assessment of the Convergence Model."

27 Dookeran, "Introducing the Convergence Model."

28 World Bank, *Caribbean Economic Review*, 7–8.

29 Porter, "Cluster and the New Economics."

30 Dookeran, "Introducing the Convergence Model.

31 SELA, *Productive Development and Industrialization*, 26–36.

32 SELA, *Productive Development and Industrialization*.

33 Clarence Henry, quoted in Curaçao Chronicle, 2 May 2013. http:// curacaochronicle.com/region/essence-spirit-of-caricom-still-relevant -ambassador-clarence-henry/.

34 Dookeran and Jantzen, "A New Leadership Challenge," 230.

9. Capturing Space in the Power of Markets

1 Central Bank of Trinidad and Tobago, compilation of speeches.

2 Dookeran, "Money Matters."

3 Te Welde, "Global Financial Crisis: Taking Stock, Taking Action."

4 Te Welde, "Global Financial Crisis: Phase 2 Synthesis."

5 See Say, *Treatise on Political Economy*; Sowell, *Say's Law*; Kates, *Say's Law and the Keynesian Revolution*.

6 Wilke, "Mutual Fund Growth Altering Economy," *Wall Street Journal*, 16 June 1996.

7 Basel Committee on Banking Supervision and International Association of Deposit Insurers, "Core Principles."

8 See Eichengreen and Hausmann, "Exchange Rates and Financial Fragility."

9 See Halifax Initiative Coalition, *Fifteen Years Is Enough*.

10 Dookeran, *Uncertainty, Stability and Challenges*.

11 Clarke and Zephirin, ed. *Essays in Honor of William Demas*.

12 Persaud, "Breaking the Anti-growth Coalition."

10. The Quest for Equality and Sustainable Growth

1 World Bank, *Building Knowledge Economies*, 98, box 5.9.

2 World Bank, *Constructing Knowledge Societies*, 8.

3 World Bank, *Constructing Knowledge Societies*, 19.

4 Global Joint Task Force, 22.

5 See Stiglitz's lecture, https://www.nobelprize.org/uploads/2018/06/stiglitz-lecture.pdf. The quote is from Snowdon, "Redefining the Role of the State," 10.

6 New Zealand Ministry of Education, *New Zealand's Tertiary Education Sector*; Renoult, *Le plan U3M en Île-de-France*; Hall, Symes, and Leucher, *The Governance of Merger in South African Higher Education*; Government of India, Planning Commission, *India as Knowledge Superpower*.

7 Kemp, "New Knowledge, New Opportunities."

8 Jamil Salmi, "Student Loans in an International Perspective: The World Bank Experience." January 2003, 15. https://documents1.worldbank.org/curated/en/149001468765578181/pdf/272950student1loans.pdf.

9 White, "Funding of Higher Education.

10 Dookeran, *Crisis and Promise*, 71–2.

11 UNESCO/OECD, *Financing Education*, 6.

12 UNESCO/OECD, *Financing Education*, 13.

13 Johnstone, Arora, and Experton, *Financing and Management of Higher Education*, 3.

14 UNESCO Education Sector, newsletter, October–December 2002.

15 Johnstone, "Funding of Higher Education."

16 Gerszon Mahler, Montes, and Newhouse, "Internet Access."

17 Court, *Financing Higher Education in Africa*, 5.

18 Court, *Financing Higher Education in Africa*, 5.

19 University of the West Indies, *Building an Entrepreneurial UWI*, May 2020, 6, https://online.flippingbook.com/view/484744/.

20 Teixeira et al., *Markets in Higher Education*; Amaral and Maglhães, "Access Policies."

21 Dookeran and Malaki, *Leadership and Governance*, chap. 3.

22 Bok, *Universities in the Marketplace*, 205, 104, 5, 6.

23 Aronowitz, *Knowledge Factory*, 164.

24 Aronowitz, *Knowledge Factory*, 164.

25 Cheng, "Beyond Economics," 37.
26 Information drawn from fastforward.tt, Ministry of Public Information, Government of the Republic of Trinidad and Tobago.
27 Chenery et al., *Redestribution with Growth*, 16.
28 Kravis, Heston, and Summers, "Real GDP per Capita."
29 In this section I ignore problems of measurement and bias created by the use of different statistics. I also assume comparability of data over the time series. I have used the household as the unit of measurement, although changes in this unit could affect specific inferences. I accept income estimates (unmodified for tax or other purposes) as given in the Household Budgetary Survey. I believe that the level of generality will not be reduced by these qualifications.
30 There may be biases in the construction of these data, and hence it is possible that the distribution may not actually depict the real situation. Apart from purely statistical problems of sample size and sampling methods there are a number of other measurement problems that must be considered. The definition of income and the treatment of non-declared income poses an immediate problem. The 1975–76 HBS survey excludes from income the following: capital gains, windfall gains, inheritances, tax refunds, "income in kind," value for "owner occupied and rent free dwellings." Usually, business expense accounts are excluded from the definition of income. These factors along with the valuation and benefits of state services (library, museum, parks, etc.) and the "pro rich" bias of the retail price system are likely to generate a statistical bias towards greater equality. Hence it is possible that the real distribution has a wider income disparity than that shown in the constructed data.
31 Harewood, "Poverty and Basic Needs."
32 This point has been reviewed in the literature. See for instance Allingham, "Measurement of Inequality"; Michal, "An Alternative Approach." Technically the situation arises because the Gini coefficient assumes a constant marginal utility of income and a straight-line social welfare function.
33 The decile ratio test is a variant of the centile ratio test, which has been extensively used in the literature. See Michal, "An Alternative Approach."
34 See Harewood, "Poverty and Basic Needs."
35 Ahiram, "Distribution of Income."
36 Ahiram, "Distribution of Income."
37 See Dookeran, "East Indians," and Harewood, "Poverty and Basic Needs."

11. Small-State Diplomacy and the Liberal Order

1 Colgan and Keohane, "The Liberal Order Is Rigged."
2 Acharya, "After Liberal Hegemony," 272.

3 Knight, "US Hegemony," 301.
4 Bew, *Realpolitik*, 6.
5 Quotes from the jacket copy of Bew, *Realpolitik*.
6 Acharya, "After Liberal Hegemony," 283.
7 Estevadeordal and Goodman, *21st Century Cooperation*.
8 Acharya, "Regionalism,"52.
9 Keohane, "Lilliputians' Dilemmas," 291.
10 Cooper and Shaw, *Diplomacies of Small States*, Abstract.
11 Baldacchino and Wivel, *Handbook*, 2.
12 Baldacchino and Wivel, *Handbook*, 2.
13 For her comments, see https://www.cepal.org/en/pressreleases/call
-renewed-inclusive-multilateralism-latin-america-and-caribbean-forefront
-new-forms.
14 This section is based on the author's notes and presentations at the conference "Competitiveness Strategies for the Small EU States: Economic and
Social Perspectives," Luxembourg, 19–20 April 2018.
15 Acharya, "After Liberal Hegemony."
16 World Economic Forum, *Global Competitiveness Report 2017–18*, 9.
17 World Bank, *Small States: A Roadmap*, 14.
18 See "The World Bank's 'Ease of Doing Business' Report Faces Tricky Questions," *The Economist*, 20 January 2018.
19 Bustillo et al., "Resilience and Capital Flows."
20 Long, "Small States, Great Power," 23.
21 See, for example, Edis, "Punching Above Their Weight," and Seitz,
"Punching Above Their Weight."
22 Long, "Small States, Great Power," 10.
23 See Allegrezza, "The Economy of Luxembourg."
24 Long, "Small States, Great Power."
25 See Estevadeordal and Goodman, *21st Century Cooperation*, 134–53; Acharya, "Regionalism."
26 Henrikson, "A Coming 'Magnesian' Age?"; Alesina and Spolaore, *The Size
of Nations*.
27 Michelle Egan, "European Regional Public Goods," 258.

12. Getting Governance and Development Right

1 Ricardo Hausmann, workshop on modified suggestions and concepts
based on complex dynamic system behaviour, July 2010, Port of Spain.
2 David Jessop is director of the Caribbean Council of Europe and a regular
commentator on Caribbean issues in several forums.
3 Stiglitz, *Making Globalization Work*.
4 Stiglitz, *Making Globalization Work*.

5 Dalrymple, "Catalyst for Development Resources."
6 Briguglio et al., *Pillars of Economic Resilience*, 11–34.
7 Katzenstein, *Small States in World Markets*.
8 Senghaas, *European Experience*.
9 Preville, "CARICOM's Orientation."
10 Venu Menon, "Governance, Leadership."
11 "Leadership for Economic Growth," *Sunday Times*, 17 August 2008, http://sundaytimes.lk/080817/Columns/eco.html.
12 The report is titled *Caribbean States in 2020: Sinking, Surviving or Prospering?*
13 See Grindle, "Good Enough Governance Revisited"; Grindle, "Good Governance"; and Lewis, "Regional and International Integration."

Epilogue

1 The quote is from the front jacket copy of Shafik, *What We Owe Each Other.*
2 Shafik, *What We Owe Each Other*, xi.
3 Year Ahead Virtual Conference 2021, held at the Norman Paterson School of International Affairs, Carleton University, and the Canadian Defense and Security Network, Ottawa, 4 December 2020.
4 "The COVID-19 Pandemic Is Forcing a Rethink in Macroeconomics," *The Economist*, 25 July 2020.
5 See Schwab and Malleret, *COVID-19: The Great Reset.*
6 Heng, "Small States," Summary, 1.
7 Heng, "Small States," 13.
8 Cohen and Fontaine, "The Case for Microlateralism."

Bibliography

Acemoglu, Daron, and James A. Robinson. *Why Nations Fail: The Origins of Power, Prosperity, and Poverty*. New York: Crown, 2012.

Acharya, Amitav. "After Liberal Hegemony: The Advent of a Multiplex World Order." *Ethics and International Affairs* 3 (Fall 2017): 271–85. https://doi.org/10.1017/S089267941700020X.

– *Constructing Global Order: Agency and Change in World Politics*. Cambridge; Cambridge University Press, 2018.

– "Regionalism in the Evolving World Order: Power, Leadership, and the Provision of Public Goods." In *21st Century Cooperation: Regional Public Goods, Global Governance, and Sustainable Development*, edited by Antoni Estevadeordal and Louis W. Goodman, 39–54. London: Routledge, 2017.

Adam, M.F., and Niels, K. *Practice Makes Perfect? The European Union's Engagement in Negotiations on a Post-2015 Framework for Development*. DIIS Report 2013:04. Copenhagen: Danish Institute for International Studies, 2013.

Ahiram, E. "Distribution of Income in Trinidad and Tobago and Comparison with Distribution of Income in Jamaica." *Social and Economic Studies* 15, no. 2 (1966): 103–20.

Aizenrnan, Joshua, "Large Hoarding of International Reserves and the Emerging Global Economic Architecture." Working Paper no. 07-08, Santa Cruz Center for International Economics, 2007.

Alesina, Alberto. *The Political Economy of High and Low Growth*. Washington, DC: World Bank, 1997.

Alesina, Alberto, and Spolaore Enrico. *The Size of Nations*. Cambridge, MA: MIT Press, 2003.

Allegrezza, Serge. "The Economy of Luxembourg." In *Small States and the European Union: Economic Perspectives*, edited by Lino Briguglio, chap. 7. Abingdon: Routledge, 2016.

Allen, Danielle, Sharon Block, Joshua Cohen, Peter Eckersley, M. Eifler, Lawrence Gostin, and Darshan Goux. *Roadmap to Pandemic Resilience*. 2020

Edmond J. Safra Center for Ethics, Harvard University, 20 April 2020.
https://ethics.harvard.edu/files/center-for-ethics/files/roadmapto
pandemicresilience_updated_4.20.20_1.pdf.

Alleyne, Dillion, and Nickolaos Karagiannis. *A New Economic Strategy for Jamaica: With Special Consideration of International Competition and the FTAA*. Kingston: Arawak, 2003.

Allingham, M.G. "The Measurement of Inequality." *Journal of Economic Theory* 5, no. 1 (1972): 163–9.

Al Omian, Khuloud. "Are We Witnessing the Awakening of a New World Order?" *Forbes – Middle East*, 7 April 2020. https://www.forbesmiddleeast.com/leadership/opinion/are-we-witnessing-the-awakening-of-a-new-world-order.

Amaral, Alberto, and António Maglhães. "Access Policies: Between Institutional Competition and the Search for Equality of Opportunities." Journal of Adult and Continuing Education 15, no. 2 (2009): 155–69. https://doi.org/10.1177%2F147797140901500203.

Andonova, L.B. "Globalization, Agency and Institutional Innovation: The Rise of Public-Private Partnerships in Global Governance." Goldfarb Center Working Paper no. 2006–004, 2006.

Arjoon, Vaalmikki. "What Drives Economic Complexity? Panel Data Evidence from Latin America and the Caribbean." Chapter 8 in *Frontiers, Flows and Frameworks: Resetting Caribbean Policy Analysis in the Aftermath of the COVID-19 Pandemic*, edited by Winston Dookeran and Raymond Izarali. Saint Andrew Parish, Jamaica: University of the West Indies Press, 2022.

Aronowitz, Stanley. *The Knowledge Factory: Dismantling the Corporate University and Creating True Higher Learning*. Boston: Beacon, 2000.

Association of Caribbean States (ACS). "Draft Declaration of Haiti." Preparatory Meeting for the 6th Extraordinary Meeting of the ACS Ministerial Council, Peton Ville, Haiti, 23–24 April 2013.

– Fifth Summit of Heads of State and/or Government of the Association of Caribbean States. "Draft Plan of Action." Barbados, 17 April 2013.

Baldacchino, Godfrey, and Anders Wivel, eds. *Handbook on the Politics of Small States*. Elgar online, March 2020.

Bárcena, Alicia. "A Development Allocation of SDRs Should Benefit All Developing Countries Irrespective of Their Income Levels." Economic Commission for Latin America and the Caribbean, 26 March 2021. https://www.cepal.org/en/articles/2021-development-allocation-sdrs-should-benefit-all-developing-countries-irrespective-their.

– "Measuring the Impact of COVID-19 with a View to Reactivation." Economic Commission for Latin America and the Caribbean, 2020. https://www.cepal.org/en/publications/45477-measuring-impact-covid-19-view-reactivation.

Basel Committee on Banking Supervision and International Association of Deposit Insurers. "Core Principles for Effective Deposit Insurance Systems." Basel: BCBS/IADI, June 2009.

Berg, Andrew B., and Jonathan D. Ostry. "Equality and Efficiency." *Finance & Development* 48, no. 3 (2011), https://www.imf.org/external/pubs/ft/fandd /2011/09/pdf/berg.pdf.

– "Inequality and Unsustainable Growth: Two Sides of the Same Coin?" IMF Staff Discussion Notes, 8 April 2011.

Berkowitz, Daniel, Hong Ma, and Shuichiro Nishioka. "Can State Owned Enterprises Restructure? Theory and Evidence from China (Preliminary, Comments welcome)." 7 April 2014. https://cep.lse.ac.uk/seminarpapers /30_04_14_SN.pdf.

– "Recasting the Iron Bowl: The Reform of China's State-Owned Enterprises." *Review of Economics and Statistics* 99, no. 4 (2017): 735–47. https://doi.org /10.1162/REST_a_00637.

Bernal, Richard. "CARICOM: Externally Vulnerable Regional Economic Integration." Paper presented at the conference Economic Integration in the Western Hemisphere: Prospects for Latin America, University of Notre Dame, Institute for International Studies, Notre Dame, IN, 17–18 April 1993.

– "Paths to the Free Trade Area of the Americas." Policy Papers on the Americas, vol. 8, study 2. Center for Strategic and International Studies, Washington, DC, 1997.

Bew, John. *Realpolitik: A History*. Oxford: Oxford University Press, 2016.

Bhagwati, Jagdish. *Regionalism and Multilateralism: An Overview*. Discussion Paper Series no. 603. Washington, DC: World Bank, 1992.

Birdsall, Nancy. "Adjustment, Reform and Growth in the Caribbean: The Missing Ingredient." In *Choices and Change: Reflections on the Caribbean*, ed. Winston Dookeran, 15–24. Washington, DC: Inter-American Development Bank, 1996.

– "The World Is Not Flat: Inequality and Injustice in Our Global Economy." UNU-WIDER Annual Lecture no. 9, Helsinki, 2006.

Bissessar, Kamala Persad, prime minister of Republic of Trinidad and Tobago, UN General Assembly Thematic Debate "The UN and the Global Economic Governance," 15 April 2013.

Bok, Derek. *Universities in the Marketplace: The Commercialization of Higher Education*. Princeton: Princeton University Press, 2004.

Bridgetown Declaration of Principles. Caribbean/United States Summit, Bridgetown, Barbados, 1997.

Briguglio, Lino, Gordon Cordina, Nadia Farrugia, and Constance Vigilance. *Small States and the Pillars of Economic Resilience*. London: Islands and Small States Institute of University of Malta/Commonwealth Secretariat, 2008.

Bustillo, Inés, Helvia Velloso, Winston Dookeran, and Daniel Perrotti. "Resilience and Capital Flows in the Caribbean." Washington, DC: ECLAC, March 2018.

Buvinić, Mayra, and Jacqueline Mazza, eds., with Ruth Anne Deutsch. *Social Inclusion and Economic Development in Latin America*. Washington, DC: IADB, 2004. https://publications.iadb.org/publications/english/document/Social-Inclusion-and-Economic-Development-in-Latin-America.pdf.

Callaghy, Thomas M. "Toward State Capability and Embedded Liberalism in the Third World: Lessons for Adjustment." In *Fragile Coalitions: The Politics of Economic Adjustment*, ed. Joan Nelson, 115–38. New Brunswick: Transaction, 1989.

Cappelletti, Mauro. "Repudiating Montesquieu? The Expansion and Legitimacy of 'Constitutional Justice.'" 35 Cath. U. L. Rev. 1 (1986). https://scholarship.law.edu/lawreview/vol35/iss1/3.

Caribbean States in 2020: Sinking, Surviving or Prospering? Report on Wilton Park Conference 900. London, March 2008. https://www.wiltonpark.org.uk/wp-content/uploads/2020/09/wp900-report.pdf.

Central Bank of Trinidad and Tobago. Compilation of speeches delivered by Winston Dookeran, governor of the Central Bank of Trinidad and Tobago, 1997–2002. Speech catalogue: "Issues and Themes." Unpublished. Port of Spain, Trinidad and Tobago, 2002.

Chenery, H., M.S. Ahluwalia, C.L.G. Bell, J.H. Duloy, and R. Jolly. *Redistribution with Growth: The Economic Framework*. Oxford: Oxford University Press, 1974.

Cheng, Yin Cheong. "Beyond Economics." *UNESCO Courier*, November 2000. https://unesdoc.unesco.org/ark:/48223/pf0000121198.

Clarke, Laurence, and M.G. Zephirin, ed. *Essays in Honor of William Demas: Towards a Caribbean Economy in the 21st Century*. Caribbean Centre for Monetary Studies, 1997. https://www.cert-net.com/files/publications/monograph_book/TowardsaCaribbeanEconomyintheTwentyFirstCentury.pdf.

Cliffe, Mark. "Pandenomics – Policymaking in a Post-Pandemic World." VOX-CEPR, 13 April 2020. https://voxeu.org/article/pandenomics-policymaking-post-pandemic-world.

Cohen, Jared, and Richard Fontaine. "The Case for Microlateralism: With U.S. Support, Small States Can Ably Lead Global Efforts." *Foreign Affairs*, 29 April 2021. https://www.foreignaffairs.com/articles/world/2021-04-29/case-microlateralism.

Colgan, Jeff D., and Robert O. Keohane. "The Liberal Order Is Rigged: Fix It Now or Watch It Wither." *Foreign Affairs*, May/June 2017, https://www.foreignaffairs.com/articles/world/2017-04-17/liberal-order-rigged.

Cooper, Andrew F., and Timothy M. Shaw, eds. *The Diplomacies of Small States at the Start of the Twenty-First Century: How Vulnerable? How Resilient?* London: Palgrave Macmillan, 2009.

Court, David. *Financing Higher Education in Africa: Makerere, the Quiet Revolution*. World Bank/Rockefeller Foundation, April 1999.

Csaba, Laszlo. "Country Study, Hungary." Paper presented to the UNU-WIDER Conference on Country Role Models, Helsinki, 13–14 June 2008.

Cui, Zhiyuan. "International Chapter 11 and SDR." In *The Financial System under Stress: An Architecture for the New World Economy*, 1, edited with an introduction by Marc Uzan, 57–63. New York: Routledge, 1996. http://ndl .ethernet.edu.et/bitstream/123456789/7965/1/4.pdf.

Dalrymple, Kelvin. "A Catalyst for Development Resources in the Caribbean." Paper presented at High-Level Roundtable on International Cooperation for Sustainable Development in Caribbean Small Island Developing States, Bridgetown, Barbados, 25–27 March 2008.

Demas, William G. *The Economics of Development in Small Countries with Special Reference to the Caribbean*. Montreal: McGill University Press, 1965.

De Melo, Jaime, and Arvind Panagariya, eds. *New Dimensions in Regional Integration*. Cambridge: Cambridge University Press, 1993.

Dominguez, Jorge. "The Caribbean in a New International Context: Are Freedom and Peace a Threat to its Prosperity?" In *The Caribbean: New Dynamics in Trade and Political Economy*, ed. A.T. Bryan, 1–23. New Brunswick: Transaction, 1995.

Dookeran, Winston. Address to the Conference on Global Governance and Reform of the International Financial System: Impact on the Americas, OAS, Washington, DC, 22 April 2013.

– "Caribbean Convergence: Revisiting Caribbean Integration." Remarks at opening ceremony of Caribbean Development Roundtable, Georgetown, Guyana, 30 May 2012.

– "Caribbean Integration: An Agenda for Open Regionalism." *The Round Table: Commonwealth Journal of International Affairs* 83, no. 330 (1994): 205–11.

– *Crisis and Promise in the Caribbean*. London: Ashgate, 2015.

– "The Distribution of Income in Trinidad and Tobago, 1957–1976," *Review of Income and Wealth* 27, no. 2 (1981): 195–206. https://doi.org/10.1111 /j.1475-4991.1981.tb00209.x.

– "East Indians and the Economy of Trinidad and Tobago." In *Calcutta to Caroni: The East Indians of Trinidad*, ed. John Gaffar La Guerre, 63–76. Longmans, 1974.

– "Facing the Issues: Turning the Economy Around: Partnering with All Our People." Budget Statement, 2010–2011.

– "Forum Looks to Set New Strategy for the Caribbean." Presented at the Forum on the Future of the Caribbean: Stimulating Radical Ideas, 2015, http://www.acs-aec.org/index.php?q=resources/galleries/2015/forum -on-the-future-of-the-caribbean-stimulating-radical-ideas.

– "Introducing the Convergence Model of Integrated Production." Paper presented at meeting of Regional Integration Bodies in the Margins of the UNECLA, Bogota, Colombia, 2013.

– "Money Matters: Emerging Challenges for Small States." Lecture delivered at the Distinguished Lecture Series, Institute of International Relations, University of the West Indies, St. Augustine, 2000.
– Plenary speech at the Caribbean Growth Forum Launch Event, 18–19 June 2012, Kingston, Jamaica.
– *Policy Reform in the Caribbean: Choices and Change.* University of Suriname, Institute for Development Policy Management, 1996.
– *Power, Politics and Performance: A Partnership Approach for Development.* Kingston: Ian Randle, 2012.
– "Preferential Trade Arrangements in the Caribbean: Issues and Approaches." In *Trade Liberalization in the Western Hemisphere*, 437–70. Washington, DC: Inter-American Development Bank/ECLAC, 1995.
– "Reflections on the COVID-19 Pandemic and the Caribbean." EUCLID Global Health, 1 April 2020. https://globalhealth.euclid.int/reflections -on-the-covid-19-pandemic-and-the-caribbean/.
– "Towards a Macro Dynamic Methodology for Transportation Planning in the Caribbean Environment." *International Journal of Transport Economics* 8, no. 1 (April 1981): 113–21.
– *Uncertainty, Stability and Challenges: Economic and Monetary Policy, a Small State Perspective.* San Juan, Trinidad: Lexicon Trinidad, 2006.
Dookeran, Winston, and Miriam Campanella, "The COVID-19 Symmetric Shock and Its Asymmetric Consequences: What Can Caribbean Countries Do They Didn't Do Before." SSRN Repository 2020.
Dookeran, Winston, and Carlos Elias, eds. *Shifting the Frontiers: An Action Framework for the Future of the Caribbean.* Kingston: Ian Randle, 2016.
Dookeran, Winston, and Manfred Jantzen. "A New Leadership Challenge." In Dookeran, *Power, Politics and Performance*, 230–35.
– "Prospectus for the Foundation for Politics and Leadership – FPL." 4 June 2008, Port of Spain, Trinidad.
Dookeran, Winston, and Akhil Malaki. *Leadership and Governance in Small States: Getting Development Right.* Saarbrucken: VDM Verlag, 2008.
Drezner, Daniel W., Ronald R. Krebs, and Randall Schweller. "The End of Grand Strategy: America Must Think Small." *Foreign Affairs*, May/June 2020. https://www.foreignaffairs.com/articles/world/2020-04-13/end -grand-strategy.
ECDPM (European Center for Development Policy Management). *Synthesis of ACP Independent Comments on the Green Paper of the European Commission on Partnership 2000.* Maastricht: ECDPM, 1997.
ECLAC (Economic Commission for Latin America and the Caribbean). "The Caribbean Forum: Shaping a Sustainable Development Agenda to Address the Caribbean Reality in the Twenty-First Century." Draft report, Bogota, 5–6 March 2013.

– *Education, Structural Change and Inclusive Growth in Latin America.* March 2015. https://repositorio.cepal.org/bitstream/handle/11362/37845 /1/S1500196_en.pdf.

– *Open Regionalism in Latin America and the Caribbean.* Santiago: United Nations ECLAC, 1994.

– *Opportunities for Convergence and Regional Cooperation: High Level Summit of Latin America and the Caribbean*, Cancun, Mexico, 21–23 February 2010.

– "The Politics of Global Financial Regulation Rulemaking." ECLAC Brief, Washington, DC, 2012.

– *Strengthening Development: The Interplay of Macro and Microeconomics.* Santiago: United Nations ECLAC, 1996.

– *Summary of Global Economic Developments 1995.* ECLAC Subregional Headquarters for the Caribbean, March 1996.

Edis, Richard. "Punching Above Their Weight: How Small Developing States Operate in the Contemporary Diplomatic World." *Cambridge Review of International Affairs* 5, no. 2 (2007): 45–53. https://doi.org/10.1080 /09557579108400066.

Egan, Michelle. "European Regional Public Goods: Insiders and Outsiders." Chap. 12 in *21st Century Cooperation: Regional Public Goods, Global Governance, and Sustainable Development*, edited by Antoni Estevadeordal and Louis W. Goodman. London: Routledge, 2017.

Eichengreen, Barry Julian, and Ricardo Hausmann. "Exchange Rates and Financial Fragility." National Bureau of Economic Research, Cambridge, MA, November 1999.

Emmerij, Louis. "Turning Points in Development Thinking and Practice." In Mavrotas and Shorrocks, *Advancing Development*, 37–49.

Estevadeordal, Antoni, and Louis W. Goodman. *21st Century Cooperation: Regional Public Goods, Global Governance, and Sustainable Development.* London: Routledge, 2017.

Etienne, Henri. "The Limits of Integration?" Charles Francis Adams Lecture Series, Fletcher School of Law and Diplomacy, Tufts University, Medford, MA, 14 October 1993.

Evans, Peter B., Harold K. Jacobson, and Robert D. Putnam, eds. *Double-Edged Diplomacy: International Bargaining and Domestic Politics.* Berkeley: University of California Press, 1993.

Floyd, Kathryn H. "Foreword: Whole of Government Approaches during COVID-19." *Diplomatic Courier*, 25 August 2020. https://www.diplomaticourier .com/posts/whole-of-government-approaches-during-covid-19.

Fornes, Gaston. "Emerging Markets: The Markets of the Future." Munich Personal RePEc Archive (MPRA) Paper no. 42315, September 2012, University Library of Munich, Germany.

Foster, Angus. "Difficult Choices Ahead for Mercosur." *Financial Times*, 19 December 1994.

Fosu, Augustin K. "Anti-growth Syndromes in Africa: A Synthesis of the Case Studies." In *The Political Economy of Economic Growth in Africa 1960–2000*, edited by Benno J. Ndulu, Stephen A. O'Connell, Robert H. Bates, Paul Collier, and Chukwuma C. Soludo, 137–72. Cambridge: Cambridge University Press, 2008.

Galbraith, John Kenneth. "The New Dialectic." *The American Prospect* 18 (1994): 9–11.

Gerszon Mahler, Daniel, Jose Montes, and David Newhouse. "Internet Access in Sub-Saharan Africa." World Bank Poverty and Equity Notes no. 13, March 2019. https://documents1.worldbank.org/curated/en/518261552658319590/pdf/Internet-Access-in-Sub-Saharan-Africa.pdf.

Ghai, Dharam. "Structural Adjustment, Global Integration, and Social Democracy." Discussion Paper no. 37. Geneva: United Nations Research Institute for Social Development, 1992.

Goldman Sachs. "Dreaming with BRICS: The Path to 2050." Global Economics Paper no. 99. Goldman Sachs, October 2003.

Gonzales, Anthony. "The Caribbean–EU Relations in a Post-Lomé World." Working paper on EU-Development Policy. Bonn: EU, 1996.

– "Europe and the Caribbean: Towards a Post-Lomé Strategy." In *The Caribbean: New Dynamics in Trade and Political Economy*, edited by A.T. Bryan, 55–71. New Brunswick: Transaction, 1995.

Gonzales, Anthony P. "Assessment of the Convergence Model of Integrated Production." Symposium to discuss the paper "Introduction to the Convergence Model of Integrated Production." ECLAC Sub-regional Headquarters for the Caribbean, Port of Spain, Trinidad and Tobago, 9 May 2013.

Government of India, Planning Commission. *India as Knowledge Superpower: Strategy for Transformation*. Task force report. June 2001. https://niti.gov.in/planningcommission.gov.in/docs/aboutus/taskforce/tk_know.pdf.

Griffith, Ivelaw. "Caribbean Security on the Eve of the Twenty-First Century." McNair Paper no. 54. Washington, DC: Institute for National Strategic Studies, 1996.

Griffith-Jones, Stephany. "Perspectives on the Governance of Global Financial Regulation." Paper presented at Commonwealth Finance Ministers Meeting, Limmasol, Cyprus, 30 September–3 October, 2009.

Grindle, Merilee S. "Good Enough Governance Revisited." *Development Policy Review* 25, no. 5 (2007): 553–74. http://courses.washington.edu/pbaf531/Grindle_GoodEnoughGovRevisited.pdf.

– "Good Governance: The Inflation of an Idea." CID Working Paper no. 202, October 2010. https://www.hks.harvard.edu/sites/default/files/centers/cid/files/publications/faculty-working-papers/202.pdf.

Halifax Initiative Coalition. *Fifteen Years Is Enough*. Ottawa: HIC, 2010.

Hall, Martin, Ashley Symes, and Thierry Leucher. *The Governance of Merger in South African Higher Education*. Research report prepared for Council of Higher Education. August 2004. https://www.researchgate .net/publication/277294844_The_Council_on_Higher_Education.

Hanson, Gordon. "The Rise of Middle Kingdoms: Emerging Economies in Global Trade." NBER Working Paper no. 17961, March 2012.

Harewood, J. "Poverty and Basic Needs." *Caribbean Issues*, ISER UWI 1978, 1978.

Hausmann, Ricardo. Based on a workshop facilitated by the finance minister at the Ministry of Finance of Trinidad and Tobago, modified suggestions and concepts of Dr. Ricardo Hausmann based on complex dynamic system behaviour, July 2010.

Heng, Yee-Kuang. "Small States." In *Oxford Research Encyclopedia of International Studies*, 2020. https://oxfordre.com/internationalstudies/view/10.1093 /acrefore/9780190846626.001.0001/acrefore-9780190846626-e-545.

Henrikson, Alan K. "A Coming 'Magnesian' Age? Small States, the Global System, and the International Community." *Geopolitics* 6, no. 3 (2001): 49–86. 2001. https://doi.org/10.1080/14650040108407729.

– "Diplomacy and Small States in Today's World." Dr. Eric Williams Memorial Lecture Series, Port of Spain, May 1998.

Huggins, George. *Green Paper on Relations between the European Union and the ACP Countries on the Eve of the Twenty–First Century*. Maastricht: ECDPM, 1996. https://op.europa.eu/en/publication-detail/-/publication/fd0026af -3614-4e2d-9330-73b2078bb9b1.

IDB. "The Fragile Path to Recovery." *Caribbean Quarterly Bulletin* 10, no. 2 (August 2021). https://publications.iadb.org/publications/english /document/Caribbean-Quarterly-Bulletin-Volume-10-Issue-2-August -2021.pdf.

IMF (International Monetary Fund). *Fund-Supported Programs, Fiscal Policy, and Income Distribution*. Washington, DC: IMF, 1986.

IMF Staff. "Globalization: A Brief Overview." May 2008. https://www.imf.org /external/np/exr/ib/2008/053008.htm.

Ito, Takotoshi. *What Can Developing Countries Learn from East Asian Economic Growth?* Washington, DC: World Bank, 1997.

Jantzen, Manfred. *One World Informational Age*. Arthur Lok Jack Global School of Business, University of the West Indies, 2012.

Jantzen, N., G. Saha, M. Nicholson, A. Curling, E. Kacal, D. Lewis, and T. Boodram. "Caribbean Future Initiative: In the Context of the Caribbean Future Forum." Paper prepared for Winston Dookeran, Minister of Foreign Affairs, August 2015.

Johnstone, D. Bruce, Alka Arora, and William Experton. *The Financing and Management of Higher Education: A Status Report on Worldwide Reforms*.

Washington, DC: World Bank, 1998. http://documents.worldbank.
org/curated/en/941721468741874640/The-financing-and-management-of
-higher-education-a-status-report-on-worldwide-reform.

– "The Funding of Higher Education." Keynote address, Salzburg Seminar, November 2002. https://www.salzburgglobal.org/multi-year
-series/general/pageId/6207.

Karim, Fazal. "Good Leadership Is About Delivering Results." Speech given at the conference Leadercast 2015. http://www.news.gov.tt/content
/karim-good-leadership-about-delivering-results.

Kates, Steven. *Say's Law and the Keynesian Revolution: How Macroeconomic Theory Lost Its Way*. Cheltenham: Eduard Elgar, 1998.

Katzenstein, Peter J. *Small States in World Markets*. Ithaca: Cornell University Press, 1985.

Keijzer, N., B. Lein, M. Negre, and N. Tissi. "ACP-EU Relations beyond 2020: Exploring European Perceptions." DIE/GDI Briefing Paper no. 11. Bonn: German Development Institute, 2013.

Kemp, David. "New Knowledge, New Opportunities: A Discussion Paper on Higher Education Research and Research Training." June 1999.
https://www.voced.edu.au/content/ngv%3A23061.

Keohane, Robert. "Lilliputians' Dilemmas: Small States in International Politics." *International Organization* 23, no. 2 (1969): 291–310.

– "Sovereignty, Interdependence, and International Institutions." In *Ideas and Ideals: Essays on Politics in Honor of Stanley Hoffman*, edited by Linda B. Miller and Michael Joseph Smith. Boulder: Westview, 1993.

Knight, W. Andy. "US Hegemony." In *International Organization and Global Governance*, edited by Thomas G. Weiss and Rorden Wilkinson, 292–303. Abingdon: Routledge, 2014.

Knight, W. Andy, and Randolph B. Persaud. "Subsidiarity, Regional Governance and Caribbean Security." *Latin American Politics and Society* 43, no. 1 (2001): 29–56. https://doi.org/10.2307/3177012.

Kravis, I.B., A.W. Heston, and R. Summers. "Real GDP per Capita for More than One Hundred Countries." *Economic Journal* 88, no. 350 (1978): 215–42. https://doi.org/10.2307/2232127.

Kumar, Ashwani, and Dirk Messner, eds. *Power Shifts and Global Governance: Challenges from South to North*. London: Anthem, 2010.

Lawson, Sandra. "Dreaming with BRICS: The Path to 2050." *CEO Confidential*, October 2003.

"Leadership for Economic Growth." *Sunday Times*, 17 August 2008.
http://sundaytimes.lk/080817/Columns/eco.html.

Lewis, Linden, ed. *Caribbean Sovereignty, Development and Democracy in an Age of Globalization*. New York: Routledge, 2013.

Lewis, Vaughn. "Regional and International Integration and Modes of Governance: The Caribbean Case." *Caribbean Dialogue* 7, nos. 1/2 (2001).

Lijphart, Arend. "The Political Consequences of Electoral Laws, 1945–1985." *American Political Science Review* 84, no. 2 (1990): 481–96.

– "Size Pluralism and the Westminster Model of Democracy: Implications for the Eastern Caribbean." In *A Revolution Aborted: The Lesson of Grenada*, edited by Jorge Heine, 321–42. Pittsburg: University of Pittsburgh Press, 1990.

Long, Tom. "Small States, Great Power? Gaining Influence through Intrinsic, Derivative, and Collective Power." *International Studies Review* 19, no. 2 (2017): 185–205. https://doi.org/10.1093/isr/viw040.

Malaki, Akhil. "A Partnership Approach to Caribbean Convergence." *Caribbean Journal of International Relations and Diplomacy* 1, no. 3 (September 2013): 83–94. https://journals.sta.uwi.edu/iir/index.asp?action =viewIssue&issueId=71.

Mannermaa, Mika. *Democracy in the Turmoil of the Future*. Parliament of Finland, Committee of the Future, 2007.

Mavrotas, George, and Anthony Shorrocks, eds. *Advancing Development: Core Themes in Global Economics*. London: Palgrave Macmillan, 2007.

McCloskey, Deirdre. *Bourgeois Dignity: Why Economists Can't Explain the Modern World*. Chicago: University of Chicago Press, 2010.

Mehdudia, Sujay. "The Way Forward: From Policy Discussions to Delivering Tangible Benefits, BRICS Nations Plan on a Wider Cooperation." *The Hindu*, 21 February 2013, https://www.thehindu.com/news/cities/Delhi/the -way-forward/article4435519.ece.

Michal, Jan M. "An Alternative Approach to Measuring Income Inequality in Eastern Europe." In *Economic Development in the Soviet Union and Eastern Europe*, vol. 2, edited by Zbigniew M. Fallenbuchl. New York: Praeger, 1976.

Moon, Suerie. "Power in Global Governance: An Expanded Typology from Global Health." *Global Health* 15, no. 74 (2019). https://doi.org/10.1186 /s12992-019-0515-5.

Morris, Stephen, and Shin, Hyun Song. "Catalytic Finance: When Does It Work?" *Journal of International Economics* 70, no. 1 (2006): 161–77. https://doi.org/10.1016/j.jinteco.2005.06.014.

Musacchio, Aldo, and Emilio I. Pineda Ayerbe, eds. *Fixing State-Owned Enterprises: New Policy Solutions to Old Problems*. New York: Inter-American Development Bank, 2019.

Nafxiger, Wayne, E. "From Seers to Sen: The Meaning of Economic Development." In Movrotos and Shorrocks, *Advancing Development*, 50–62.

National Planning Commission. *Medium Term Macro Planning Framework 1989– 1995: Restructuring for Economic Independence*. 1 January 1990. https://www .amazon.com/Medium-planning-framework-1989-1995-economic -independence/dp/B0000EEJZV.

Ndii, David. "Memo to #UpperDeckPeopleKE: Coronavirus Economic Shock Is Coming and It Has Your Names on It." *The Elephant*, 16 April 2020.

https://www.theelephant.info/op-eds/2020/04/16/memo-to
-upperdeckpeopleke-coronavirus-economic-shock-is-coming-and-it-has
-your-names-on-it/.

New Zealand Ministry of Education. *New Zealand's Tertiary Education Sector: Profile and Trends 1998*. December 1999. https://www.educationcounts.govt
.nz/__data/assets/pdf_file/0019/9244/PT-1998.pdf.

Norton, Roger D. "Agricultural Issues in Structural Adjustment Programs." FAO Economic and Social Development Paper no. 66, Rome, 1987.

OECD. "Evaluating the Initial Impact of COVID-19. Containment Measures on Economic Activity." 10 June 2020. https://www.oecd.org/coronavirus
/policy-responses/evaluating-the-initial-impact-of-covid-19-containment
-measures-on-economic-activity-b1f6b68b/.

– *OECD Guidelines on Corporate Governance of State-Owned Enterprises*, 2015. https://www.oecd.org/corporate/guidelines-corporate-governance-soes
.htm.

Ohmae, Kenichi. *The End of the Nation State: The Rise of Regional Economies*. New York: Free Press, 1995.

Osmani, S.R. "The Sen System of Social Evaluation." In *Arguments for a Better World: Essays in Honour of Amartya Sen*, vol. 1: *Ethics, Welfare and Measurement*, edited by Kaushik Basu and Ravi Kanbur, 15–34. Oxford: Oxford University Press, 2009.

Ostry, Jonathan D., Andrew Berg, and Prakash Loungani. *Confronting Inequality: How Societies Can Choose Inclusive Growth*. New York: Columbia University Press, 2019.

Ostry, Jonathan D., Andrew Berg, and Charalambos G. Tsangarides. *Redistribution, Inequality, and Growth*. IMF Staff Discussion Note, February 2014. https://www.imf.org/external/pubs/ft/sdn/2014/sdn1402.pdf.

Ostry, Sylvia. *The Post–Cold War Trading System*. Chicago: University of Chicago Press, 1997.

Pantin, Dennis. *Industrial Policy for CARICOM*. United Nations ECLAC, 1995.

Patterson, P.J. Foreword to *Power, Politics and Performance: A Partnership Approach for Development*, by Winston Dookeran, xi–xii. Kingston: Ian Randle, 2012.

– Keynote speech at book launch of Sir Sridath Ramphal's *Caribbean Challenges*, Jamaica, 18 June 2012.

Payne, Anthony. "Westminster Adapted: The Political Order of the Commonwealth Caribbean." In *Democracy in the Caribbean: Political, Economic, and Social Perspectives*, edited by Jorge Dominguez, Robert A. Pastor, and DeLisle Worrell, 57–73. Baltimore: Johns Hopkins University Press, 1993.

Persaud, Avinash. "Breaking the Anti-growth Coalition: Solutions for Caribbean and CARICOM Development." In Dookeran, *Power, Politics and Performance*, 190–229.

Piketty, Thomas. *Capital in the Twenty-First Century*. Cambridge, MA: Belknap, 2014.

Polanyi, Karl. *The Great Transformation: The Political and Economic Origins of Our Time*. 2nd ed. Boston: Beacon, 2001.

Porter, Michael. "Cluster and the New Economics of Competition." *Harvard Business Review*, November–December 1998.

Prebisch, Raúl. *El desarollo económico de América Latina: Problemas, teóricos y práticos*. CEPAL, 1973.

– *El desarrollo económico de América Latina y sus principales problemas*. Santiago: CEPAL, 1949.

– *Problemas practicos y teoricos del crecimiento económico*. Santiago: CEPAL, 1973.

– *Problemas teóricos y prácticos del crecimiento económico*. Santiago: CEPAL, 1973.

Preville, Claudius. "CARICOM's Orientation in External Trade Negotiations and Resilience Building." In *Small States and the Pillars of Economic Resilience*, edited by Lino Briguglio, Gordon Cordina, Nadia Farrugia, and Constance Vigilance, 119–128. London: Islands and Small States Institute of University of Malta/Commonwealth Secretariat, 2008.

Putnam, Robert D. "Diplomacy and Domestic Politics: The Logic of Two-Level Games." *International Organization* 42, no. 3 (1988): 427–60. https://doi.org/10.1017/S0020818300027697.

– *Making Democracy Work: Civic Traditions in Modern Italy*. Princeton: Princeton University Press, 1994.

– "The Prosperous Community: Social Capital and Public Life." *The American Prospect* 13 (1993): 35–42.

Ramphal, Sridath. "Vision and Leadership: The Infinite Unity of Caribbean Needs." In *Caribbean Challenges: Sir Shridath Ramphal's Collected Counsel*, 157–73. London: Hansib, 2012.

Ramsaran, Ramesh. "Aspects of Growth and Adjustment in Post-Independence Trinidad and Tobago." *Journal of Social and Economic Studies* (Special Issue on Monetary Studies) 48, no. 1/2 (1999): 215–86.

– *The Challenge of Structural Adjustment in the Commonwealth Caribbean*. New York: Praeger, 1992.

Renoult, Daniel. "Le plan U3M en Île-de-France: Perspectives 2000–2006." *Bulletin des bibliothèques de France*, no. 2, 2002, 4–11. https://bbf.enssib.fr/consulter/bbf-2002-02-0004-001.

Sabia, Michael. "In This Pandemic, Governments Will Face Three Tests – Including How Best to Restart the Economy." *Globe and Mail*, 12 April 2020.

Sachs, Jeffrey. *Common Wealth: Economics for a Crowded Planet*. New York: Penguin, 2008.

Salmi, Jamil. "Student Loans in an International Perspective: The World Bank Experience." January 2003. https://documents1.worldbank.org/curated/en/149001468765578181/pdf/272950student1loans.pdf.

Saunders, Ronald. "Tied to No One's Apron Strings: The Caribbean in an Emerging New World." Caribbean News Global, 7 May 2020. https://www.caribbeannewsglobal.com/tied-to-no-ones-apron-strings-the-caribbean-in-an-emerging-new-world/.

Say, Jean-Baptiste. A Treatise on Political Economy; or the Production, Distribution, and Consumption of Wealth. Translated from the 4th edition of the French by C.R. Prinsep. Kitchener: Batoche Books, 2001.

Scalapino, Robert A. The Politics of Development: Perspectives on Twentieth-Century Asia. Cambridge, MA: Harvard University Press. 1989.

Schwab, Klaus, and Thierry Malleret. COVID-19: The Great Reset. World Economic Forum, Geneva, 2020.

Seitz, Sam. "Punching Above Their Weight: Theorizing Smaller State Behaviour." Politics in Theory and Practice (blog), 7 September 2017. https://politicstheorypractice.com/2017/09/07/punching-above-their-weight-theorizing-smaller-state-behavior/.

SELA (Latin American and Caribbean Economic System). Productive Development and Industrialization in Latin America and the Caribbean. Caracas: SELA, 2012.

Sen, Amartya. Development as Freedom. Oxford: Oxford University Press, 1999.

– "Identity and Justice." In The Face of Man, vol. 2, Dr. Eric Williams Memorial Lecture Series, 101–17. Central Bank of Trinidad and Tobago, 2005.

Senghaas, Dieter. The European Experience: A Historical Critique of Development Theory. Dover: Berg, 1985.

Shafik, Minouche. What We Owe Each Other: A New Social Contract for a Better Society. New York: Penguin Random House, 2021.

Shankarjha, Prem. "Modi's 'Stimulus Package' Is a Gigantic Confidence Trick Played on the People of India." The Wire, 18 May 2020. https://thewire.in/political-economy/modis-stimulus-package-is-a-gigantic-confidence-trick-played-on-the-people-of-india.

Smith, Adam. The Wealth of Nations. Introduction by Robert Reich. New York: Modern Library, 2000.

Smith, M.G. The Plural Society in the West Indies. Berkeley: University of California Press, 1965.

Snowdon, Brian. "Redefining the Role of the State: Joseph Stiglitz on Building a 'Post-Washington.'" World Economics 2, no. 3 (2001): 45–86. https://www8.gsb.columbia.edu/faculty/jstiglitz/sites/jstiglitz/files/2001_World_Economics.pdf.

Sowell, T. Say's Law: A Historical Analysis. Princeton: Princeton University Press, 1972.

Spolaore, Enrico. "Small States and the Future of Globalization." Key note address. Luxembourg, 19–20 April 2018.

Stephen, Matthew D. "Emerging Powers and Emerging Trends in Global Governance." Global Governance 23, no. 3 (2017): 483–502. http://dx.doi.org/10.1163/19426720-02303009.

Stewart, Frances. "Do We Need a New 'Great Transformation'? Is One Likely?" In Mavrotas and Shorrocks, *Advancing Development*, 616–38.

Stiglitz, Joseph E. *An Agenda for Development for the Twenty-First Century*. Washington, DC: World Bank, 1997.

– *Making Globalization Work*. New York: W.W Norton, 2007.

– "The State, the Market and Development." WIDER Working Paper 2016 /1. https://www.wider.unu.edu/sites/default/files/wp2016-1.pdf.

Teixeira, Ben Jongbloed, David Dill, and Alberto Amaral, eds. *Markets in Higher Education: Rhetoric or Reality?* Dordrecht: Kluwer, 2004.

Te Welde, D.W. "The Global Financial Crisis and Developing Countries: Phase 2 Synthesis." Overseas Development Institute briefing paper 316, London, 2009.

– "The Global Financial Crisis and Developing Countries: Taking Stock, Taking Action." Overseas Development Institute briefing paper 54, London, 2009.

Turner, Adair. "Monetary Finance Is Here." *Project Syndicate*, 20 April 2020. https://www.project-syndicate.org/commentary/monetary-finance-of -covid19-fiscal-deficits-by-adair-turner-2020-04.

UNESCO/OECD. *Financing Education – Investments and Returns: Analysis of the World Education Indicators*. Paris: UNESCO/OECD, 2002. https://www .oecd.org/education/skills-beyond-school/2494749.pdf.

Unger, Roberto Mangabeira, and Zhiyuan Cui. "China in the Russian Mirror." *New Left Review* 208, November/December 1994, 1–10.

Venu Menon, Sudha. "Governance, Leadership and Economic Growth in Singapore." Munich Personal RePEc Archive (MPRA) paper no. 4741, University Library of Munich, Germany.

Verrest, Hebe, and Rhoda Reddock. "Poverty and Statistics in Trinidad and Tobago: An Introduction." *Caribbean Dialogue* 9, no. 4 (2004): 1–11. https://journals.sta.uwi.edu/cd/index.asp?action=viewPastAbstract &articleId=195&issueId=28.

Weder, Beatrice, and Rolf Weder. "Switzerland's Rise to a Wealthy Nation: Competition and Contestability as Key Factors." Paper presented at UNU-WIDER Conference on Country Role Models, 2008.

Wenner, Mark. "Caribbean Diaspora: How Can They Finance Development in the Region?" Caribbean DEV Trends (IDB blog), 25 January 2016. https://blogs.iadb.org/caribbean-dev-trends/en/caribbean-diaspora-how -can-they-finance-development-in-the-region/.

West Indian Commission. *Time for Action: Report of the West Indian Commission*. St. Michael, Barbados: West Indian Commission Secretariat, 1992.

White, Tony. "The Funding of Higher Education: A Record of Universities Project Symposium." Presented at Salzberg Seminar, November 2002.

"WHO Director General's Opening Remarks at the Media Briefing on COVID-19, 11 March 2020." https://www.who.int/director-general /speeches/detail/who-director-general-s-opening-remarks-at-the-media -briefing-on-covid-19---11-march-2020.

Wilke, John R. "Mutual Fund Growth Altering Economy." *Wall Street Journal*, 16 June 1996.

Wolf, Martin. "Myth of Empty Sovereignty." *Financial Times*, 5 December 1994.

– *The Shifts and the Shocks: What We've Learned – And Have Still to Learn – From the Financial Crisis*. Penguin, 2015.

– "The World Economy Is Now Collapsing: A Microbe Has Overthrown Our Arrogance and Sent Global Output into a Tailspin." *Financial Times*, 14 April 2020. https://www.ft.com/content/d5f05b5c-7db8-11ea-8fdb -7ec06edeef84.

World Bank. *Annual World Bank Conference on Development Economics*. Edited by Boris Pleskovic and Joseph E. Stiglitz. World Bank, 2000.

– *Building Knowledge Economies: Advanced Strategies for Development*. Washington, DC: World Bank, 2007.

– *Caribbean Economic Review*. Report no. 20460-LAC, June 2000. https://web .worldbank.org/archive/website00951/WEB/PDF/CG_ECON_.PDF.

– *Constructing Knowledge Societies: New Challenges for Tertiary Education*. Washington, DC: World Bank, 2002. http://hdl.handle.net/10986/15224.

– *Financing Higher Education in Africa: Makerere: The Quiet Revolution*. Report no. 22883. Washington, DC: World Bank, April 1998. https://documents1 .worldbank.org/curated/en/759471468760210734/pdf/multi0page.pdf.

– *The Growth Report: Strategies for Sustained Growth and Inclusive Development*. Commission on Growth and Development. 2008. http://www .growthcommission.org.

– *Multipolarity: The New Global Economy*. Washington, DC: World Bank, 2011.

– "The Role of Emerging Market Economy Demand during the Post-2005 Boom." Contribution to the G20 Commodity Markets Sub-working Group 71266, April 2012.

– *Small States: A Roadmap for World Bank Group Engagement*. Washington, DC: World Bank, 2017.

– *World Development Report 2006: Equity and Development*. Washington, DC: World Bank, 2005.

World Bank Joint Task Force. *Small States: Meeting Challenges in the Global Economy*. Commonwealth Secretariat, Washington, DC, 2003.

World Bank, UNESCO, and Task Force on Higher Education and Society. *Higher Education in Developing Countries: Peril and Promise*. Washington, DC: Task Force on Higher Education and Society/World Bank, 2000. https://documents1 .worldbank.org/curated/en/345111467989458740/pdf/multi-page.pdf.

World Economic Forum. *Global Competitiveness Report 2017–18*. Geneva: WEF, 2017. https://www.weforum.org/reports/the-global-competitiveness -report-2017-2018.

Yao, Yang. "The Disinterested Government: An Interpretation of China's Economic Success in the Reform Era." Paper presented to the UNU-WIDER

Conference on Country Role Models for Development Success, Helsinki, 13–14 June 2008. http://hdl.handle.net/10419/45124.

Young Professionals. "Resetting T&T's Economy – A Sustainable Response to the COVID-19 Crisis." 24 April 2020. https://www.scribd.com/document /478525209/Resetting-T-T-s-Economy-A-Sustainable-Response-to-the -Covid-19-Crisis-REVISED-Version-pdf.

Zoellick, Robert B. "After the Crisis." Development Outreach, World Bank Institute, Washington, DC, December 2009.

Zuchoff, Mitchell. "At GATT's Core: A Debate about Money, Sovereignty." *Boston Globe*, 27 November 1994.

Index

Page numbers in italic represent figures and tables; *b* represents boxes.

CPSIA information can be obtained
at www.ICGtesting.com
Printed in the USA
BVHW040220241022
649959BV00003B/5/J